D1273844

ULTIMATE
AMERICAN
CARS

FIVE-VIEW SERIES

ULTIMATE AMERICAN CARS

General Editor:
Craig Cheetham

MOTORBOOKS

This edition published in 2006 by Motorbooks, an imprint of MBI Publishing Company, Galtier Plaza, Suite 200, 380 Jackson Street, St. Paul, MN 55101-3885 USA

Copyright © 2006 International Masters Publishers AB
Introduction text copyright © 2006 Amber Books Ltd

All rights reserved. With the exception of quoting brief passages for the purposes of review, no part of this publication may be reproduced without prior written permission from the Publisher.

The information in this book is true and complete to the best of our knowledge. All recommendations are made without any guarantee on the part of the author or Publisher, who also disclaim any liability incurred in connection with the use of this data or specific details.

This publication has been prepared solely by Amber Books Ltd. and MBI Publishing Company and is not approved or licensed by any other entity. We recognize that some words, model names, and designations mentioned herein are the property of the trademark holder. We use them for identification purposes only. This is not an official publication.

MBI Publishing Company titles are also available at discounts in bulk quantity for industrial or sales-promotional use. For details write to Special Sales Manager at MBI Publishing Company, Galtier Plaza, Suite 200, 380 Jackson Street, St. Paul, MN 55101-3885 USA

ISBN: 978-0-7603-2570-4

Produced by
Amber Books Ltd
Bradley's Close
74–77 White Lion Street
London N1 9PF
United Kingdom
www.amberbooks.co.uk

Printed in Thailand

All photographs © International Masters Publishers AB except
Richard Dredge: 6, 8, 9, 11

Contents

Introduction

For well over a century, America has been involved in a love affair. A love affair that sprang up from the smoking ashes of the industrial revolution, began in Europe and over time became the key to the automation and independence that today we not only rely on, but take for granted.

The story of the automobile began in 1885 when a young German engineer called Karl Benz

Below: The 'T-Ford' was the car that got America motoring, and is regarded as the automobile that brought motoring to the masses. Over 15 million were sold in total.

demonstrated the first 'horseless carriage' to be powered by an internal combustion engine. Its propulsion, which ignited gasoline by means of a spark, and forced air and fuel to mix in its combustion chamber, was quickly proven to not only be much cheaper than steam power, but also much more reliable.

Five years later, America's automobile industry was born. Charles Duryea of Massachussetts, pioneered the USA's first internal combustion chamber and went on to sell his devices to wealthy landowners, who had the means to enjoy his creation to the full.

While Duryea might have been credited with creating the first self-propelled American automobile, though, it would be another 16 years before the country's car industry really took off.

Henry Ford

Henry Ford, the son of an Irish potato farmer who had migrated to Michigan in the 1860s to teach agriculture in the Northern States, had long been fascinated with how things were made. He designed and built his own machinery to use on his father's farm, and by 1903 had built his very first car. The two-seat racer was crude and unrefined, and Ford had to demolish the wall of the barn he'd built it in to get it out, but little did commentators of the time know that young Henry was about to turn America's fledgling automobile industry on its head.

At a trade fair in 1906, Henry showed his plans for a production line system, where cars could be built in bulk rather than one at a time. "I will build a car for the multitudes," he told prospectors, and as a

Above: Not all cars were for all people, and the Auburn Speedster was very much a model for the higher echelons of society. It wooed Hollywood film stars and gangsters, until the Great Depression eroded demand for luxury cars.

result achieved financial backing from a group of local businessmen. Later that year, the Ford Motor Company was founded and within two years the Model T was put into production. Within five years, a car took just one and a half hours to build, compared to a week for models built before the turn of the century, and by keeping costs to a minimum (offering 'any colour as long as it's black') and ordering parts from external suppliers that could be stockpiled and used along the line, Ford achieved his dream of offering a car for under $100.

The auto industry owes a lot to his mould-breaking idea. His brainwave single-handedly led to massive industrial growth across the North-East states, with huge steel mills and parts factories springing up across his home city of Detroit.

Above: Chevrolet had the Corvette, and Ford had the T-Bird. The iconic American sports car debuted in 1955, and the name continues to this day.

Because of the wide availability of steel and components, Detroit became a magnet for the country's automakers, and within a decade it became known as the Motor City, or 'Motown'.

Sprawling city

Joining Ford in what became the global hub of the Auto Industry were General Motors (GM), Dodge, Chrysler, Plymouth, DeSoto and Studebaker to name but a handful. Today, a century after Henry Ford planted that first seed, Detroit remains the administrative and manufacturing headquarters for three of the biggest automakers in the world, and while

economic changes, a growth in imported vehicles and market forces dictate that it isn't the industrial powerhouse it once was, the sprawling city is still a spectacular sight for any enthusiast with gasoline running through his veins.

As in all industry, competition was rife, and only the strongest would survive, and following the great depression of the 1930s carmakers had been forced to pull together to weather the storm. The smaller makers were swallowed up by the larger ones, and by the end of that decade the American industry consisted of just three primary manufacturers – Ford, GM and Chrysler.

Ford's corporation included marques such as Mercury and Lincoln, GM owned Chevrolet, Cadillac, Buick, Oldsmobile and Pontiac, while Chrysler incorporated Dodge, Plymouth and Willys.

Others, such as Duesenberg, Cord and Auburn made their money from wealthy customers, and as demand dropped from the top end of the market they folded, never to be seen again. A crying shame, for among them were some of the true innovators of the automobile world, and while they may no longer be with us, their contributions still are. Cord, for example, was the first manufacturer to offer front-wheel-drive and pop-up headlights, both of which are in common use today.

The great world war of 1939–45 in Europe also hit the car industry hard, as all of America's big three had manufacturing facilities in Great Britain. When the conflict ended, so did Ford's monopoly of the car market. GM became the biggest carmaker in the world – a position it retains today, with manufacturing plants now located in over 200 countries and a global model range incorporating some 600-plus vehicles.

By the 1950s, though, America was entering an era of newfound prosperity, and the car industry entered something of a golden era. Fins, chrome and a brand new car for each model year were the order of the day, while newly-liberated young adults discovered rock 'n' roll and drive-in movie houses, both of which influenced the style of the era.

New innovations

Sports cars, such as the Chevy Corvette and Ford Thunderbird, made their debuts on American soil, while in other areas of the market it was more about elegant style and panache. Cars such as the Chevy Bel Air, Cadillac Eldorado, Ford Skyliner and Oldsmobile Starfire wowed the masses with their

Below: The muscle car era saw family sedans modified into thundering hot rods. The Dodge Charger has a 428ci V8 engine and found fame in the TV series The Dukes of Hazzard.

Above: Ford's Mustang was an instant success, selling over four million between 1966 and 1971. The Boss 429 model seen here is the ultimate performance incarnation.

Right: The Chevrolet Corvette was the first car to use a glassfibre monocoque in its construction, meaning it wouldn't rust. This style of Corvette dates from the late 1970s.

new innovations. Power-assisted steering, power roofs, in-car entertainment centres, electric windows and air brakes were suddenly commonplace.

By the Sixties, the glitz and glamour were replaced by brute force, as the Ford Mustang ushered in the era of the muscle car.

Ford's newcomer was a little piece of history repeating itself, as, like the iconic Model T, it soon established itself as the best selling car in the world, available in all shapes and sizes from an economy-based six-cylinder notchback to a growling V8 Shelby-powered coupe.

The power and performance ethic promoted by the Mustang quickly followed through to the rest of America's big three, and in 1966 Pontiac unveiled the GTO. Based on the stock Tempest sedan or

convertible, the 'Goat' was incredible. Powered by a 440ci engine, it offered power to match a modern supercar in the body of a 1960s stock sedan. Others soon followed, including such legendary names as the Oldsmobile 4-4-2, Plymouth Roadrunner and Dodge Charger, to name but a few.

Sadly, the Muscle Car era was short-lived, but not before its culture had ingratiated itself on a whole generation of American auto enthusiasts. By the 1970s, the impact of the Vietnam War and the Gulf Oil Crisis meant economy models were growing ever more important, and American makers struggled to fend off the tide of inexpensive, four-cylinder imports from European and Japanese manufacturers that were starting to creep into the sales charts. Restrictive emissions and safety legislation also caused designers headaches, and led to a period where performance and style were drained out of much of Detroit's car manufacturing. It was a bleak period, but there was the odd highlight, with cars such as the AMC AMX and Ford Boss Mustang proving that enthusiasts were still at work.

What the period did see, though, were massive advances in environmental and safety technology that now make today's cars safer than ever, with crumple zones, multiple airbags, anti-skid braking systems and ever-more stringent crash testing.

Environmentally conscious

Today, diversity is back in the market, and more recent designs such as the Saturn Sky, Chrysler Crossfire and 2005 Pontiac GTO show that the spirit that made America's cars great is once again on the agenda. The Sports Utility vehicle, such as the Chevy Suburban or Ford Explorer, is still a huge phenomenon in American motoring, but today's buyers are becoming ever more environmentally conscious and automakers are still leading the field in technological development, with both GM and

Ford committed to developing hydrogen power systems and dual-fuel hybrid cars that are not only environmentally aware, but are also as bold and innovative as those models that were around in the very early days of motoring.

This book aims to take you as closely as possible to over a century of American motoring history. It isn't simply a history of the automobile, but a detailed analysis of over 75 of America's most significant models, with stunning plan photography, real-life testers' notes and comprehensive technical specifications that put you as close as possible to the driving seats of the most famous cars ever to come out of Detroit, be them icons such as the Corvette, GTO and Mustang, or failures such as the Edsel Citation and Tucker Torpedo.

Above all, this work celebrates the automobile and its role in American life. From the first seedlings sowed by Charles Duryea to the birth of mass production courtesy of Henry Ford, right up to the present day, our aim is to show that despite the pressures the car industry faces on a daily basis, America's automakers still have a lot to be proud of!

AC **COBRA**

When Texan racing driver Carroll Shelby wanted a real performance sports car, he put a Ford V8 into AC's Ace chassis and produced a legend—the mighty Cobra. Engines grew, power outputs soared and the Cobra reached supercar status.

"...oozing raw power."

"Turn the key and the huge V8 rumbles into life, shaking the car and oozing raw power. The driving position and seats are comfortable, which is just as well because you'll be working hard. The Cobra is almost all engine and the chassis had to be strengthened to take the 7-liter V8. Despite the wider tires of the 427, there's still a huge surplus of power over grip. Power oversteer is available whenever you want it. When 100 mph can come up in 10 seconds it's hard to breathe."

Hang on tight! Hair raising performance is what the Cobra is all about. The interior is comfortable, but very windy at 150 mph.

Milestones

1962 Carroll Shelby installs a 260-cubic inch Ford V8 into an AC Ace chassis to create the first Cobra, shown at the New York Motor Show, and production begins.

Cobra was based on the AC Ace.

1963 The original 260 V8 engine is replaced with 289 V8 that makes 271 bhp.

1964 Shelby builds the Daytona coupe and a prototype 427 Cobra. Having outgrown the Venice facility building Cobras, Shelby Mustangs and Sunbeam Tigers, Shelby American moves to the Los Angeles airport.

Massive performance made the Cobra a natural for racing.

1965 The Daytona Cobras win the World Sports Car Championship ahead of Ferrari. This is the first championship of its kind won by an American car. The 427 Cobra goes into production.

1966 Shelby American liquidates its Cobra inventory at its famous 'fire sale' and closes its doors in February.

UNDER THE SKIN

Beef it up

To take the bigger engine and its massive power output, the two main longitudinal chassis tubes were replaced by larger diameter, thicker section tube. Suspension pick-up points were strengthened. Original 260 and 289 Cobras retain the Ace's leaf-sprung rear end, but the MkII versions gained more sophisticated coil-sprung suspension which improved handling.

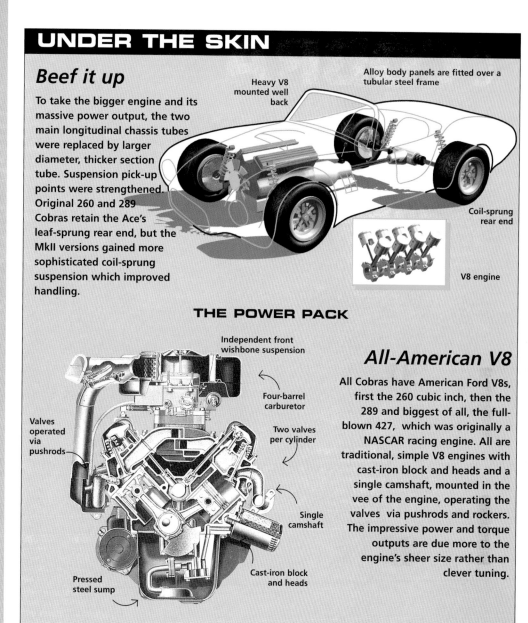

Heavy V8 mounted well back

Alloy body panels are fitted over a tubular steel frame

Coil-sprung rear end

V8 engine

THE POWER PACK

Independent front wishbone suspension

Four-barrel carburetor

Two valves per cylinder

Valves operated via pushrods

Single camshaft

Pressed steel sump

Cast-iron block and heads

All-American V8

All Cobras have American Ford V8s, first the 260 cubic inch, then the 289 and biggest of all, the full-blown 427, which was originally a NASCAR racing engine. All are traditional, simple V8 engines with cast-iron block and heads and a single camshaft, mounted in the vee of the engine, operating the valves via pushrods and rockers. The impressive power and torque outputs are due more to the engine's sheer size rather than clever tuning.

Baby Cobra

It's not as powerful as the 427 and it uses the leaf-spring chassis, but the early Cobra 289, built from 1963 is capable of 138 mph and 0-60 mph in 5.7 seconds. Because the body is so light, the little car had no problem getting the power to the ground.

Not as powerful as the 427, the 289 still has enough performance to thrill.

AC **COBRA** 🇺🇸

Brash and completely over the top, the 427 looks like a caricature of a sports car. Thanks to Shelby American and Ford's massive American V8 engines, the Ace finally has an edge to be competitive in road racing.

Flared wheel arches

To cover the much larger wheels and tires of the 427 model, the wheel arches are drastically flared rather than the whole body being redesigned.

427-cubic inch big block V8

The 427 engine is 97 lbs. heavier than the 289 but much more powerful. Its this engine that gave the Cobra its legendary status.

Side exhausts

Side exhausts make the 427 look even more muscular. They are a feature of the 427 S/C (Street/Competition) models, which are basically racing models sold as road cars.

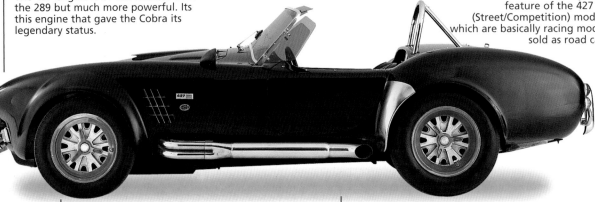

Halibrand alloy wheels

These wheels were very popular in the U.S. where the Ace was transformed into the Cobra. Although the original Cobras run on wire wheels, they cannot handle the power of Ford's potent 427 engine.

Tubular steel chassis

The Cobra's chassis features two main tubular steel chassis members connected by cross braces.

Quick-release fuel filler

Practical as well as stylish, the big alloy fuel filler cap can be opened in a split second for refueling during a race.

Roll-over hoop

This 427 has a roll-over hoop to protect the driver in the event of an accident, but standard Cobras do without it.

Wide track

When the Ace first appeared it was a small and quite narrow car, but the track was widened for the Cobra conversion to fit its massive wheels and tires.

Alloy bodywork

To be as light as possible, all Cobra bodies are made of alloy, and were hand-built at AC's Thames Ditton factory.

Coil spring suspension

The leaf-spring chassis of the original Cobra was updated for the 427 model and more modern coil-spring suspension is installed at the front and rear.

Specifications
1965 AC Cobra 427

ENGINE
Type: V8
Construction: Cast-iron block and heads
Valve gear: Two valves per cylinder operated by single block-mounted camshafts via pushrods and rockers
Bore and stroke: 4.24 in. x 3.78 in.
Displacement: 427 c.i.
Compression ratio: 10.5:1
Induction system: Holley 750 CFM four-barrel carburetor
Maximum power: 425 bhp at 6,000 rpm
Maximum torque: 480 lb-ft at 3,700 rpm

TRANSMISSION
Borg-Warner four-speed manual

BODY/CHASSIS
Tubular steel ladder frame with cross braces and alloy two-door, two-seat convertible

SPECIAL FEATURES

Large chrome side grill vents hot air from the 427's crowded engine compartment.

Quick-release fuel filler cap was a style as well as practical feature.

RUNNING GEAR
Steering: Rack-and-pinion
Front suspension: Double wishbones with coil springs and telescopic shocks
Rear suspension: Double wishbones with coil springs and telescopic shocks
Brakes: Discs, 11.6 in. dia. (front), 10.8 in. dia. (rear)
Wheels: Alloy 15 in. x 7.5 in.
Tires: 7.3 in. x 15 in. (front), 7.7 in. x 15 in. (rear)

DIMENSIONS
Length: 156 in.   **Width:** 68 in.
Height: 49 in.
Wheelbase: 90 in.
Track: 156 in. (front), 56 in. (rear)
Weight: 2,530 lbs.

AMC **AMX**

American Motors struggled to establish the sort of market identity that the other manufacturers had gained. Its 'character' car, possibly aimed at the Chevrolet Corvette, was the curious AMX two-seat coupe.

"...serious performance."

"Turn the V8's starter motor and your senses awaken—this really sounds like a muscle machine. The deep reserves of torque make driving very easy, and there is plenty of power for fast takeoffs. Add in the optional quick-rack power steering, front disc brakes and limited-slip differential and you have a serious performance machine that is just as capable of tackling twisty mountain roads as taking part in a traffic light drag race."

The dashboard is trimmed with wood grain trim which was very stylish in the late 1960s.

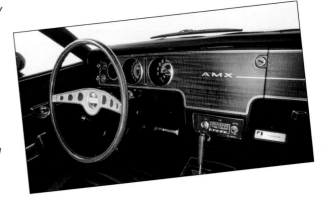

Milestones

1968 Mid-season, AMC launches its new compact sports coupe with a choice of three V8 engines.

Another of AMC's compact muscle cars of the period was the Hurst SC Rambler.

1969 This year the AMX remains very much as the previous year.

1970 A mild restyle includes moving the spotlights to the front grill and adding a prominent hump to the hood. The standard engine expands to 390 cubic inches and power outputs rise. This is the last year of AMX sales.

Due to its design, many thought the AMX was supposed to compete with the Corvette.

1971 The AMX name is reduced to an option package on a larger and curvier Javelin. After 1973 it is more show than go.

UNDER THE SKIN

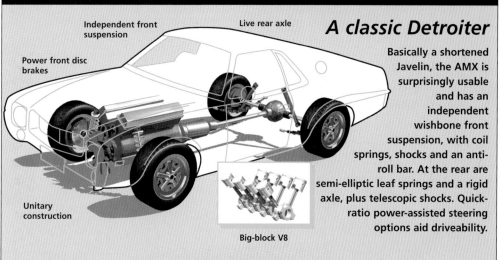

Independent front suspension

Power front disc brakes

Unitary construction

Live rear axle

Big-block V8

A classic Detroiter

Basically a shortened Javelin, the AMX is surprisingly usable and has an independent wishbone front suspension, with coil springs, shocks and an anti-roll bar. At the rear are semi-elliptic leaf springs and a rigid axle, plus telescopic shocks. Quick-ratio power-assisted steering options aid driveability.

THE POWER PACK

Muscle car V8

The standard engine in the AMX is a 225-bhp, 290-cubic inch V8, although larger 343 and 390-V8s were optional. The 390 has a forged steel crankshaft and connecting rods, and a Carter AFB four-barrel carburetor. Its 315 bhp power output is more than adequate and the 425 lb-ft of torque gives it pulling power which modern cars can only dream of. Though very underrated, this two-seat machine is one of the most potent cars to ever have seen action on American pavement.

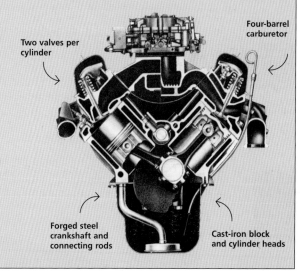

Two valves per cylinder

Four-barrel carburetor

Forged steel crankshaft and connecting rods

Cast-iron block and cylinder heads

Super rare

Few changes occurred in 1969, but the 1970 AMX received a new grill with air vents, plus an improved interior, revised graphics and optional 15-inch wheels. Just 4,116 of the 1970 model were built, making it the rarest and most desirable of all AMXs.

The 1970 AMC AMX muscle cars are the most sought-after by collectors.

AMC **AMX**

By shortening the Javelin, AMC produced a cheap all-American two-seater sports coupe. Just 19,134 AMXs were built, making it a highly desirable muscle car today.

Bulging hood

A popular and sporty option on the AMX was the performance hood complete with dual air scoops. In 1968 the hood bulge was only decorative, but in 1970 the 'Go' package included a fully functional ram air system.

Sporty rear styling

The rear end is styled to give the car a smooth side profile but a ridged-out appearance from behind.

Chrome sills

With AMC's move toward flashier styling, the AMX featured chrome-plated sill covers. Later, these sills gained mock vents, mimicking a side-mounted exhaust.

Short wheelbase

Riding on a 97-inch wheelbase, the AMX is 12 inches shorter than the Javelin. This is even shorter than the Corvette, and qualified the AMX as one of the most compact American cars on the market at the time.

Two-seat interior

Shortening the bodyshell of the 2+2 Javelin means the AMX has room for just two passengers sitting on bucket seats, although there is a large space behind the seats for extra luggage.

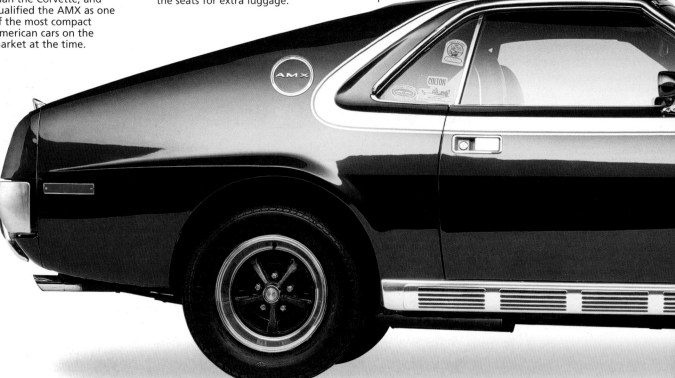

Racing paintwork

The typical paint scheme for the AMX in its first two years was twin racing stripes running down the center. Late 1970 models lose the hood stripes but have side stripes instead.

V8 power

Emphasizing its sporty role, the AMX was only ever sold with V8 engines. It was the only AMC at the time not to be offered with a straight-six engine as standard.

Specifications

1968 AMC AMX

ENGINE

Type: V8

Construction: Cast-iron block and cylinder heads

Valve gear: Two valves per cylinder operated by a single camshaft, pushrods and rockers

Bore and stroke: 4.16 in. x 3.57 in.

Displacement: 390 c.i.

Compression ratio: 10.2:1

Induction system: Single four-barrel carburetor

Maximum power: 315 bhp at 4,600 rpm

Maximum torque: 425 lb-ft at 3,200 rpm

TRANSMISSION

Three-speed automatic or four-speed manual

BODY/CHASSIS

Integral with two-door steel coupe body

SPECIAL FEATURES

AMX meant something special after AMC showed a stunning mid-engined sports car with the AMX badge.

The 390-cubic inch V8 was AMC's biggest engine in the late 1960s.

RUNNING GEAR

Steering: Recirculating ball

Front suspension: Wishbones with coil springs and shocks

Rear suspension: Rigid axle with leaf springs and shocks

Brakes: Drums (front and rear)

Wheels: Steel, 14-in. dia.

Tires: E70 x 14 in.

DIMENSIONS

Length: 177 in.   **Width:** 71.5 in.

Height: 51.7 in.   **Wheelbase:** 97 in.

Track: 58.8 in. (front), 57 in. (rear)

Weight: 3,400 lbs.

AMC REBEL MACHINE

After the overachieving little SC/Rambler of 1969, AMC returned to the muscle car market with the Rebel Machine. It still sported loud graphics, but thanks to a 390-cubic inch, 340-bhp V8, it was more than capable of outshining the competition and backing up its flashy appearance.

THE MACHINE

"...built to be a performer."

"It may have a horizontal-sweep speedometer, but a four-on-the-floor and bucket seats assure you that this car was built to be a performer. The 390-cubic inch V8 is a lot more tractable than some others in everyday driving, and although throttle control is required to really get the Machine moving, the end result is worth it. Through corners, the AMC feels quite nimble for its size, with much less understeer than you would expect."

A four-speed transmission with a cue-ball shifter is nestled between the front seats.

Milestones

1968 American Motors releases

photographs of a menacing mid-size Rebel. It has semi-gloss dark paint with matching bumpers and wheels. Called the Machine, it is intended for production in 1969, but none are actually sold.

The SC/Rambler was American Motors' first serious muscle car.

1969 With help

from Hurst Performance, AMC stuffs its biggest engine in the compact Rogue, resulting in the Hurst SC/Rambler. Packing 315 bhp and capable of 14.3-second quarter miles, 1,512 of these patriotic-looking cars are built.

The two-seater AMX could also get the big 390-c.i. V8.

1970 Replacing the

SC/Rambler is a new, larger Rebel Machine. Packing 340 bhp from a 390 V8, it is a potent performer too, but lasts for only one model year.

UNDER THE SKIN

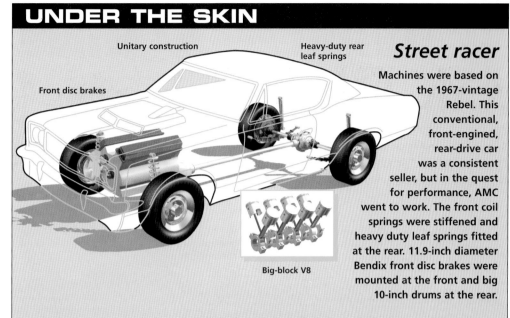

Unitary construction

Heavy-duty rear leaf springs

Front disc brakes

Big-block V8

Street racer

Machines were based on the 1967-vintage Rebel. This conventional, front-engined, rear-drive car was a consistent seller, but in the quest for performance, AMC went to work. The front coil springs were stiffened and heavy duty leaf springs fitted at the rear. 11.9-inch diameter Bendix front disc brakes were mounted at the front and big 10-inch drums at the rear.

THE POWER PACK

AMC's biggest

In order to compete with the big three, American Motors realized that the best way was to stuff its largest engine in a mid size car. The 390-cubic inch mill that powered all Machines is an enlarged version of the 343 unit. It followed customary practice with a cast-iron block and heads, plus two valves per cylinder. Where the 343 has cast-iron rods and crankshaft, the 390 has forged-steel items and larger bearings. The 390 is a moderate performer, producing its 340 bhp at 5,100 rpm.

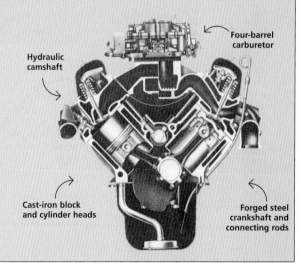

Four-barrel carburetor

Hydraulic camshaft

Cast-iron block and cylinder heads

Forged steel crankshaft and connecting rods

Patriotic

Rebel Machines were offered for only one year, and with a production total of 2,326 are not exactly common. The first 1,000 cars built had a special white, blue and red color scheme, making them particularly sought-after in AMC circles.

Later Machines could be ordered in any Rebel factory color.

AMC REBEL MACHINE

Although AMC stated 'The Machine is not that fast,' the car could give many muscle cars from the big three a run for their money, particularly with an experienced driver behind the wheel.

King of the cubes

In 1970, the 390-cubic inch V8 was the biggest engine offered by American Motors. With a big four-barrel carburetor and functional hood scoop, it produces a credible 340 bhp and 430 lb-ft of torque, good enough for mid-14-second ¼-mile ETs.

Strong transmission

Like the AMX and Javelin, the Machine was offered with a Borg-Warner T-10 four-speed manual transmission and a Hurst shifter. This enabled lightning-quick getaways from the lights.

Twin-Grip

Transmitting power to the rear tires is a Twin-Grip differential with standard 3.54:1 final drive. Steeper gearing was offered over the counter—up to an incredible 5.00:1 for hardcore drag-racer types.

Power steering

Manual steering was standard, but many buyers considered it too heavy and thus ordered the optional power setup. It was, however, boosted and contemporary road testers wrote that it was 'grossly over-assisted.'

Stiff suspension

Rebel Machines rode on some of the stiffest suspension from Detroit. Fitting the Rebel wagon's heavy-duty rear leaf springs gave a street racer stance, and although handling is good for a muscle car, the jacked-up rear results in severe wheel hop if the gas is floored from a standing start.

Hood scoop

Besides having an interesting look, the vacuum-operated hood scoop is functional too, forcing cooler, denser air into the engine. The scoop assembly also contains an integrated 8,000-rpm tachometer, which can be difficult to read in harsh sunlight or rain.

Specifications

1970 AMC Rebel Machine

ENGINE

Type: V8

Construction: Cast-iron block and heads

Valve gear: Two valves per cylinder operated by pushrods and rockers

Bore and stroke: 4.17 in. x 3.57 in.

Displacement: 390 c.i.

Compression ratio: 10.0:1

Induction system: Four-barrel carburetor

Maximum power: 340 bhp at 5,100 rpm

Maximum torque: 430 lb-ft at 3,600 rpm

TRANSMISSION

Borg-Warner T-10 four-speed manual

BODY/CHASSIS

Steel unitary chassis with two-door coupe body

SPECIAL FEATURES

In 1970, the 390 was the largest engine in AMC's inventory.

The functional hood scoop houses an integrated tachometer.

RUNNING GEAR

Steering: Recirculating ball

Front suspension: Unequal-length A-arms with coil springs, telescopic shock absorbers and stabilizer bar

Rear suspension: Live axle with semi-elliptic leaf-springs, telescopic shock absorbers and stabilizer bar

Brakes: Discs front, drums rear

Wheels: 7 x 15 in. pressed steel

Tires: Goodyear Polyglas E60-15

DIMENSIONS

Length: 199.0 in. **Width:** 77.2 in.

Height: 56.2 in. **Wheelbase:** 114.0 in.

Track: 59.7 in. (front), 60.0 in. (rear)

Weight: 3,650 lbs.

Auburn **SPEEDSTER**

Auburn's 851 Speedster was the sleekest car on American roads in the 1930s. It followed the lead of the big Mercedes SSK of the 1920s with its supercharged engine, and its eight cylinders were enough to give a guaranteed top speed of more than 100 mph.

"The faster the better."

"That was the opinion of road testers in 1935. In America that year there was nothing to touch the Auburn Speedster for the price. The supercharged 280-cubic inch eight-cylinder engine gives lots of smooth power, and thanks to the two-speed axle and three-speed transmission, the driver has six gears to play with. The hydraulic brakes are man enough to haul the heavy car down, and the handling is impressive for its day. Because of its low-geared steering and excessive body roll, the car shows its age around tight corners."

The Auburn Speedster offered a high level of comfort as well as serious art-deco fittings.

Milestones

1928 First Auburn 'boat tail' Speedster is
introduced. It has a similar tiny swept-back windshield, but an upright grill and open fenders. Most powerful is the eight-cylinder, 125-bhp 8-125, produced in 1930.

This 1929 Model 115 evolved into the 120 and the 125.

1932 By adding a 160-bhp Lycoming V12 to
the speedster chassis, Auburn creates the similarly styled 12-160 Speedster. Top speed is 117 mph but it is not a success and is dropped for 1934.

1935 The Speedster 851 is introduced.
Restyled by new designer, Gordon Buehrig, it uses a 150-bhp supercharged version of the Lycoming straight-eight engine.

Auburn's dynamic president, Errett Lobban Cord, arrived at Auburn in 1924.

1936 Name changes to 852 from 851. Sales are
slow and production ends. The total number of 851/852 Speedsters built is just over 500.

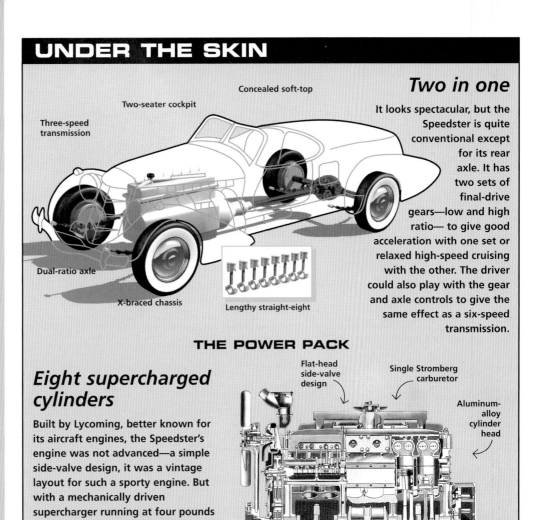

Concealed soft-top

Two-seater cockpit

Three-speed transmission

Dual-ratio axle

X-braced chassis

Lengthy straight-eight

Two in one

It looks spectacular, but the Speedster is quite conventional except for its rear axle. It has two sets of final-drive gears—low and high ratio— to give good acceleration with one set or relaxed high-speed cruising with the other. The driver could also play with the gear and axle controls to give the same effect as a six-speed transmission.

THE POWER PACK

Eight supercharged cylinders

Built by Lycoming, better known for its aircraft engines, the Speedster's engine was not advanced—a simple side-valve design, it was a vintage layout for such a sporty engine. But with a mechanically driven supercharger running at four pounds of boost, the straight-eight engine gives a good deal of low-end torque. Although the centrifugal supercharger runs at six times crankshaft speed, the limited amount of boost means the engine is hardly over-stressed.

Flat-head side-valve design

Single Stromberg carburetor

Aluminum-alloy cylinder head

2.4 gallon oil pan

Five bearing crankshaft

Auburn record

In 1935, the classy Auburn Speedster became the first American production car to exceed 100 mph for more than 12 hours, averaging 102.9 mph. It was driven by racing driver Ab Jenkins. He also set a new record in the flying mile with a top speed of 104.17 mph.

Using a centrifugal supercharger, the Speedster really lives up to its name.

Auburn SPEEDSTER

Auburn's famous designer Gordon Buehrig wanted the Speedster to appear to be the fastest car on the road. He succeeded, using features like the low V windshield, sloping grill and flowing wing-line to give a streamlined look to the car.

Teardrop headlights

The Auburn's styling is supposed to suggest speed. The streamlined lights, with bulging convex lenses, help achieve this impression.

Supercharged engine

The Auburn's mechanically driven supercharger runs at six times engine-speed and helps the Lycoming engine generate 150 bhp—35 bhp more than without the supercharger.

Top cover

The Auburn's top folds away neatly under this rigid cover to maintain the car's sleek lines.

Flexible exhaust headers

Each of the four flexible exhaust headers serve two cylinders. The conventional rigid pipes are hidden under the flexible tubes.

Dual-ratio rear axle

The driver could switch from a low- to a high- axle ratio, and with a three-speed transmission that gave six gears overall. In high-ratio top gear, the Speedster's engine rotated at only 2,250 rpm at 60 mph.

Winged mascots

Each of the side 'flying lady' mascots was made by slicing the radiator mascot in two.

Luggage hatch

A carriage key opens this hatch. The compartment is just large enough to take a set of golf clubs, a feature much appreciated by the typical playboy Speedster owner.

Hydraulic lever-arm shocks

Before telescopic shocks were introduced, cars like the Auburn used hydraulic lever arms to replace the previous friction shocks.

Drum brakes

All the cars in the 1930s had drum brakes, but the Auburn's hydraulically-operated drums were more modern than most.

Boat-tail design

From above, the description is obvious. The style was popular in the 1920s and '30s and here it is mirrored in in its rearend styling.

Specifications
1935 Auburn Speedster 851

ENGINE

Type: In-line eight
Construction: Cast-iron block and light alloy cylinder head
Valve gear: Side-valve with two valves per cylinder and single block-mounted camshaft
Bore and stroke: 3.06 in. x 4.75 in.
Displacement: 280 c.i.
Compression ratio: 6.5:1
Induction system: Single downdraft Stromberg carburetor with Schwitzer-Cummins supercharger
Maximum power: 150 bhp at 4,000 rpm
Top speed: 108 mph
0–50 mph: 10.0 sec.

TRANSMISSION

Three-speed manual with dual-ratio rear axle

BODY/CHASSIS

Steel two-door, two-seat speedster body with steel box-section ladder-type chassis rails

SPECIAL FEATURES

Each Speedster has a signed plaque guaranteeing it has been tested to more than 100 mph.

Mechanically-driven supercharger is used to boost power.

RUNNING GEAR

Steering: Worm-and-peg
Front suspension: Solid axle with semi-elliptic leaf springs and Delco hydraulic shock absorbers
Rear suspension: Live axle with semi-elliptic leaf springs and Delco hydraulic shock absorbers
Brakes: Four-wheel Lockheed drums, hydraulically operated with Bendix vacuum booster
Wheels: Pressed steel or wire spoke, 6.5 in. x 15 in.
Tires: Crossply 6.5 in. x 16 in.

DIMENSIONS

Length: 194.4 in.   **Width:** 71.5 in.
Height: 56.5 in.   **Wheelbase:** 127 in.
Track: 59 in. (front), 62 in. (rear)
Weight: 3,753 lbs.

Buick GSX

If the 1970 mid-size GS™ 455 wasn't wild enough, Buick raised the muscle car ante with the fearsome GSX. It had all the power of the regular GS 455, but included a better suspension and wild appearance package. When ordered with the optional 455 Stage I engine the GSX became lethal.

"...the Velvet Hammer."

"Unlike most other muscle cars of the era, Buick's GSX offered creature comforts that were mostly associated with luxury cars. Included in the package was a brutal 455 V8. The GSX combined luxury with high performance, earning it the nickname the 'Velvet Hammer.' With more than 510 lb-ft of torque, its low-end power was nothing short of insanity. Thanks to its heavy duty suspension and 15-inch wheels, the GSX handled great for such a heavy car."

Although one of the quickest muscle cars built, the GSX is definitely not a stripped-out racer.

Milestones

1970 Buick unveils

a restyled Skylark™. The Gran Sport (GS) model receives a 455-V8. The GSX option package also appears but the cars are only available painted in Apollo White or Saturn Yellow. Production for the model year is just 687 units.

Although overshadowed by the GSX, regular GS models continued into 1972.

1971 The GS and the GSX option continue.

A wider assortment of colors is now available. GM drops the compression ratio in the 455 engines down to 8.5:1 to meet stricter emission standards. The regular 455 now makes 315 bhp while the Stage 1 engine makes 345 bhp.

When Buick launched the GN™ in the 1980s, it made one of the fastest late model street cars.

1972 The GS reverts

to an option package on the Skylark models. The GSX package is still available, but only 44 cars are ordered. The Stage 1 455 only makes 270 bhp.

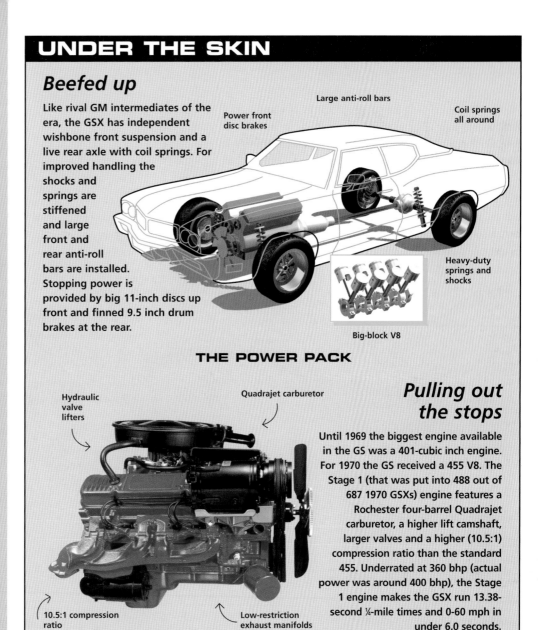

UNDER THE SKIN

Beefed up

Like rival GM intermediates of the era, the GSX has independent wishbone front suspension and a live rear axle with coil springs. For improved handling the shocks and springs are stiffened and large front and rear anti-roll bars are installed. Stopping power is provided by big 11-inch discs up front and finned 9.5 inch drum brakes at the rear.

Large anti-roll bars

Power front disc brakes

Coil springs all around

Heavy-duty springs and shocks

Big-block V8

THE POWER PACK

Hydraulic valve lifters

Quadrajet carburetor

10.5:1 compression ratio

Low-restriction exhaust manifolds

Pulling out the stops

Until 1969 the biggest engine available in the GS was a 401-cubic inch engine. For 1970 the GS received a 455 V8. The Stage 1 (that was put into 488 out of 687 1970 GSXs) engine features a Rochester four-barrel Quadrajet carburetor, a higher lift camshaft, larger valves and a higher (10.5:1) compression ratio than the standard 455. Underrated at 360 bhp (actual power was around 400 bhp), the Stage 1 engine makes the GSX run 13.38-second ¼-mile times and 0-60 mph in under 6.0 seconds.

Still potent

Although the GSX was Buick's muscle flagship for 1970, regular GS models were just as powerful and could also be ordered with the 360-bhp, 455-cubic inch Stage 1 V8. Only 1,416 GS convertibles with this package were built for the 1970 model year.

Standard GS 455s may have a more subtle appearance, but they are still fast.

Buick GSX

With its loud paintwork, spoilers, scoops and graphics, plus a monstrous 455 engine, the GSX is Buick's finest muscle car and comes complete with all the trimmings.

Front disc brakes

With so much performance just a stab of the throttle away, the GSX needs powerful brakes. It uses 11-inch diameter disc brakes at the front, but made do with finned drum brakes at the rear.

Awesome power

1970 marked the introduction of 455-cubic inch engines in GM intermediates. A standard Buick GS 455 churns out 350 bhp, but the optional Stage 1 produces 360 bhp due to a more aggressive cam and a higher compression ratio.

Transmissions

Three different transmissions were available: three- or four-speed manual, or a TurboHydramatic 400 automatic transmission with a Hurst gear shifter.

Suspension upgrades

The GSX has heavy-duty suspension and powered front disc brakes, plus uprated shock absorbers and stiffer springs for better handling.

Color availability

Introduced halfway through the model year, the 1970 GSX was available in only two colors: Apollo White or Saturn Yellow.

Chrome wheels

The GSX package included a handsome set of 7-in wide Magnum 500 chrome-plated steel wheels and Goodyear Polyglas GT series tires.

Restyled body

Some people criticized the 1968-1969 GS for looking out of proportion. For the 1970 model year, the Skylark received an attractive facelift and full rear wheel cut-outs.

Specifications
1970 Buick GSX

ENGINE

Type: V8

Construction: Cast-iron block and heads

Valve gear: Two valves per cylinder operated by pushrods and rockers

Bore and stroke: 4.33 in. x 3.9 in.

Displacement: 455 c.i.

Compression ratio: 10.5:1

Induction system: Rochester four-barrel Quadrajet carburetor

Maximum power: 360 bhp at 4,600 rpm

Maximum torque: 510 lb-ft at 2,800 rpm

TRANSMISSION

Four-speed close-ratio manual

BODY/CHASSIS

Steel coupe body on separate chassis

SPECIAL FEATURES

A hood-mounted tachometer came standard on all GSX models.

The rear spoiler and black accent stripes are some of the GSX's styling features.

RUNNING GEAR

Steering: Power-assisted recirculating ball

Front suspension: Independent wishbones with coil springs, telescopic shocks and heavy-duty roll bar

Rear suspension: Live axle fitted with 3.64:1 axle gears, heavy-duty coil springs, telescopic shocks and anti-roll bar

Brakes: Vented discs, 11-in. dia. (front), finned drums, 9.5-in. dia. (rear)

Wheels: Magnum 500, 7 x 15 in.

Tires: Goodyear Polyglas GT G60-15

DIMENSIONS

Length: 202 in.   **Width:** 75.9 in.

Height: 53 in.   **Wheelbase:** 112 in.

Track: 60.1 in. (front), 58.9 in. (rear)

Weight: 3,561 lbs.

Buick **LIMITED**

For 1958, Buick decided bigger was better and added the lengthened Limited to the range. Along with it came advances such as air suspension and alloy brake drums. However, by 1959 Buick had discontinued it.

"...the softest of rides."

"You don't so much drive the air-suspended Limited as set sail. Be prepared for the softest of rides, as the springs cannot keep up with the motion of the very long body on its comparatively short wheelbase. Sharp corners have the Buick heeling hard over, although it sticks adequately. The good news is the more effective braking from the alloy drums, which helps make up for the lack of response from the Flight-Pitch Dynaflow three-speed automatic."

The large cabin of the Limited glistens thanks to copious amounts of chrome.

Milestones

1957 Buick introduces a new X-braced chassis with deep side rails available with either a 122- or 127.5-inch wheelbase.

The 1958 Roadmaster was priced below the Limited.

1958 The longer-wheelbase chassis is chosen as the basis for the new Limited model, which revives an old Buick nameplate. It comes with the new Flight-Pitch automatic transmission as standard and optional air springs. It is built in three body-styles: two- and four-door hardtop, or two-door convertible.

In later years, the Limited became a trim option on a wide variety of Buicks like this 1983 Century.

1959 The Limited does not prove a success (with just 7,436 sold) and is discontinued for the 1959 model year. The Limited name reappears as a trim option on up-market Buicks in the mid-1970s.

UNDER THE SKIN

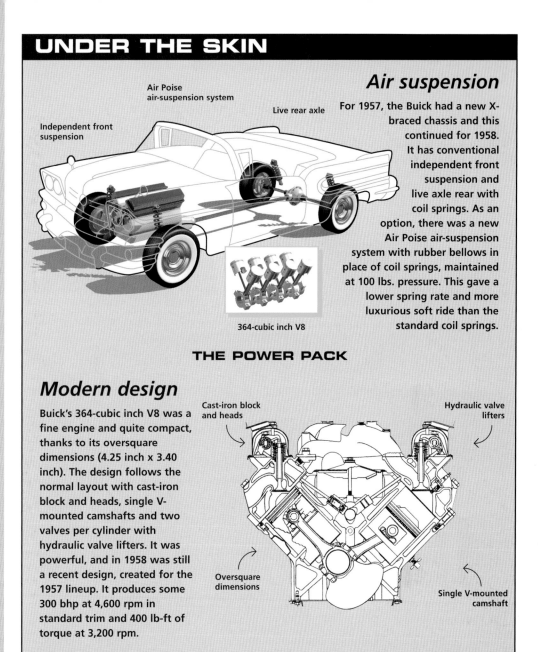

Air Poise air-suspension system

Live rear axle

Independent front suspension

364-cubic inch V8

Air suspension

For 1957, the Buick had a new X-braced chassis and this continued for 1958. It has conventional independent front suspension and live axle rear with coil springs. As an option, there was a new Air Poise air-suspension system with rubber bellows in place of coil springs, maintained at 100 lbs. pressure. This gave a lower spring rate and more luxurious soft ride than the standard coil springs.

THE POWER PACK

Modern design

Buick's 364-cubic inch V8 was a fine engine and quite compact, thanks to its oversquare dimensions (4.25 inch x 3.40 inch). The design follows the normal layout with cast-iron block and heads, single V-mounted camshafts and two valves per cylinder with hydraulic valve lifters. It was powerful, and in 1958 was still a recent design, created for the 1957 lineup. It produces some 300 bhp at 4,600 rpm in standard trim and 400 lb-ft of torque at 3,200 rpm.

Cast-iron block and heads

Hydraulic valve lifters

Oversquare dimensions

Single V-mounted camshaft

Collectible

The Limited to choose is the convertible, with its power top and leather upholstery. It is very rare, with only 839 made. This accounts for its high price in the collector-car market where they can cost $40,000. The four-door hardtop will cost you about $20,000.

Rarest of all Limiteds is the two-door convertible.

Buick LIMITED

The attraction of the Limited is its sheer scale, extravagant length and excessive chrome, but it was already as doomed as the dinosaurs when it came out, destined to be replaced by Buick's superbly styled 1959 range.

Alloy front brakes

One real advance for 1958 were the new front brakes. They are very large finned alloy castings, with a vented iron insert on which the larger-than-usual brake shoes rub. They performed exceptionally in brake-fade tests. The rear has conventional drums.

V8 engine

For the heavyweight Limited models, Buick used the 364-cubic inch V8 in its most advanced state of tune, which consists of a higher, 10.0:1 compression ratio (instead of 9.5:1) and a Carter or Rochester four-barrel carburetor. This increased power to 300 bhp at a slightly higher 4,600 rpm, with an excellent torque output of 400 lb-ft.

Flight-Pitch Dynaflow

New for 1958 was a revised form of Buick's Dynaflow automatic transmission. This has three rather than two turbines inside, with variable pitch, and was designed to give a smoother transition across the range of gears. It also features a 'G' (grade-retarding) gear for use when going down steep hills.

Huge rear overhang

The Limited is really an example of size just for the sake of it. The extra length, compared with even the standard big Buicks like the Roadmaster™, is all in the tail, with a rear overhang of more than 60 inches. Despite this great length, rear legroom is still very poor.

Variable ride height

One feature of the air suspension is that it can be used to raise the car's ride height by 5 inches. A manual override knob on the dash activates a compressor, which inflates the springs.

Bigger radiator

Because the V8 had to work hard hauling huge cars like the Limited around, in 1958 the radiator was made wider by 3 inches. There was another change to the cooling system: fan speed became independent of the engine's speed.

Specifications

1958 Buick Limited

ENGINE
Type: V8

Construction: Cast-iron block and heads

Valve gear: Two valves per cylinder operated by a single V-mounted camshaft with pushrods, rocker arms and hydraulic lifters

Bore and stroke: 4.25 in. x 3.40 in.

Displacement: 364 c.i.

Compression ratio: 10.0:1

Induction system: Single Carter or Rochester four-barrel carburetor

Maximum power: 300 bhp at 4,600 rpm

Maximum torque: 400 lb-ft at 3,200 rpm

TRANSMISSION
Three-speed automatic Flight-Pitch Dynaflow

BODY/CHASSIS
Separate steel X-braced chassis frame with steel two-door hardtop body

SPECIAL FEATURES

The Limited's gas cap is tucked away under the rear bumper.

These angled rear taillights set the Limited apart from the other Buicks.

RUNNING GEAR
Steering: Recirculating-ball

Front suspension: Unequal length A-arms with coil springs, telescopic shock absorbers and anti-roll bar

Rear suspension: Live axle with coil springs, trailing arms, Panhard rod and telescopic shock absorbers

Brakes: Alloy-cased drums (front), drums (rear)

Wheels: Stamped steel disc, 15-in. dia.

Tires: 8.00 x 15

DIMENSIONS
Length: 227.1 in. **Width:** 79.8 in.

Height: 59.4 in. **Wheelbase:** 127.5 in.

Track: 60.0 in. (front), 61.0 in. (rear)

Weight: 4,691 lbs.

Buick RIVIERA GRAN SPORT

Bigger and heavier for 1971, Buick's personal luxury coupe also got dramatic new styling—especially at the rear, which gave rise to its 'boat-tail' nickname. Some saw it as the ultimate land yacht, but the GS™ model's 330 bhp made for fast, executive-style driving.

"...easy and effortless ."

"When viewed from the outside, the Riviera looks positively huge, but take your place behind the wheel and it feels much smaller. Easy and effortless to drive, this big Buick is at its best on long, straight roads, but with the GS package it will corner hard, ultimately only let down by its tires and sheer girth. The V8 is another matter; with the GS option it packs 330 bhp and 455 lb-ft of torque. This car will reach 60 mph quicker than many other personal luxury cars of its era."

A radiused gauge cluster and close-mounted console garnish the Riviera's lavish interior.

Milestones

1971 Replacing the 1966 vintage
Riviera is a new, larger model, with a wheelbase three inches longer and swoopy styling. Weighing about 100 lbs. more, sales drop to 33,810 due in part to its controversial rear end.

The Riviera was reborn as a personal luxury coupe in 1963.

1972 Chrome side spears
and a new grill mark the 1972 model. The Gran Sport package is still around, though power is down because of its low-lead, 8.5:1 compression ratio. The big 455-c.i. V8 makes 225 bhp—250 in GS tune.

1974 saw the heaviest Riviera yet, weighing in at 4,572 lbs.

1973 A bigger front bumper
and toned down rear deck styling give the Buick's personal luxury car a less distinctive look. Sales creep up slightly to 34,080.

UNDER THE SKIN

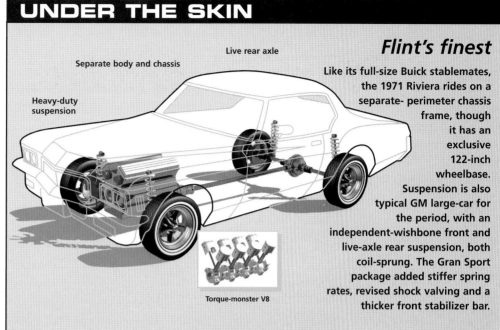

Live rear axle

Separate body and chassis

Heavy-duty suspension

Torque-monster V8

Flint's finest

Like its full-size Buick stablemates, the 1971 Riviera rides on a separate-perimeter chassis frame, though it has an exclusive 122-inch wheelbase. Suspension is also typical GM large-car for the period, with an independent-wishbone front and live-axle rear suspension, both coil-sprung. The Gran Sport package added stiffer spring rates, revised shock valving and a thicker front stabilizer bar.

THE POWER PACK

Mammoth motor

With fuel selling for around 30 cents per gallon in 1971, the Riviera naturally came with Buick's largest V8. Displacing 455-cubic inches, it was an outgrowth of the 1967 430. A very long (3.90-inch) stroke makes it a torque monster; it thumps out a whopping 455 lb-ft at just 2,800 rpm. Driving such a car as the Riviera Gran Sport, it is possible to entice drivers of smaller and lighter muscle cars to a traffic light duel. Though it has a lot of torque, the engine is still well behaved and will provide relaxed high-speed cruising.

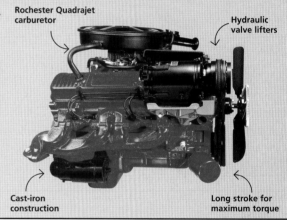

Rochester Quadrajet carburetor

Hydraulic valve lifters

Cast-iron construction

Long stroke for maximum torque

Speed boat

Although large and unique, the boat-tail Riviera does have a following. The 1971-1972 models have the unusually styled rear end, which was toned down for 1973. The 1971 GS is also the most sporty version and luckily can still be bought at reasonable prices.

1971 is the pinnacle year for boat-tails in terms of styling and performance.

Buick RIVIERA GRAN SPORT

Penned by Jerry Hirschberg, the 1971 Riviera was a unique design because it broke away from the conservative luxury so often associated with Buick cars. This is what elevated this short-lived car to cult status in later years.

Giant V8

Powering one of the largest and heaviest Rivieras is Buick's largest passenger car engine. Displacing a monster 455-cubic inches, this giant packs 330 bhp in Gran Sport trim and 455 lb-ft of torque. The Riviera GS was the perfect street sleeper for those who were looking for something different.

Heavy-duty suspension

Ordering the Gran Sport package in 1971 brought with it stiffer coil springs and shock absorbers, plus a thicker stabilizer bar. It made for one of the most sporty luxury coupes then on sale.

Body-on-the-frame construction

Rivieras in 1971 had their own E-body chassis but shared their separated chassis structure with the other GM B- and C-body full-size cars.

Boat-tail deck styling

Riviera stylist Hirschberg gave the new Riviera a very dramatic rear deck style which extended right to the bumper. This necessitated an offset rear license plate bracket.

Cornering lights

Costing just $36 in 1971, cornering lights are mounted in the front fenders. These come on with the turn signals. At night, the front and side signals flash alternately instead of in time.

Dual exhaust

Initially, Rivieras had dual exhaust, each with individual mufflers. This system prevailed until 1975, when the adoption of a catalytic convertor necessitated the need for a single setup.

Counterbalanced hood

Like most U.S. cars of the period, the 1971 Riviera has a counterbalancing hood. When opened, heavy-duty hinges support it, eliminating the need for a prop rod. The hood latch is located in the front-grill assembly.

Specifications

1971 Buick Riviera Gran Sport

ENGINE
Type: V8
Construction: Cast-iron block and heads
Valve gear: Two valves per cylinder operated by pushrods and rockers
Bore and stroke: 4.31 in. x 3.90 in.
Displacement: 455 c.i.
Compression ratio: 8.5:1
Induction system: Rochester Quadrajet four-barrel carburetor
Maximum power: 330 bhp at 4,600 rpm
Maximum torque: 455 lb-ft at 2,800 rpm
Top speed: 120 mph
0-60 mph: 8.1 sec.

TRANSMISSION
GM TurboHydramatic 400 three-speed automatic

BODY/CHASSIS
Steel-perimeter chassis with separate two-door coupe body

SPECIAL FEATURES

Pillarless styling is a feature of Rivieras built up to 1974.

1971–72 models are the only true boat-tail-styled Rivieras.

RUNNING GEAR
Steering: Recirculating ball
Front suspension: Unequal-length A-arms with coil springs, telescopic shock absorbers and stabilizer bar
Rear suspension: Live axle with coil springs and telescopic shock absorbers
Brakes: Discs (front), drums (rear)
Wheels: Steel 7 x 15
Tires: G70-15 in.

DIMENSIONS
Length: 217.4 in.   **Width:** 79.9 in.
Height: 56.4 in.   **Wheelbase:** 122.0 in.
Track: 60.4 in.
Weight: 4,325 lbs.

Buick ROADMASTER

The combination of just about the most comfortable ride in any large sedan and the total convenience of the pioneering two-speed Dynaflow transmission made the 1949 Roadmaster a huge success.

"...comfortable and relaxing."

"Its incredibly soft suspension may not give the Roadmaster the best hand-ling, but it does mean that it is blissfully comfortable and relaxing. This is enhanced by the quiet, refined, and strong straight-eight engine. The pioneering and impressively smooth Dynaflow transmission comes into its own as you accelerate to around 30 mph, when it performs really well. You just select 'Drive' and forget the rest—the Buick can easily soak up hundreds of miles in a day."

The view of the gauges through the large steering wheel is excellent.

Milestones

1945 Buick production gets underway again after WWII. Its cars changed from the 1942 models. Among the range is a Roadmaster.

By 1953, the Roadmaster had an OHV V8 engine.

1949 There is a fundamental restyle for the Roadmaster, with the top line of the front fender carried all the way through the doors to the top of the rear fender. The modern look complements the pioneering two-speed automatic transmission, with Dynaflow-drive.

1958 is the last year for the Buick Roadmaster.

1953 The straight-eight engine is replaced by a new, overhead-valve, pushrod 322-cubic inch V8 producing 188 bhp.

1958 The name Roadmaster is discontinued. It is resurrected in 1991.

UNDER THE SKIN

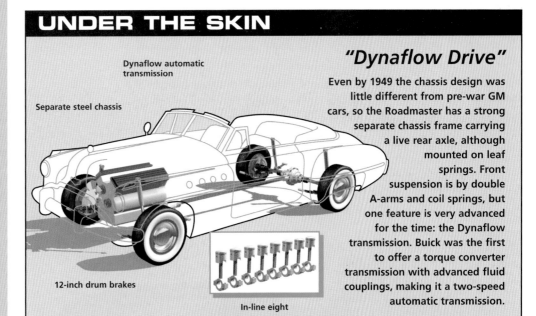

Dynaflow automatic transmission

Separate steel chassis

12-inch drum brakes

In-line eight

"Dynaflow Drive"

Even by 1949 the chassis design was little different from pre-war GM cars, so the Roadmaster has a strong separate chassis frame carrying a live rear axle, although mounted on leaf springs. Front suspension is by double A-arms and coil springs, but one feature is very advanced for the time: the Dynaflow transmission. Buick was the first to offer a torque converter transmission with advanced fluid couplings, making it a two-speed automatic transmission.

THE POWER PACK

Pre-war power

Buick's fine straight-eight engine, with its cast-iron block and cylinder head has its origins in the pre-war period. With the use of long crankshafts mounted on five bearings, by 1936 the capacity had increased to 320 cubic inches. A single block-mounted camshaft operates in-line overhead valves with pushrods and rockers. It is very unstressed and has a small 6.9:1 compression ratio. The engine is tuned for torque rather than outright power with its long stroke. The maximum power output of 150 bhp and 260 lb-ft of torque are produced, at 3,600 rpm and 2,400 rpm respectively.

Open-top joy

The two-door convertible is the most sought-after Roadmaster. At the time, it was more affordable than the two-door coupe. This helped account for its popularity, with over 8,200 sold in the model year— almost twice as many as the Riviera coupe.

The open-top Roadmaster is the ideal model for cruising.

Buick ROADMASTER

For 1949, the Roadmaster's new flatter side styling and the first appearance of portholes in the front fenders were an instant hit. Buick sales increased by more than 100,000.

Straight-eight engine

The design of Buick's straight-eight engine dates back to 1931. Straight-eights were built for prestige and, although very smooth, had drawbacks, such as length and the very long crankshaft, which limited engine speeds.

Foot starter

To start the Roadmaster, the ignition is switched on and then, with the transmission in 'Park' or 'Neutral,' the throttle is pressed right to the floor, activating the starter button.

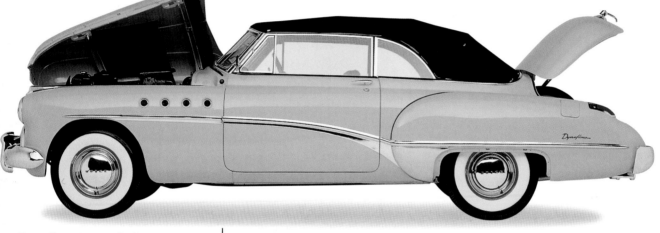

Dynaflow transmission

Buick was not the first to offer an automatic transmission but was the first to have a torque converter. It called its new transmission dynaflow. It is a much more sophisticated version of a fluid coupling, which magnifies the effect of the torque produced by the engine, so Drive is the only selection really needed.

Rear wheel covers

The 1949 Buicks, including the Roadmaster, were the last to have enclosed rear wheels. A removable panel allows the wheel to be changed.

Split windshield

The 1949 Roadmaster was one of the last Buicks to have a split windshield. Soon technology enabled curved, one-piece windshields to be produced.

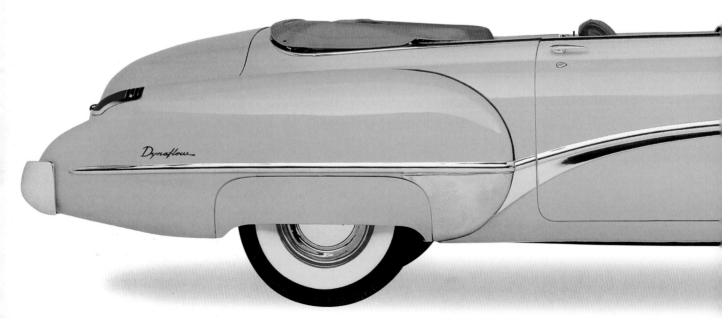

Recirculating-ball steering

The Roadmaster is a big and very heavy car, so the recirculating-ball steering needed more than five turns to go from lock to lock. This was improved with the power steering introduced in 1952. By 1954, there were 4.5 turns lock to lock, but the steering was still vague.

Drum brakes

Large, cast-iron drums give the Roadmaster good stopping power and can halt the car from 60 mph in 240 feet. Brake fade soon sets in if the car is driven hard.

A-arm front suspension

Coil-sprung double A-arm suspension and an anti-roll bar are used at the front to give the best possible ride.

Specification

1949 Buick Roadmaster

ENGINE

Type: In line eight-cylinder

Construction: Cast-iron block and head

Valve gear: Two valves per cylinder operated by a block-mounted camshaft.

Bore and stroke: 3.44 in. x 4.25 in.

Displacement: 320.2 c.i.

Compression ratio: 6.9:1

Induction system: One two-barrel Stromberg carburetor/ or carter carburetor

Maximum power: 150 bhp at 3,600 rpm

Maximum torque: 260 lb-ft at 2,400 rpm

Top speed: 100 mph

0-60 mph: 17.1 sec.

TRANSMISSION

Two-speed Dynaflow automatic with a torque converter

BODY/CHASSIS

Separate steel chassis with two-door convertible body

SPECIAL FEATURES

The Roadmaster has four portholes compared to the three of other Buicks.

The Dynaflow transmission was the first torque-converter automatic on a production car.

RUNNING GEAR

Steering: Recirculating-ball

Front suspension: Double A-arms with coil springs, telescopic shock absorbers and anti-roll bar

Rear suspension: Live axle with leaf springs, torque arm and telescopic shock absorbers

Brakes: Drums, 12-in. dia. (front and rear)

Wheels: Steel disc, 15-in. dia.

Tires: 8.20 x 15

DIMENSIONS

Length: 214.1 in.   **Width:** 80.0 in.

Height: 63.2 in.   **Wheelbase:** 126.0 in.

Track: 59.1 in. (front), 62.2 in. (rear)

Weight: 4,370 lbs.

Buick SKYLARK

One of Harley Earl's long-standing projects, the Skylark was an exclusive convertible that arrived in Buick's 50th anniversary year and sold for just two seasons. It was the ideal car for the wealthy.

"...a cut above the rest."

"Buicks of this period ooze refinement and civility, and the Skylark is one of the shining examples. The 200-bhp V8, coupled to the Dynaflow transmission means the car has more than enough power, but it is more of a fast cruiser than sportster. Fit and finish are top rate, with quality materials inside and out. As a top-of-the-line car, the Skylark is laden with luxury features and pampers its driver and passengers, making them feel a cut above the rest."

Skylarks came with a four-way power bench seat, power windows and a Selectronic radio.

Milestones

1953 In its 50th year, Buick gets its first overhead-valve V8 and a new top-level offering, the Skylark. Based on the Roadmaster™ chassis, it has a custom coachbuilt body and standard Dynaflow transmission. Priced at $5,000, only 1,690 are sold this year.

Five other convertibles were offered in 1954; this is a Super.

1954 The Skylark returns but as a regular production model, now based on the shorter Century™ chassis. The price is trimmed to $4,883, but sales are even less than in 1953, totaling 836. The 322-cubic inch Buick V8 now puts out 200 bhp.

The Skylark nameplate lasted up until 1998. Its final incarnation was the N-body compact.

1961 Skylark is revived, but as a top-level hardtop on the new 112-inch wheelbase Special™ compact.

UNDER THE SKIN

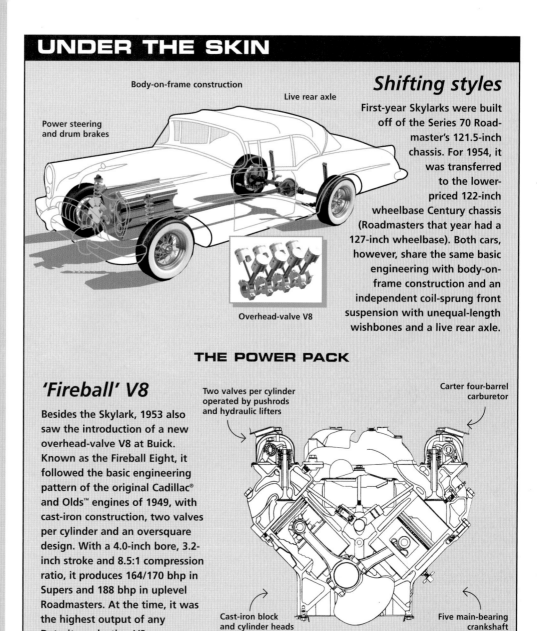

Body-on-frame construction

Power steering and drum brakes

Live rear axle

Overhead-valve V8

Shifting styles

First-year Skylarks were built off of the Series 70 Roadmaster's 121.5-inch chassis. For 1954, it was transferred to the lower-priced 122-inch wheelbase Century chassis (Roadmasters that year had a 127-inch wheelbase). Both cars, however, share the same basic engineering with body-on-frame construction and an independent coil-sprung front suspension with unequal-length wishbones and a live rear axle.

THE POWER PACK

'Fireball' V8

Besides the Skylark, 1953 also saw the introduction of a new overhead-valve V8 at Buick. Known as the Fireball Eight, it followed the basic engineering pattern of the original Cadillac® and Olds™ engines of 1949, with cast-iron construction, two valves per cylinder and an oversquare design. With a 4.0-inch bore, 3.2-inch stroke and 8.5:1 compression ratio, it produces 164/170 bhp in Supers and 188 bhp in uplevel Roadmasters. At the time, it was the highest output of any Detroit-production V8.

Two valves per cylinder operated by pushrods and hydraulic lifters

Carter four-barrel carburetor

Cast-iron block and cylinder heads

Five main-bearing crankshaft

Sky's the limit

Of the 1950s Skylarks, the 1953 models are the most special, with their custom-built bodies. The 1954 models are lighter and more powerful, with 200 bhp versus 188. Despite being more ostentatious, the 1954 versions are much rarer.

Only 836 Skylarks were built in 1954, despite the drop in price.

Buick SKYLARK

Rare and exclusive, the Skylark was a short-lived image maker for General Motors' other premium division. It showed that the cars from Flint could compete with the best luxury automobiles that Lincoln had to offer.

Fireball power

A 200-bhp, 322-cubic inch version of Buick's famed 'Fireball' overhead-valve V8 powers the 1954 Skylark. This engine was stroked to 364 cubic inches in 1957 and remained as an option until 1967, in 401- and 425-cubic inch forms.

Changing chassis

When introduced in 1953, the Skylark rode a 121.5-inch Roadmaster chassis. For 1954, as a cost-saving measure, this was changed to the 122-inch Series 60 Century chassis.

Dynaflow

While some critics called it the Dynaslush, Buick's fully automatic Dynaflow transmission was, for the most part, well received. In 1953, an improved twin-turbine unit was introduced and proved more responsive. It was standard on all Skylarks.

Drum brakes

The Skylark used four-wheel drum brakes. A power brake booster was standard, but repeated firm applications on the pedal could result in fading.

Special touches

Skylarks have a number of distinguishing features, including the absence of fender vents, unique wheel well styling (flared at the rear), special front fenders and big chrome fins grafted on the rear quarter panels.

1954 Buick Skylark

ENGINE
Type: V8

Construction: Cast-iron block and heads

Valve gear: Two valves per cylinder operated by a single V-mounted camshaft via pushrods and rockers

Bore and stroke: 4.00 in. x 3.20 in.

Displacement: 322 c.i.

Compression ratio: 8.5:1

Induction system: Carter four-barrel carburetor

Maximum power: 200 bhp at 4,100 rpm

Maximum torque: Not quoted

TRANSMISSION
Dynaflow two-speed automatic

BODY/CHASSIS
Separate steel chassis with two-door convertible body

SPECIAL FEATURES

Skylarks even have their own special steering wheel boss.

The stylish Kelsey-Hayes 15-inch wire wheels have knock off spinners.

RUNNING GEAR
Steering: Recirculating ball

Front suspension: Unequal-length wishbones with coil springs and telescopic shock absorbers.

Rear suspension: Live axle with semi-elliptic leaf springs and lever-arm shock absorbers

Brakes: Drums (front and rear)

Wheels: Kelsey-Hayes wire, 15-in. dia.

Tires: 6.70 x 15 in.

DIMENSIONS
Length: 206.3 in. **Width:** 69.8 in.

Height: 55.8 in. **Wheelbase:** 122.0 in.

Track: 59.0 in. (front and rear)

Weight: 4,260 lbs.

Luxurious interior

Power steering, brakes, four-way front bench seat and a power convertible top are all standard equipment. A Selectronic radio, which automatically searches for stations at the touch of a button, and 'Easy-Eye' tinted glass are also included.

Cadillac **62/DEVILLE**

In response to Chrysler's tail-finned cruisers General Motors fielded all-new C-body cars in 1959—all with outrageous styling. The 1959 Cadillac was the most flamboyant of all and became etched in the public's imagination because of its classy styling and large tail fins.

"...the definitive Cadillac."

"For its size the 1959 Cadillac is quick in a straight line, with lots of low rpm torque to get it moving. It's easily capable of maintaining a smooth, silent 80 mph. Feather-light power steering makes for easy turning, but over-enthusiastic cornering reveals the Caddy's tendency to pitch and roll in an unsettling manner. But as we already know, this isn't designed to be a race car. Rather it's a sleek and sophisticated luxury cruiser. And to most people, it's the definitive Cadillac."

The emphasis is on luxury. This car has power everything, including cruise control.

Milestones

1955 Eldorados get a revised body with a new gold anodized grill and larger, more protruding fins than the Series 62s.

In 1953 the Series 62 was the entry-level Cadillac.

1957 The ultra-exclusive Eldorado Brougham, costing $13,074, is a new flagship built to challenge the Lincoln Continental. Among a huge list of luxuries this model previews the air suspension available on the 1959 cars. The fins are made larger too.

By 1964, fins on Cadillacs had become quite modest.

1959 Totally restyled on a massive 130-inch wheelbase, the 1959 has some of the wildest fins ever, plus a huge chrome grill. All Cadillacs are powered by a V8 stretched to 390 cubic inches. The 1960 models have cleaner styling.

UNDER THE SKIN

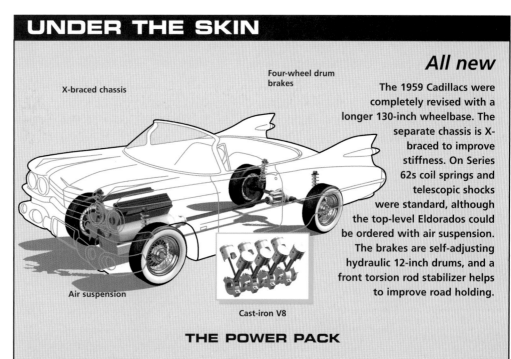

X-braced chassis

Four-wheel drum brakes

Air suspension

Cast-iron V8

All new

The 1959 Cadillacs were completely revised with a longer 130-inch wheelbase. The separate chassis is X-braced to improve stiffness. On Series 62s coil springs and telescopic shocks were standard, although the top-level Eldorados could be ordered with air suspension. The brakes are self-adjusting hydraulic 12-inch drums, and a front torsion rod stabilizer helps to improve road holding.

THE POWER PACK

Enduring V8

By 1959, the Cadillac V8 had been enlarged to 390 cubic inches and was offered in two states of tune. Series 62s, DeVilles, Sixty-Specials and 75s came with a 325-bhp unit and a Carter four-barrel carburetor. The Eldorado models were fitted with a 345-bhp version and three Rochester two-barrel carburetors. The V8 is a conventional unit, constructed from cast iron, with two valves per cylinder and hydraulic lifters. Each engine was run in before being fitted in the car.

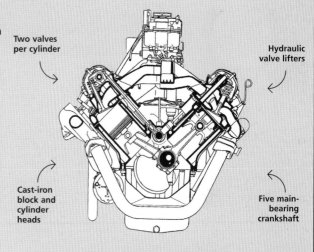

Two valves per cylinder

Hydraulic valve lifters

Cast-iron block and cylinder heads

Five main-bearing crankshaft

Biarritz special

Next up the scale from the series 62 is the DeVille, offered in hardtop coupe and sedan form. The four window sedan De Ville may not have quite the allure of a drop top but it is distinctive nonetheless and presently is cheaper to buy than a convertible.

in 1959 Sedan DeVilles came in either four- or six-window forms.

Cadillac 62/DEVILLE

The 1959 Cadillacs were at their most glamorous in convertible form, either as Series 62 models or the flagship Eldorado Biarritz. As one of the world's premier luxury cars of the late 1950s, they were almost unchallenged.

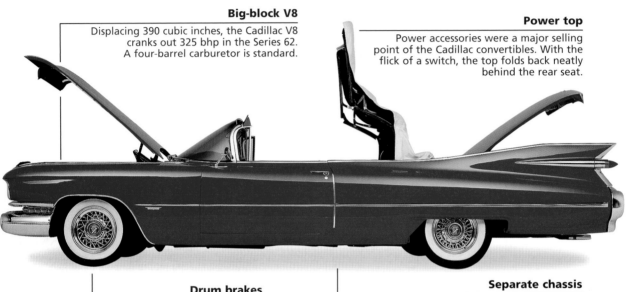

Big-block V8
Displacing 390 cubic inches, the Cadillac V8 cranks out 325 bhp in the Series 62. A four-barrel carburetor is standard.

Power top
Power accessories were a major selling point of the Cadillac convertibles. With the flick of a switch, the top folds back neatly behind the rear seat.

Drum brakes
Although it accelerates quickly, the Series 62 is not an all-out performer. Repeated heavy braking from high speed may cause the four-wheel drums to lock and quickly fade.

Separate chassis
A separate chassis provides greater ride comfort, which is essential for a luxury cruiser. The frame is X-braced for greater stiffness.

Mass-produced quality
For a mass-produced vehicle, the 1959 Cadillac was well put together. Only the finest quality materials were used during the manufacturing process.

Flamboyant styling
The 1959 Caddy was one of the last cars styled by the legendary Harley Earl and marked the end of an era.

Automatic headlights

Cadillac's 'Twilight Sentinel' headlights switch on automatically at dusk and also switch from high to low beams for oncoming traffic.

Chromed bumper

In the 1950s, designers looked to the space program for inspiration. The 1959 Cadillac has a heavy, full-width chromed rear bumper with back-up lights built into the center of its fins.

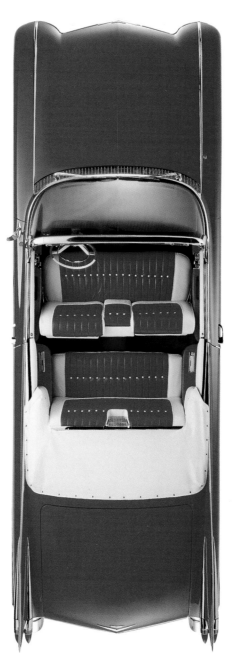

Specifications

1959 Cadillac Series 62

ENGINE

Type: V8

Construction: Cast-iron block and heads

Valve gear: Two valves per cylinder operated by a single camshaft via pushrods and rockers

Bore and stroke: 4.00 in. x 3.88 in.

Displacement: 390 c.i.

Compression ratio: 10.5:1

Induction system: Carter four-barrel carburetor

Maximum power: 325 bhp at 4,800 rpm

Maximum torque: 435 lb-ft at 3,400 rpm

Top speed:, 110 mph

0-60 mph: 11.4 sec.

TRANSMISSION

GM TurboHydramatic automatic

BODY/CHASSIS

Steel body on steel X-frame chassis

SPECIAL FEATURES

By 1959, quad headlights were in fashion. For the ultimate in excess, all 1959 Cadillacs have dual parking lights in chrome housings which form the lower part of the bumper.

The most recognizable feature are the fins—the tallest ever on a production car. Huge chrome bumpers further accentuate its advanced styling.

RUNNING GEAR

Steering: Recirculating ball

Front suspension: Wishbones with coil springs and telescopic shock absorbers

Rear suspension: Live axle with coil springs and telescopic shock absorbers

Brakes: Drums, 12-in. dia. (front and rear)

Wheels: Steel discs, 15-in. dia.

Tires: 8.20-15

DIMENSIONS

Length: 224.8 in.   **Width:** 79.9 in.

Height: 55.9 in.   **Wheelbase:** 130.0 in.

Track: 61.0 in. (front), 60.2 in. (rear)

Weight: 4,885 lbs.

Cadillac **ELDORADO**

The most expensive Cadillac of the 1950s, the Eldorado Brougham is a huge four-door hardtop derived from a show car. Each one was hand built and came with just about every conceivable option. However, its steep price resulted in it being dropped in 1960.

"...you can feel its quality."

"The most luxurious of all 1950s Cadillacs, the Eldorado Brougham is glitzy but not overtly so. You can almost feel the quality in the massive hand-stitched bench seat and door panels. The best part about this car is that it's whisper quiet at speed and the air suspension makes you feel like you're floating on a cloud. The automatic transmission is amazingly precise for a 1950s car. The steering is exceedingly light, while the brake pedal has almost no feel."

Buyers could choose from 44 trim and color combinations, including lamb's-skin seats.

Milestones

1956 In December, the Eldorado Brougham is announced for 1957. A total of 400 are built in its first year.

The Eldorado Seville was the next most expensive Cadillac after the Brougham.

1958 While regular Cadillacs receive an exterior facelift, the Brougham remains externally unchanged, although the interior door panels are now leather instead of metal.

1959-1960 Broughams were larger and sharper looking.

1959 All Cadillacs are new this year, and standard models have Detroit's tallest fins. The Brougham returns with more power and a new, four-door, hardtop body built by Pininfarina in Italy.

1960 As a result of high production costs and slow sales, the Brougham is dropped. Its styling previews 1961 Cadillacs.

UNDER THE SKIN

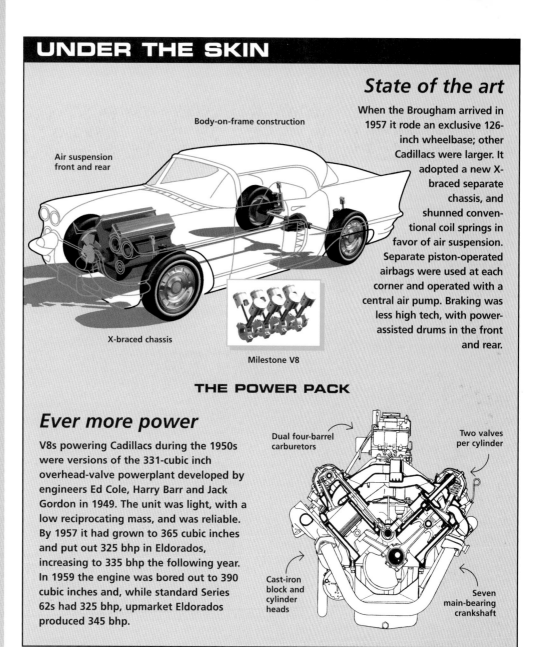

Body-on-frame construction

Air suspension front and rear

X-braced chassis

Milestone V8

State of the art

When the Brougham arrived in 1957 it rode an exclusive 126-inch wheelbase; other Cadillacs were larger. It adopted a new X-braced separate chassis, and shunned conventional coil springs in favor of air suspension. Separate piston-operated airbags were used at each corner and operated with a central air pump. Braking was less high tech, with power-assisted drums in the front and rear.

THE POWER PACK

Ever more power

V8s powering Cadillacs during the 1950s were versions of the 331-cubic inch overhead-valve powerplant developed by engineers Ed Cole, Harry Barr and Jack Gordon in 1949. The unit was light, with a low reciprocating mass, and was reliable. By 1957 it had grown to 365 cubic inches and put out 325 bhp in Eldorados, increasing to 335 bhp the following year. In 1959 the engine was bored out to 390 cubic inches and, while standard Series 62s had 325 bhp, upmarket Eldorados produced 345 bhp.

Dual four-barrel carburetors

Two valves per cylinder

Cast-iron block and cylinder heads

Seven main-bearing crankshaft

U.S.-built

Broughams can be divided into two distinct series, the 1957-1958 cars, hand-built in Detroit, and the later 1959-1960 models. These Pininfarina-built cars are larger and have much sleeker styling that other Cadillacs. Collectors tend to prefer the earlier models.

Earlier Broughams have proved to be very popular with collectors.

Cadillac ELDORADO

Cadillac was the 'Standard of the World' back in the 1950s and the Brougham was the ultimate expression of luxury on wheels. At a staggering $13,075 in 1957, however, few could afford it.

Powerful V8

By 1957 the 1949 vintage Cadillac V8 had been stroked to 365 cubic inches and produced a muscular 325 bhp on Eldorados (300 bhp on other models). All Cadillacs got an extra 10 bhp for 1958.

Air suspension

A state-of-the-art feature, air suspension, was introduced on the Brougham. It basically consisted of a rubber diaphragm and piston at each wheel controlled by a central compressor. The system was not very reliable and many owners chose to replace it with coil springs.

Suicide doors

Another feature unique to the 1957-1958 Eldorado Brougham are the suicide doors. Those at the front open in the normal manner, but the back doors are hinged at the rear. This allows easy access for passengers and also means that the Brougham was a pillarless four-door sedan that allowed the elimination of the rear quarter windows.

Modest fins

Cadillac pioneered fins among domestic manufacturers as far back as 1948. In 1955 Eldorados gained tall blade-like items, and these were adopted for the Brougham when it was launched in 1958. Interestingly, although regular Cadillacs had fins of gigantic proportions for 1959, Broughams had fairly small fins with dagger-shaped taillight lenses.

Sumptuous interior

Eldorado Broughams were laden with luxury options inside, including power steering, brakes and windows, plus air-conditioning, electric memory seats and cruise control. Buyers also had the choice of 44 interior and exterior trim and color combinations.

Huge chrome grill

Broughams have a unique eggcrate mesh-pattern grill which is neater than those on other Cadillacs. Broughams were also the first to get quad headlights.

Smooth styling

Panoramic windshields were first seen on the limited production Eldorado convertible in 1953. By 1958 all Cadillacs had them. They offered good visibility, but were costly to replace and necessitated a front dog-leg A-pillar which could make entry into the car rather difficult.

Specifications

1957 Cadillac Eldorado Brougham

ENGINE

Type: V8

Construction: Cast-iron block and heads

Valve gear: Two valves per cylinder operated by a single camshaft via pushrods and rockers

Bore and stroke: 4.00 in. x 3.63 in.

Displacement: 365 c.i.

Compression ratio: 10.0:1

Induction system: Two four-barrel carburetors

Maximum power: 325 bhp at 4,800 rpm

Maximum torque: 435 lb-ft at 3,400 rpm

Top speed: 110 mph

0-60 mph: 11.4 sec.

TRANSMISSION

Three-speed automatic

BODY/CHASSIS

Separate chassis with two-door steel convertible body

SPECIAL FEATURES

A full-length stainless-steel roof was standard on 1957-1958 Broughams—a feature lifted virtually intact from the Eldorado show car of 1954.

A gold anodized air cleaner is mounted atop the 365-cubic inch V8.

RUNNING GEAR

Steering: Recirculating ball

Front suspension: Wishbones with airbags and shock absorbers

Rear suspension: Live axle with airbags and shock absorbers

Brakes: Drums (front and rear)

Wheels: Steel, 15-in. dia.

Tires: 8.0 x 15.0 in.

DIMENSIONS

Length: 216.3 in.   **Width:** 78.5 in.

Height: 55.5 in.   **Wheelbase:** 126.0 in.

Track: 61.0 in. (front and rear)

Weight: 5,315 lbs.

Checker **A11**

For more than 30 years, the Checker was an unmistakable sight on the streets of Manhattan. Its familiar bulbous shape has been etched, not only in the minds of New Yorkers, but in people all over the world.

"...built for the human race."

"Picture the scene. It's Saturday night in midtown Manhattan and you and your Checker are experiencing one of the busiest nights of the week. The high-set driving position gives you a commanding view of the pot-holed avenues, and the huge bumpers mean other drivers stay clear of your path. This car is built like a tank and with more than 30 years of severe duty, the Checker's sturdy design and tough suspension proved it was built for the human race."

Primitive but hard-wearing, the A11's interior has everything a cabbie needs.

Milestones

1956 Checker Motors launches its A8 taxicab. It has slab-sided yet fairly restrained styling and a coil-sprung front suspension.

From 1964, Checkers were called Marathons.

1958 This year, quad headlights and a 125-bhp engine are featured.

1959 The A10 series replaces the A8 and is offered in passenger trim as the Superba Special.

Chevrolet's Impala was the main rival to the Checker in terms of NYC taxicab sales.

1963 Checker's A11 makes its debut.

1969 A 350-cubic inch Chevrolet V8 is optional.

1974 Big aluminum bumpers are fitted to comply with federal legislation. Production ends in 1982.

UNDER THE SKIN

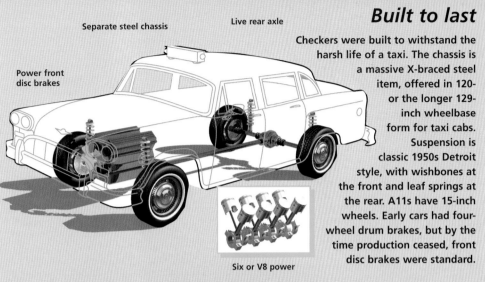

Separate steel chassis   Live rear axle

Power front disc brakes

Built to last

Checkers were built to withstand the harsh life of a taxi. The chassis is a massive X-braced steel item, offered in 120- or the longer 129-inch wheelbase form for taxi cabs. Suspension is classic 1950s Detroit style, with wishbones at the front and leaf springs at the rear. A11s have 15-inch wheels. Early cars had four-wheel drum brakes, but by the time production ceased, front disc brakes were standard.

Six or V8 power

THE POWER PACK

Myriad of options

Checker never built its own engines for the A11, but obtained them from outside sources. Initially, the A11 was powered by a 226-cubic inch Continental six, although from 1967 Chevy small-block V8s became available in 327-cubic inch form at first and in 350-cubic inch form from 1969. During the 1970s, the Checker's only full decade of production, engine choice centered around the Chevy 250-cubic inch six and 350 V8, although a debored 305 arrived for 1977. By 1980, a 229-cubic inch Chevy V6 was the base engine found in the majority of New York Cabs, but 327 and 350 V8s were offered for those who craved more torque.

New York taxi

Having led demanding and harsh lives, particularly in major U.S. cities, it is rare to find a decommissioned cab in great shape. Checkers do not command much money, but with fewer cabs out there, finding a genuine, running New York taxi that's not beat to death is rare.

This A11 is one of the last working Checkers in the Big Apple.

Checker **A11**

Although operated by cab companies in many different cities across the U.S., New York is considered the Checker's natural habitat. Big Apple cabs even had their own special NYC package.

V6 or V8

By 1980, when this cab left the factory, engine choices were 229-cubic inch V6s or V8s displacing 267 or 305 cubic inches. A diesel V8 was also listed on the order form.

Heavy-duty suspension

Traveling thousands of miles over cratered and broken pavement requires heavy-duty suspension. The Checker's proven setup of stiff coils and leaf springs is well up to the job.

Propane

Although most Checkers run on gas, some have been converted to use propane. These cars are identified by a fairing over the gas cap on the rear valance.

Spacious interior

Two different wheelbases were available (120 or 129 inches). The longer A11E version has rear-facing jump seats and can seat up to eight instead of six passengers.

New York certified

Manhattan cabs are operated under the control of the NYC Taxi and Limousine Commission. Official cabs have yellow paint and a medallion number, which is assigned to each driver and marked on the roof, rear doors and license plates. A driver is not allowed to pick up fares in the Big Apple without it.

Bumper guards

Due to heavy traffic in New York, many cabs were fitted with bumper guards to keep wayward motorists at bay.

Specifications

1980 Checker A11

ENGINE
Type: V8

Construction: Cast-iron block and heads

Valve gear: Two valves per cylinder operated by pushrods and rockers

Bore and stroke: 3.74 in. x 3.48 in.

Displacement: 305 c.i.

Compression ratio: 8.6:1

Induction system: Rochester four-barrel carburetor

Maximum power: 155 bhp at 3,800 rpm

Maximum torque: 250 lb-ft at 2,400 rpm

TRANSMISSION
GM Turbohydramatic 350 three-speed automatic

BODY/CHASSIS
Steel-perimeter chassis with separate four-door sedan body

SPECIAL FEATURES

Cabs working 24 hour or night shifts were required to have a glass divider.

All official New York taxis have a medallion number on the roof sign.

RUNNING GEAR
Steering: Recirculating ball

Front suspension: Unequal-length wishbones with telescopic shock absorbers and anti-roll bar

Rear suspension: Live axle with semi-elliptic leaf springs and telescopic shock absorbers

Brakes: Discs (front), drums (rear)

Wheels: Pressed steel, 15-in. dia.

Tires: 155/70 R15

DIMENSIONS
Length: 201.0 in.   **Width:** 79.5 in.

Height: 71.6 in.   **Wheelbase:** 120.0 in.

Track: 64.6 in. (front and rear)

Weight: 3,830 lbs.

Chevrolet CAMARO PACE CAR

Chevrolet's Mustang fighter debuted in 1967 and, also that year, served as the pace car for the Indianapolis 500. Two years later, the Camaro was again pacing this prestigious race. This time, however, a greater number of replicas were offered for sale—all in white with orange interiors and stripes.

"...unbeatable experience."

"It's easy to see why this is one of the all-time great American classics. The hound's tooth upholstered seats may have little support and the thin wheel may almost slip through your fingers, but turn the key dangling from the column, put her in gear and hit the road. The V8 has a pure, unadulterated sound and the driving experience soon becomes all enveloping. The shifter feels good in your hand, and with the top down the experience is unbeatable."

The Pace Car package added an orange interior with hound's tooth seat inserts.

Milestones

1966 Introduced in September, the Camaro is Chevrolet's answer to the Ford Mustang. It was also selected to pace the Indy 500 race. Four Camaro RS/SS convertibles—all have white with blue stripes and are powered with modified 396 V8s—were used. To give the pubic a chance to own this pacing legend, Chevrolet built 100 replicas which were sold through select dealers.

The most fearsome of all 1969 Camaros was the ZL-1™.

1968 After building 220,906 copies for 1967, Chevy makes a few changes to its pony car. V8 models get multi-leaf springs. An Astro ventilation system results in the elimination of the front vent windows.

The second-generation Camaro was only available as a coupe.

1969 Camaros pace the Indy 500 again. The 1969 pace car—like the 1967—was painted white but has orange instead of blue stripes. 3,675 replicas are sold.

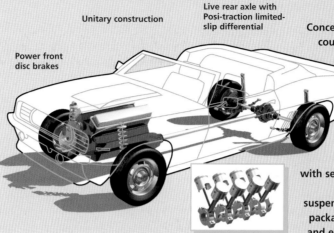

Unitary construction

Live rear axle with Posi-traction limited-slip differential

Power front disc brakes

Small-block V8

Uniframing

Conceived as a budget-wise sports coupe, the Camaro shared many parts with the Nova™. They include its unitary body/chassis design, a front bolt-on subframe carrying the engine and double wishbone front suspension. At the back was a live axle with semi-elliptic multi-leaf springs. Pace Cars have a heavy-duty suspension (which is part of the SS package), power front disc brakes and either a four-speed manual or an automatic transmission.

THE POWER PACK

Mighty mouse, roarin' rat

Camaro entered its third season for 1969 and still the base engine was a 230-cubic inch, six-cylinder unit. The Z11 Pace Car replicas, however, were only offered with two different V8s. The majority (like this one) came with the 350-cubic inch V8 and some came with the stout 396. Sharing many features with the original small-block of 1965, including its cast-iron block and five-main-bearing crankshaft, the 350 put out 300 bhp and a credible 380 lb-ft of torque. Approximately 100 of the Z11 Pace Cars used the 396-cubic inch Turbo Jet V8, which was available in three different states of tune. The top L-78 version thumped out a mighty 375 bhp.

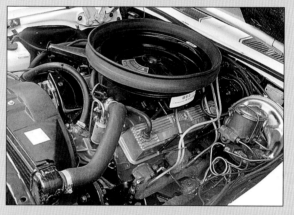

Vintage year

1969 models are possibly the most coveted Camaros of all and the Pace Car replicas are highly desirable machines. Excellent examples trade hands for up to $45,000. A small number of coupes under the code RPO Z10 were also built.

1969 is considered the pinnacle year among Camaro afficionados.

Chevrolet CAMARO PACE CAR

Driven by 1960 Indy 500 winner Jim Rathmann at the Brickyard, the actual Pace Car was powered by a 375-bhp, 396-cubic inch big-block, but in the interests of driveability most of the replicas had small-block engines.

Pace Car package

To get a 1969 Camaro Pace Car, you had to check off the Regular Production Order (RPO) Z11 on the order form. This put you behind the wheel of a hot Camaro decorated with white paint and orange stripes on the hood and decklid. Pace Car decals for the doors were dealer-installed at the owner's request.

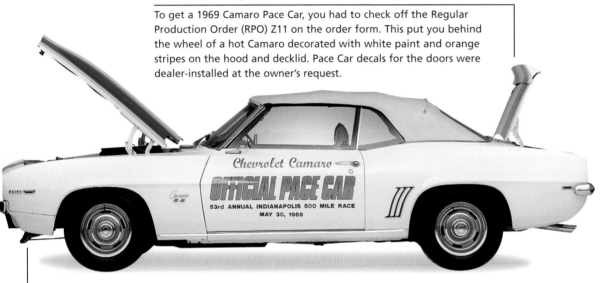

One-year wonder

Although they were based on the 1967-1968 cars, the 1969 Camaros received new sheet metal with sweeping fender lines.

RS/SS package

The price of $37 for the Z11 option was deceiving because you also had to order the SS package, Z/28 cowl induction hood and rear spoiler, plus the hidden headlight RS grill.

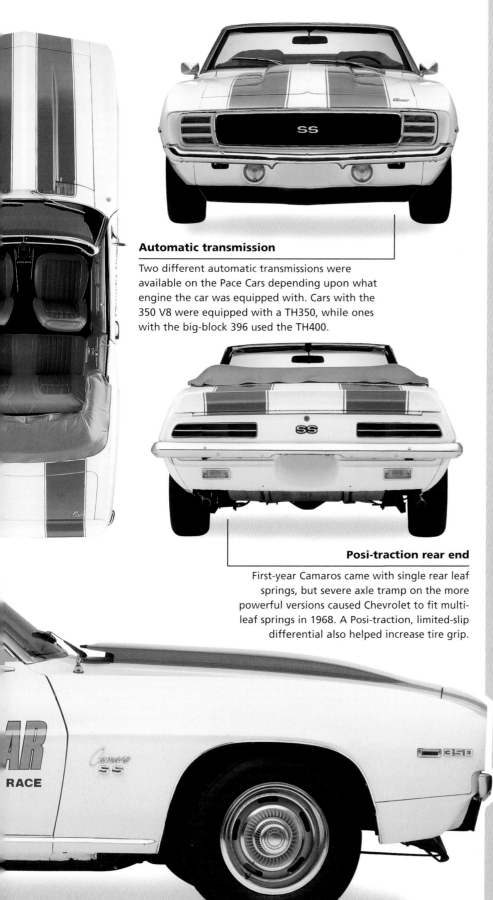

Automatic transmission

Two different automatic transmissions were available on the Pace Cars depending upon what engine the car was equipped with. Cars with the 350 V8 were equipped with a TH350, while ones with the big-block 396 used the TH400.

Posi-traction rear end

First-year Camaros came with single rear leaf springs, but severe axle tramp on the more powerful versions caused Chevrolet to fit multi-leaf springs in 1968. A Posi-traction, limited-slip differential also helped increase tire grip.

Specifications

1969 Chevrolet Camaro Pace Car

ENGINE

Type: V8

Construction: Cast-iron block and heads

Valve gear: Two valves per cylinder operated by a single V-mounted camshaft with pushrods and rockers

Bore and stroke: 4.00 in. x 3.48 in.

Displacement: 350 c.i.

Compression ratio: 10.25:1

Induction system: Rochester Quadrajet four-barrel carburetor

Maximum power: 300 bhp at 4,800 rpm

Maximum torque: 380 lb-ft at 3,200 rpm

TRANSMISSION

Turbo 350 automatic

BODY/CHASSIS

Steel unitary chassis with two-door convertible body

SPECIAL FEATURES

Convertibles were sold with pace car decals in the trunk ready to stick on.

The actual pace car used in the race was fitted with Chevy rally wheels like these.

RUNNING GEAR

Steering: Recirculating ball

Front suspension: Unequal length A-arms with coil springs, telescopic shock absorbers and anti-roll bar

Rear suspension: Live axle with semi-elliptic leaf springs and telescopic shock absorbers

Brakes: Discs (front), drums (rear)

Wheels: Steel Rally, 7.0 x 14 in.

Tires: Goodyear Polyglas, G-70 14

DIMENSIONS

Length: 186.0 in.   **Width:** 74.0 in.

Height: 51.0 in.   **Wheelbase:** 108.0 in.

Track: 59.6 in. (front) 59.5 in. (rear)

Weight: 3,395 lbs.

Chevrolet CAMARO ZL-1

GM supported the Automotive Manufacturers Association (AMA) ban in the 1960s by only using its 400 cubic-inch and larger engines in full size cars and Corvettes. Through the Central Office Production Order system Vince Piggins, one of Chevrolet's officers, found a loop hole with the ban and created the ultimate Camaro—the ZL-1.

"...the apex of Chevy muscle."

"This is the apex of Chevy's muscle cars. In the driver's seat the car resembles a typical six-cylinder Camaro. When you start it up and listen to the aggressive engine you soon realize you've slid behind the wheel of a true factory-built racer. With the addition of tubular headers, drag slicks and a super tune, one of these nasty Camaros could run the ¼ mile in 11.68 seconds at more than 120 mph. Few cars come close to offering the level of thrill that a ZL-1 can."

Most ZL-1s had stripped cabins, but this one has a deluxe interior with woodgrain trim.

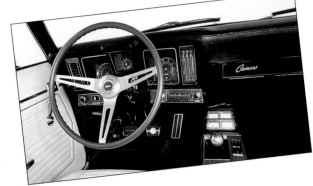

Milestones

1967 In response to the Mustang,

Chevrolet launches the Camaro. The most powerful engine available is the 375 bhp, 396 V8. Because of the AMA ban, GM's intermediates weren't available with engines larger than 400 cubic inches. Meanwhile, a handful of Chevy dealers were installing 427 V8s into these cars, especially Camaros.

In 1967 car dealers were installing 427 V8s into new Camaros.

1968 Don Yenko of

Yenko Sports Cars becomes the largest dealer converting these Camaros. GM's Vince Piggins takes notice. Later that year, Piggins and Yenko get together to offer the conversion package from GM's COPO (Central Office Production Order) department for 1969.

Don Yenko's YSC Camaros got the ball rolling for the ZL-1.

1969 A few hundred COPO Camaros are

built. While most come with cast iron 427s, 69 versions known as ZL-1s are built with aluminum big-block engines. Tuned ZL-1s made 500+ bhp and could cover the ¼ mile in just under 12 seconds.

UNDER THE SKIN

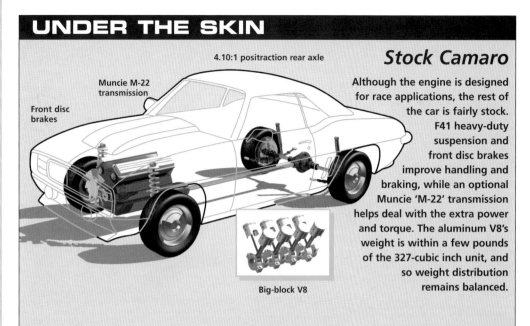

4.10:1 positraction rear axle

Muncie M-22 transmission

Front disc brakes

Big-block V8

Stock Camaro

Although the engine is designed for race applications, the rest of the car is fairly stock. F41 heavy-duty suspension and front disc brakes improve handling and braking, while an optional Muncie 'M-22' transmission helps deal with the extra power and torque. The aluminum V8's weight is within a few pounds of the 327-cubic inch unit, and so weight distribution remains balanced.

THE POWER PACK

Exotic big-block

The ZL-1 was unlike any other engine that GM made at that time. The engine is roughly equivalent to the L88 Corvette racing V8 but has an aluminum instead of cast-iron block. The reciprocating assembly consisted of a forged steel crankshaft, forged pistons that slide in steel cylinder liners and four-bolt main bearing caps. The aluminum cylinder heads have closed chambers and rectangle intake ports. A Holley 850-cfm four-barrel carburetor fed the massive engine the fuel it required.

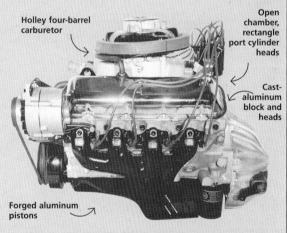

Holley four-barrel carburetor

Open chamber, rectangle port cylinder heads

Cast-aluminum block and heads

Forged aluminum pistons

Pure racer

ZL-1s are ranked with the Hemi Cuda convertible and Ram Air IV™ GTO® as one of the most desirable muscle cars ever produced. With only 69 built with the all-aluminum engine, they attract a premium price and often trade hands for $150,000 or more.

To this day, Chevrolet hasn't built a more powerful production car than the ZL-1.

Chevrolet CAMARO ZL-1

Most ZL-1s had plain bodies with skinny steel wheels—they didn't even have any badging to designate their model or engine size. This unique ZL-1 has the RS appearance package, vinyl top and 427 badging.

ZL2 cowl hood

All ZL-1s came with cowl induction hoods. It forced cool air into the engine from the high pressure area just below the windshield.

Expensive engine

You had to have a healthy bank account to be able to afford a ZL-1 Camaro. The engine's all-aluminum construction saved 160 lbs. over the cast-iron 427. Because it is virtually hand built, the engine alone cost $4,160—more than most cars of the period.

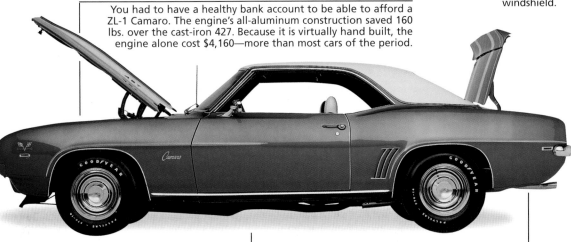

Better balance

Although it is a big-block unit, the ZL-1 engine weighs about 500 lbs. which is roughly the same as a 327, and so these special Camaros actually handle better than the stock SS 396™. However, these cars were designed for use in NHRA Super Stock drag racing events.

Standard exhaust system

ZL-1s left the factory with lots of mismatched parts because the owners were expected to do a lot of race development themselves. The stock exhaust manifolds restrict the flow of exhaust gases and were usually among the first items to be replaced.

The ZL-1 option package

All ZL-1s began life as SS 396s, but the engine and Super Sport™ option were deleted. Instead, the special cars received the ZL-1 option package which included the aluminum engine, F41 suspension, front discs and a cowl induction hood.

Heavy duty suspension components

All ZL-1s were equipped with the heavy duty F41 suspension and front disc brakes. To better handle the 450 lb-ft of torque from the powerful engines, ZL-1s were equipped with 12-bolt rear ends with 4.10 gears.

Performance transmission

Only two transmissions were strong enough to cope with the ZL-1 V8: the Muncie M-22 'Rock Crusher' four-speed or the equally stout TurboHydramatic 400 automatic.

Specifications

1969 Chevrolet Camaro ZL-1

ENGINE

Type: V8

Construction: Aluminum block and cylinder heads

Valve gear: Two valves per cylinder operated by a single camshaft

Bore and stroke: 4.25 in. x 3.76 in.

Displacement: 427 c.i.

Compression ratio: 12.0:1

Induction system: Holley four-barrel carburetor

Maximum power: 430 bhp at 5,200 rpm

Maximum torque: 450 lb-ft at 4,400 rpm

TRANSMISSION

Muncie M-22 four-speed manual

BODY/CHASSIS

Unitary steel chassis with two-door hardtop coupe body

SPECIAL FEATURES

Each ZL-1 engine has a special sticker on the valve cover.

Most ZL-1s have exposed headlights, but this car has the RS package.

RUNNING GEAR

Steering: Recirculating ball

Front suspension: Double wishbones with coil springs, telescopic shock absorbers and anti-roll bar

Rear suspension: Live axle with semi-elliptic leaf springs and telescopic shock absorbers

Brakes: Discs (front), drums (rear)

Wheels: Steel, 6 x 15 in.

Tires: Goodyear Wide Tread GT, E70-15

DIMENSIONS

Length: 186.0 in.   **Width:** 74.0 in.

Height: 51.0 in.   **Wheelbase:** 108.0 in.

Track: 59.6 in. (front), 59.5 in. (rear)

Weight: 3,300 lbs.

Chevrolet CHEVELLE SS 454

In 1970, Chevrolet introduced the ultimate powerhouse for its midsize muscle car. It was also the year GM lifted its displacement ban on all of its midsize cars. For the Chevelle, it meant 450 bhp from a stout LS-6 454 V8 for the Super Sport model. Today, it is regarded as one of the most fearsome muscle cars of all time.

"...all-out performance."

"This is not a toy—it's an LS-6 Chevelle SS. It's one of those cars GM built just to show up Ford and Mopar. For years, the SS used semi-powerful 396 V8s, but when Chevy® released the LS-6 454, the competition shuddered. The all-out performance engine has a factory rating of 450 bhp—no other muscle car production engine had a higher rating. The LS-6 Chevelle's only limitation was its tires. But even with the stock tread, the SS could be power shifted to 13.7 seconds in the ¼ mile."

While most Chevelle Super Sports were ordered with custom buckets, this one has a bench seat.

Milestones

1969 SS is an option package. Top-of-the-line engine continues to be the L78 396 with 375 bhp. However, Vince Piggins, GM's performance products manager, had 323 COPO (Central Office Production Order) Chevelles built with L72 427 V8s. They produce 425 bhp, and run the ¼ mile in 13.3 seconds at 108 mph.

Earlier Chevelles had much boxier styling.

1970 General Motors unleashes its wildest muscle cars yet, with revised styling. The LS-5 (360 bhp) and LS-6 (454 bhp) 454 V8s join the 396 in the Chevelle SS line up as a regular production order.

In 1970, the smaller-engined SS 396 was still available.

1971 The SS 454 returns, though the LS-6 option is dropped. The less powerful LS-5 actually gains 5 bhp, to 365. Only 9,402 SS 454s are built. A new Chevelle arrives for 1973.

UNDER THE SKIN

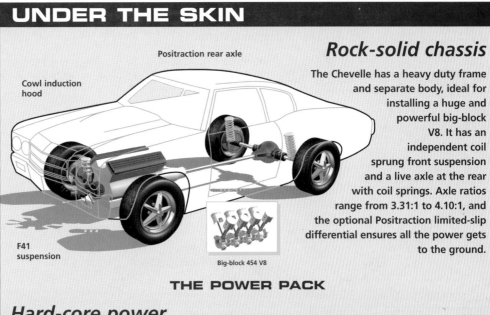

Positraction rear axle

Cowl induction hood

F41 suspension

Big-block 454 V8

Rock-solid chassis

The Chevelle has a heavy duty frame and separate body, ideal for installing a huge and powerful big-block V8. It has an independent coil sprung front suspension and a live axle at the rear with coil springs. Axle ratios range from 3.31:1 to 4.10:1, and the optional Positraction limited-slip differential ensures all the power gets to the ground.

THE POWER PACK

Hard-core power

The lightning and thunder raging under the hood of the highest performance Chevelle SS—the infamous LS-6—produces 450 bhp and 500 lb-ft of torque. The block shares the same 4.25-inch bore as the 427 V8, but the stroke was increased to 4.00 inches. The longer stroke helps produce gobs of low end power. The powerful LS-6 uses high (11.25:1) compression forged pistons, steel crankshaft, high-lift camshaft with mechanical lifters and closed-chamber, rectangle-port cylinder heads. It uses an aluminum intake manifold and a Holley 800 cfm carburetor. This engine means business.

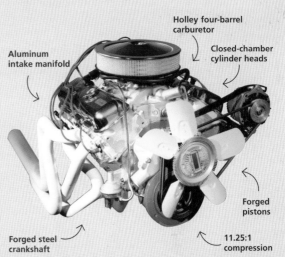

Holley four-barrel carburetor

Closed-chamber cylinder heads

Aluminum intake manifold

Forged pistons

11.25:1 compression

Forged steel crankshaft

Collector's cars

The 1970 Chevelle Super Sport was restyled from the 1969 model and again in 1971. A 1970 SS with the LS-6 is as rare as it is powerful. Only 4,475 of these venomous vehicles were produced, making them popular and valuable among auto collectors.

Not many muscle cars come close to the tire-shredding power of the LS-6 SS.

Chevrolet **CHEVELLE SS 454**

The LS-6 Chevelle was one of the most powerful muscle cars ever produced. It combined Chevrolet's largest engine with its sporty midsize car to give outrageous results.

Body stripes

By 1970 style was every bit as important as performance, and SS Chevelles were available with twin stripes running over the hood and rear decklid.

LS-6 454-cubic inch V8

The biggest performance option in 1970 was the LS-6 engine. It produces 450 bhp at 5,600 rpm and 500 lb-ft of torque at 3,600 rpm. It has high compression pistons, rectangle port cylinder heads, and solid valve lifters. Few other muscle machines could rival the power of the LS-6.

M-22 'Rock crusher' transmission

With 500 lb-ft of torque, only two transmissions were strong enough to cope with the LS-6 engine. This one has a Muncie M22 'Rock crusher' four-speed. This stout unit has a 2.20:1 straight-cut first gear.

Magnum 500 wheels

Magnum 500 steel wheels were used on all 1970 Chevelle Super Sports. The Polyglas F70x14 could barely handle the engine's torque.

Hardtop body

While all LS-6 engines were supposed to be installed in hardtops only, it's rumored that a few found their way into convertibles.

Upgraded suspension

The SS package included the F41 suspension which has stiffer front springs to compensate for the weight of the big-block engine.

Cowl induction hood

A vacuum-controlled flap at the top of the hood draws air in from the high-pressure area at the base of the windshield to help the engine exploit its power. This is known as cowl induction.

Dual exhaust

A full-length 2.5-inch dual exhaust system enables the LS-6 to optimize the engine's performance.

Specifications
1970 Chevrolet Chevelle SS 454

ENGINE
Type: V8
Construction: Cast-iron block and heads
Valve gear: Two valves per cylinder operated by pushrods and rockers
Bore and stroke: 4.25 in. x 4.00 in.
Displacement: 454 c.i.
Compression ratio: 11.25:1
Induction system: Holley four-barrel carburetor and aluminum intake manifold
Maximum power: 450 bhp at 5,600 rpm
Maximum torque: 500 lb-ft at 3,600 rpm
Top speed: 125 mph
0-60 mph: 6.1 sec

TRANSMISSION
Manual four-speed, close-ratio M-22

BODY/CHASSIS
Steel body on separate steel chassis

SPECIAL FEATURES

All Chevelle Super Sports came with Magnum 500 steel wheels and Polyglas F70x14 tires in 1970.

These NASCAR-style tie down hood pins were a popular item and helped keep the hood from lifting at high speed.

RUNNING GEAR
Steering: Recirculating ball
Front suspension: Independent with wishbones, anti-roll bar, coil springs and telescopic shock absorbers
Rear suspension: Live axle with coil springs and telescopic shock absorbers
Brakes: Disc, 11-in. dia. (front), drum 9-in. dia. (rear)
Wheels: Magnum 500, 14-in. dia.
Tires: Polyglas F70x14

DIMENSIONS
Length: 189 in.   **Width:** 70.2 in.
Height: 52.7 in.   **Wheelbase:** 112 in.
Track: 56.8 in. (front), 56.9 in. (rear)
Weight: 4,000 lbs.

Chevrolet **CORVAIR**

It was supposed to be a new, small Chevrolet in response to foreign imports, but the Corvair turned into a giant controversy regarding its safety. Later models were remedied of the handling problem and some were even fitted with turbochargers.

"...unbelievable power."

"The Corvair is a simple car to enter and all the instruments are very easy to read. While suspension problems plagued the first generation Corvairs, by 1965 this was all in the past. The handling from the four-wheel independent suspension is outstanding. It doesn't roll and there is just a slight hint of understeer. The Corsa®, optioned with a 180 bhp, turbocharged flat-six engine, was the most desirable Corvair and offered unbelievable power."

Corsas were available with a deluxe interior complete with a full set of instruments.

Milestones

1960 Chevrolet announces its Corvair, with a 140-cubic inch rear engine and three levels of specification (500, 700 and 900 Monza®) to compete with imported compacts.

Corvair (here a 700) was the most revolutionary of the big three compacts for 1960.

1962 Suspension improvements attempt to answer handling criticisms, and a convertible is added to the range. The most exciting debutante, however, is the turbocharged Monza Spyder®.

1965 A radically overhauled second-generation Corvair is launched. A new Corsa coupe and convertible displaces the Monza as the top of the range.

Second generation Corvairs included a hardtop sedan.

1969 Production finally comes to an end.

UNDER THE SKIN

Radical Chevy

Beneath its new swoopy styling, the second-generation Corvair embodied many improvements. The swing axle rear suspension is replaced by a fully independent set up with coils on both sides and double control arms, the uppers being the axle half-shafts. The front suspension is also tuned to match the rear with stiffer springs. Drum brakes are standard all around.

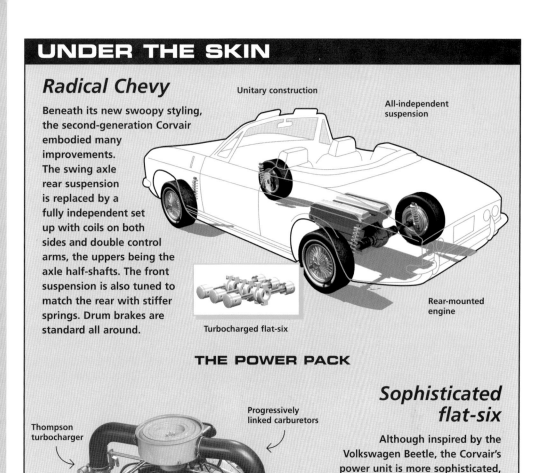

Unitary construction

All-independent suspension

Rear-mounted engine

Turbocharged flat-six

THE POWER PACK

Thompson turbocharger

Progressively linked carburetors

Individual cylinder barrels

Aluminum block with divided crankshaft

Sophisticated flat-six

Although inspired by the Volkswagen Beetle, the Corvair's power unit is more sophisticated, perhaps echoing engineer Ed Cole's background in aviation. It has six separate cylinder barrels with cast-iron walls mounted in an aluminum block with a divided crankshaft. Outputs initially varied from 80 to 95 bhp, but the addition of a Thompson turbocharger in 1962 resulted in 150 bhp. This rose to 180 bhp for the revised 1965 models, making this one of the most powerful sixes in production.

Choice Corsa

With the 1965-1966 Corsa, Chevrolet thought it had a winner on its hands. Alas, it proved to be short-lived; the Corsa and turbocharged engine were dropped after 1966. Today, not surprisingly, the Corsa is the most collectible of all Corvairs.

The Corsa only lasted for two model years and offered the most power.

Chevrolet **CORVAIR**

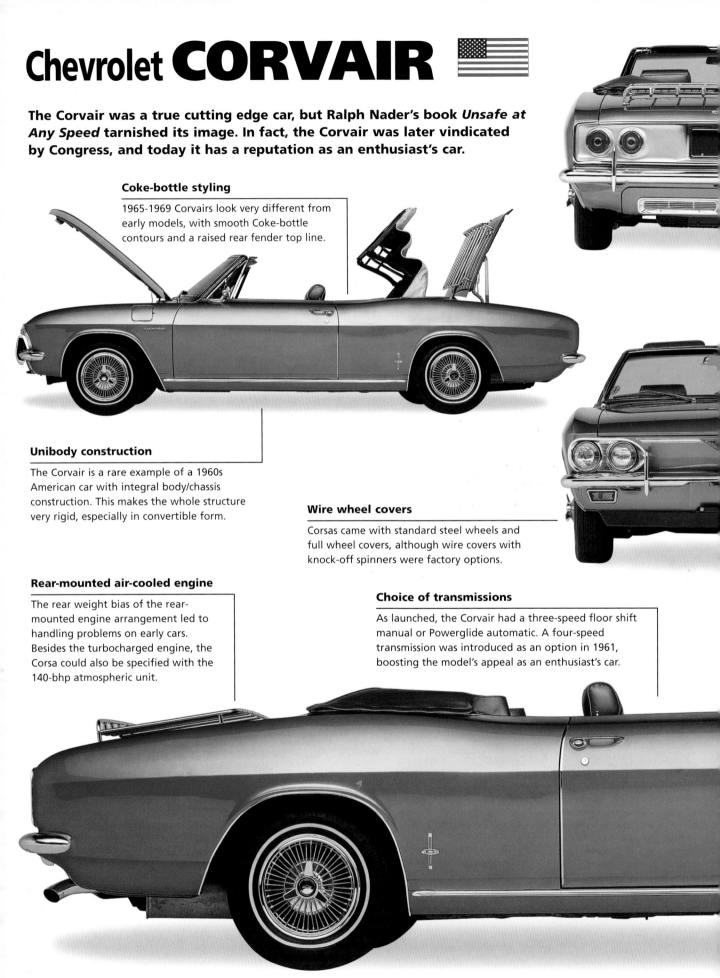

The Corvair was a true cutting edge car, but Ralph Nader's book *Unsafe at Any Speed* tarnished its image. In fact, the Corvair was later vindicated by Congress, and today it has a reputation as an enthusiast's car.

Coke-bottle styling

1965-1969 Corvairs look very different from early models, with smooth Coke-bottle contours and a raised rear fender top line.

Unibody construction

The Corvair is a rare example of a 1960s American car with integral body/chassis construction. This makes the whole structure very rigid, especially in convertible form.

Wire wheel covers

Corsas came with standard steel wheels and full wheel covers, although wire covers with knock-off spinners were factory options.

Rear-mounted air-cooled engine

The rear weight bias of the rear-mounted engine arrangement led to handling problems on early cars. Besides the turbocharged engine, the Corsa could also be specified with the 140-bhp atmospheric unit.

Choice of transmissions

As launched, the Corvair had a three-speed floor shift manual or Powerglide automatic. A four-speed transmission was introduced as an option in 1961, boosting the model's appeal as an enthusiast's car.

Revised suspension

For 1965, the Corvair received a revised rear suspension employing upper and lower control arms to better monitor wheel movement. Rods connect the lower arms to the main rear cross-member to absorb longitudinal forces.

Grill-less nose

Like the Beetle, the Corvair does not have a front grill. The headlights are set back in chrome bezels, which results in a striking and attractive appearance.

Specifications
1966 Chevrolet Corvair Corsa

ENGINE

Type: Horizontally-opposed six-cylinder
Construction: Aluminum block and heads
Valve gear: Two valves per cylinder operated by a single camshaft
Bore and stroke: 3.44 in. x 2.94 in.
Displacement: 164 c.i.
Compression ratio: 9.25:1
Induction system: Four carburetors
Maximum power: 180 bhp at 4,000 rpm
Maximum torque: 232 lb-ft at 3,200 rpm

TRANSMISSION

Three-speed manual, four-speed manual or optional two-speed automatic

BODY/CHASSIS

Integral chassis with two-door steel body

SPECIAL FEATURES

High-back buckets were a feature not too many people ordered on the Corsa.

The highest performance engine was the turbocharged flat six with 180 bhp.

RUNNING GEAR

Steering: Recirculating ball
Front suspension: Wishbones with coil springs, shock absorbers and anti-roll bar
Rear suspension: Multi-link with coil springs and shock absorbers
Brakes: Drums (front and rear)
Wheels: Steel, 13-in. dia.
Tires: 6.50 x 13

DIMENSIONS

Length: 183.3 in.   **Width:** 69.7 in.
Height: 51.3 in.   **Wheelbase:** 108.0 in.
Track: 55.0 in. (front), 57.2 in. (rear)
Weight: 2,720 lbs.

Chevrolet CORVETTE

Chevrolet was the first major car company in the world to dare to make a regular production car out of fiberglass. It was a crude affair at first but the sleek body and throaty engine captured the hearts of the American public, kick-starting the Corvette legend.

"...impressive in its day."

"You forget the modified sedan car origins of the Blue Flame Special six-cylinder engine when the throttle is floored and it roars to life. Despite the handicap of the two-speed Powerglide automatic, its 11 second 0-60 mph time is impressive for the day. Dynamically, the Corvette was closer to its traditional British sports car rivals than anything else made in the U.S. at the time, with stiff springs and a taut ride."

The interiors on early Corvettes were a bit confined and had a simple dashboard Layout.

Milestones

1952 The first full-size plaster model of the Corvette is presented to the GM president Harlow Curtice by Harley Earl. Curtice likes it and the Corvette is all set for production.

By 1957 the Corvette's V8 had gained optional fuel injection.

1953 The public sees the Corvette for the first time at the GM Motorama Show. Production begins later in the year and all cars are painted Polo White. Changes are made for the 1954 model year with more colors and increased power.

A major facelift came for the Corvette in 1961.

1954 For the 1955 model year Chevrolet's proposed facelift is shelved and the car's future is in doubt until the new V8 engine is used.

1955 It's the end of of the line for the six-cylinder Corvette. The small block V8 is now the preferred power unit.

UNDER THE SKIN

Something old, something new

With the decision made to have a fiberglass body, the Corvette had a separate chassis. It is an X-braced perimeter steel section affair, given extra stiffness once the one-piece fiberglass floor molding is added. Having the semi-elliptic leaf springs for the rear axle mounted outside the chassis rails was a Corvette innovation.

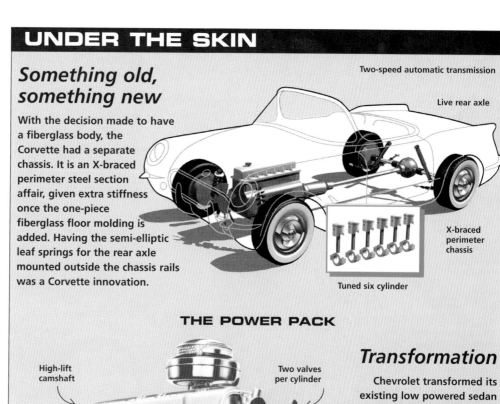

Two-speed automatic transmission

Live rear axle

X-braced perimeter chassis

Tuned six cylinder

THE POWER PACK

High-lift camshaft

Two valves per cylinder

Cast-iron construction

Pushrod valve actuation

Transformation

Chevrolet transformed its existing low powered sedan engine into the Corvette's impressive 3.9-liter Blue Flame Special. A high-lift, long duration camshaft was used in the simple pushrod engine, the cylinder head was modified, compression ratio increased, and double valve springs, along with solid valve lifters, were fitted to deal with higher rpm. Induction was transformed by fitting three Carter sidedraft carburetors on a much improved alloy manifold.

Rare original

Although the six-cylinder Chevrolet Corvettes aren't the best performing examples of the breed, they're now very valuable. Collectors value the 1953 and 1954 cars for their relative rarity, historical importance and purity of shape.

The early six-cylinder Corvettes are highly collectable today.

Chevrolet CORVETTE

Because of poor sales, GM almost gave up on the little sports car. In 1955 it got a husky V8 engine and the car was making the power it lacked. Luckily, sales picked up and the Corvette has been in Chevrolet's line up ever since.

Wishbone front suspension

The Corvette's double wishbone and coil spring front suspension was a modified version of the contemporary Chevrolet sedans, with different spring rates to suit the sports car.

Six-cylinder engine

The first Corvettes used a modified Chevrolet sedan engine. Tuning made it an effective sports car powerplant with 150 bhp.

Whitewall tires

Whitewall tires were very fashionable in the 1950s. One advantage was that they broke up the high-sided look of the tall sidewalls.

Fiberglass body

Although there were a number of fiberglass-bodied specialty and kit cars around in the U.S. in the early 1950s General Motors was the first to make a regular production car out of the material. In production the fiberglass panels used were about half as thick as the prototype's.

Two-speed transmission

Incredibly, the only available GM transmission which would take the power and torque of the modified engine was the two-speed Powerglide automatic. A three-speed manual became available for the 1955 model year cars.

Wrap-around windshield

The wrap-around style of windshield was popular in the early 1950s. Apart from looking great, it improved three-quarter vision compared with a conventional flat front glass with thick pillars.

Live rear axle

Because it was a limited-production car, the first Corvettes had to use many off-the-shelf Chevrolet components and the engineering had to be as simple as possible.

Specifications

1954 Chevrolet Corvette

ENGINE

Type: Inline six cylinder

Construction: Cast iron block and head

Valve gear: Two valves per cylinder operated by single block-mounted camshaft via pushrods and solid valve lifters

Bore/stroke: 3.56 in. x 3.94 in.

Displacement: 235 c.i.

Compression ratio: 8.0:1

Induction system: Three Carter YH sidedraft carburetors

Maximum power: 150 bhp at 4,200 rpm

Maximum torque: 233 lb-ft at 2,400 rpm

TRANSMISSION

Two-speed Powerglide automatic

BODY/CHASSIS

X-braced steel chassis with fiberglass two-seater convertible body

SPECIAL FEATURES

The first Corvettes have very curvaceous rear ends with subdued fins and prominent taillights.

Stone guards over the front headlights were purely a styling feature and unnecessary on ordinary roads.

RUNNING GEAR

Steering: Worm-and-sector

Front suspension: Double wishbones with coil springs, telescopic shocks and anti-roll bar

Rear suspension: Live axle with semi-elliptic leaf springs and telescopic shocks

Brakes: Drums (front and rear), 11-in. dia.

Wheels: Steel disc, 15-in. dia.

Tires: Crossply 5.5 x 15

DIMENSIONS

Length: 167 in. **Width:** 72.2 in.

Height: 51.3 in. **Wheelbase:** 102 in.

Track: 57 in. (front), 59 in. (rear)

Weight: 2,851 lbs.

Chevrolet CORVETTE STING RAY

When Chevrolet® introduced the Corvette Sting Ray in 1963, it was the quickest roadster Detroit had ever made. Its 327-cubic-inch V8 gave the new Corvette serious muscle, and for the first time, an American sports car could out-gun its European rivals.

"America's favorite sports car."

"Off the line, this Vette™ has the kind of low-end grunt that will leave most modern sports cars in a cloud of dust and burning rubber. First you hear the throaty rumble of the big-shouldered 427 V8, then the three two-barrel carbs snarl to life and you can feel the power throb through the chrome shifter. Both the steering and clutch are heavy, while the handling and brakes are crude by today's standards. But that snap-your-head-back lunge of power still makes the Sting Ray America's favorite sports car."

The cockpit is spartan and functional with a classic hot rod feel often imitated but never quite equaled.

Milestones

1953 The first Motorama Corvette
show car enters production with a six-cylinder engine.

1955 Zora Arkus-Duntov,
father of the Sting Ray, becomes head of the Corvette program, a position he held until retirement in 1982. Under him, manual transmission and the V8 engine are offered as options (1955) and fuel injection becomes available (1957).

1957 The Vette is the fastest
real production car in the world, showing what can be done when conventional engineering is applied well.

The 1963 convertible. Soft top is stored under a panel behind the seats.

1963 The first Sting Ray
production car is built, with all-independent suspension and the first coupe body. Its styling is based on a racing car design originally developed in 1958 by Bill Mitchell.

1965 Big-block
engine and disc brakes are available. The 396-cubic inch V8 with a solid cam is introduced with 425 bhp.

1967 Pinnacle of performance
is the L88 427-cubic inch V8. This also marks the last year of this body style.

UNDER THE SKIN

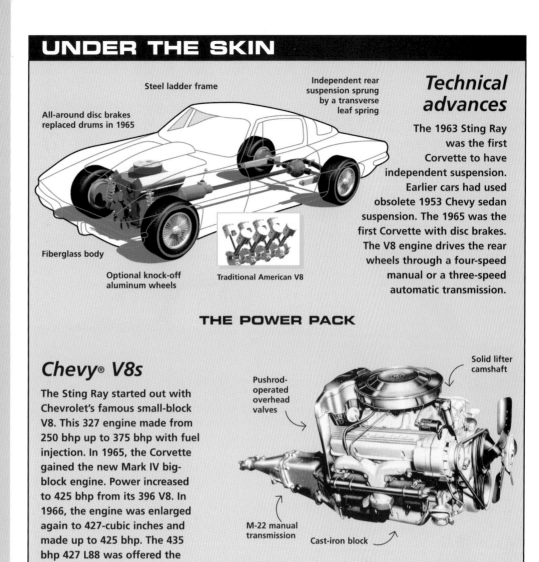

Steel ladder frame

Independent rear suspension sprung by a transverse leaf spring

All-around disc brakes replaced drums in 1965

Fiberglass body

Optional knock-off aluminum wheels

Traditional American V8

Technical advances

The 1963 Sting Ray was the first Corvette to have independent suspension. Earlier cars had used obsolete 1953 Chevy sedan suspension. The 1965 was the first Corvette with disc brakes. The V8 engine drives the rear wheels through a four-speed manual or a three-speed automatic transmission.

THE POWER PACK

Chevy® V8s

The Sting Ray started out with Chevrolet's famous small-block V8. This 327 engine made from 250 bhp up to 375 bhp with fuel injection. In 1965, the Corvette gained the new Mark IV big-block engine. Power increased to 425 bhp from its 396 V8. In 1966, the engine was enlarged again to 427-cubic inches and made up to 425 bhp. The 435 bhp 427 L88 was offered the very next year.

Pushrod-operated overhead valves

Solid lifter camshaft

M-22 manual transmission

Cast-iron block

Split rear window

The most sought-after Sting Ray is the 1963 split rear window coupe model. The designer, Bill Mitchell, intended it to form a visual connection with the central raised sections on the hood. The feature was dropped because it spoiled rear vision. Some later cars have been retro-fitted with the center pillar in an attempt to raise their values.

The split rear window coupe was only available in 1963.

Chevrolet CORVETTE STING RAY

The Sting Ray was introduced in 1963, 10 years after the Corvette's first appearance. The engine is set well back in the frame, giving nearly 50/50 weight distribution and excellent handling for the day.

Fiberglass body

Like all Corvettes, the Sting Ray has a body made from a number of fiberglass panels mounted on a traditional separate frame.

Disc brakes all around

Vented discs with dual-pot calipers on each wheel were fitted from 1965. While old stocks lasted, buyers could opt for the discontinued drums to save money.

V8 engine

Apart from the very early models, all Corvettes are powered by V8 engines. There is a wide variety of displacements and states of tune. The 327-cubic inch engine in 350-bhp tune is typical.

Optional side exhausts

The Sting Ray's enormous options list included the Side Mount Exhaust System. The side pipes are covered with a perforated shield to prevent the driver or passengers from burning themselves. Side exhausts were chosen mainly for visual effect.

No trunk lid

To preserve the contour of the car, there is no trunk lid and access to the luggage compartment is from behind the seats.

Foldaway top

The Corvette's convertible top folds away completely when not in use and is stored beneath a flush-fitting fiberglass panel behind the driver. Optional hard top cost $231.75 in 1966.

Alloy gearbox and clutch housing

To save weight, the Sting Ray was given an alloy clutch housing and an alloy-cased gearbox. This also improved weight distribution.

Flip-up headlights

The headlights are rotated by two reversible vacuum operated motors—a postwar first for an American car.

Triple side vents

Side vent arrangement, like many minor details, changed over the years. The 1965 and '66 models like this one have three vents.

Independent rear suspension

Another Corvette first, the Sting Ray has a crude but effective system with a transverse leaf spring mounted behind the differential.

Specifications
1966 Chevrolet Corvette Sting Ray

ENGINE
Type: V8, 90°

Construction: Cast-iron block and heads; Single cam, pushrods

Bore and stroke: 4.0 in. x 3.25 in.

Displacement: 327 c.i.

Compression ratio: 11:1

Induction system: Rochester fuel injection or one/two Carter four-barrel carbs

Maximum power: 375 bhp at 6,200 rpm

Maximum torque: 350 lb-ft at 4,000 rpm

Top speed: 135 mph

0-60 mph: 5.6 sec.

TRANSMISSION
Three-speed automatic (optional four-speed manual)

BODY/CHASSIS
Steel ladder frame with two-door convertible or coupe fiberglass body

SPECIAL FEATURES

Innovative retractable headlights.

Soft top folds away neatly into compartment behind seats, with luggage space below.

RUNNING GEAR
Front suspension: Double wishbone, coil springs, anti-roll bar
Rear suspension: Semi-trailing arms, half-shafts and transverse links with transverse leaf spring
Brakes: Vented discs with four-pot calipers (optional cast-iron drums)
Wheels: Five-bolt steel (knock off aluminum optional) 6 in. x 15 in.
Tires: 6.7 in. x 15 in. Firestone Super Sport 170

DIMENSIONS
Length: 175.3 in. **Width:** 69.6 in.
Height: 49.8 in. **Wheelbase:** 98 in.
Track: 56.3 in. (front), 57 in. (rear)
Weight: 3,150 lbs.

Chevrolet IMPALA

Bigger than the crisp 1955-1957 models, the 1958 Chevrolet was significant in being the first to offer a W-Series V8. A 348-engined Impala was just about the quickest and most stylish low-priced car that year.

"...nostalgic yet evocative."

"The 1958 Impala was the first Chevy® to use this now-common name on one of its cars. It was powered with a W Series 348 V8. Upon startup, the engine releases a nostalgic yet evocative sound. The Impala's primary role is that of a cruiser. Give it a little gas and the car will accelerate faster than most other cars in 1958. With drum brakes at all four corners, gentle, progressive braking is the best way to stop it."

Even though it dates from the 1950s, the interior is not as glitzy as other cars of this era.

Milestones

1957 The third and final

incarnation of the 1955-vintage Chevrolet arrives with complete new styling. Three variations are offered—the 150, 210 and Bel Air®. The 265-cubic inch V8 is bored out to 283-cubic inches; the top version makes 290 bhp.

1958 Impalas are popular to customize.

1958 All-new Chevrolets

have quad headlights and the model lineup is altered with the Delray® and Biscayne replacing the 150 and 210. Joining the Bel Air lineup is the new Impala. Supplanting the 283 as the top engine is a new W-Series 348 V8 with 250 or 315 bhp.

By 1959, the Impala lost its 1950s styling.

1959 Radically changed,

this year's Chevys are longer and lower with bat-like fins and cat's eye taillights.

UNDER THE SKIN

Air-sprung suspension

Separate steel X-frame chassis

Four-wheel drum brakes

Big-block V8

Softly sprung

Chevrolet wanted a new, lower look for 1958 and this required a redesigned chassis, changed from the traditional perimeter rail type to an all-new (and stronger and stiffer) X-frame in which the main chassis rails join in the middle. Although the double A-arm front and live axle rear suspension were retained, the previous coil and leaf springs were replaced by an optional compressor-controlled bellows. Braking is by four-wheel drums.

THE POWER PACK

Fire-breathing 348

For 1958, Chevrolet introduced the W-Series V8. Designed primarily for use in light trucks, it was a classic design with a cast-iron block and cylinder heads and two valves per cylinder. With a 4.13-inch bore and 3.25-inch stroke, it was fairly compact for its day and initially made 250 bhp with a four-barrel carburetor or an impressive 315 bhp if equipped with three two-barrel carburetors. A fairly low 9.5:1 compression ratio meant that, unlike the versatile small block, the 348 was not ideal for hot rodding.

Two valves per cylinder

Rochester four-barrel carburetor

Cast-iron block and heads

Five-main-bearing crankshaft

First year

As the first of the legendary Impalas, the 1958 model has a special significance. While all are highly prized today, the most collectable are those equipped with the W-Series 348 engines, especially with the Tri-Power induction setup.

Around 60,000 Impalas were built in its debut year.

Chevrolet IMPALA

More glitzy than ever, the 1958 Chevrolet was among the more stylish Detroit cars that year, especially in Impala form. With the brand-new W-Series engine, it also broke new ground for low-priced performance.

V8 engine

Although pretty potent in standard 250-bhp Turbo Thrust form, the 348 could be specified in greater states of tune. The Super Turbo Thrust V8, with three two-barrel carburetors, took power up to 280 bhp, while another version with solid lifters and a higher (11.0:1) compression gave 315 bhp.

Optional Air suspension

Another pioneering feature for the 1958 Chevrolet was an air suspension. Four rubber bellows replaced the usual steel springs and there was an air compressor to keep the pressure up in each bellows. The pressure increased as the load increased, regulated by height control valves.

Drum brakes

Chevrolet fitted the Impala with good size brakes—11.5-inch diameter drums on all four wheels. Power assistance was available for $38 and was a desirable option.

Front vent windows

With a more pronounced wraparound windshield, the front vent windows look like they are mounted upside down. The extreme rake of the A-pillar also results in a severe dog leg design which was a popular style in the late 1950s.

Stiffened body

As the side bodywork is not connected to the chassis rails the structure needed to be reinforced to compensate for it. Extra mounting points result in much greater torsional rigidity compared to the 1957 model.

Four-link axle

The air springs give no axle location so the live axle required additional arms. There are two angled trailing arms that run out from the chassis rails and two shorter upper arms.

Specifications

1958 Chevrolet Impala

ENGINE

Type: V8

Construction: Cast-iron block and heads

Valve gear: Two valves per cylinder operated by a single V-mounted camshaft with pushrods, hydraulic lifters and rockers

Bore and stroke: 4.13 in. x 3.25 in.

Displacement: 348 c.i.

Compression ratio: 9.5:1

Induction system: Rochester four-barrel carburetor

Maximum power: 250 bhp at 4,400 rpm

Maximum torque: 355 lb-ft at 2,800 rpm

TRANSMISSION

Three-speed manual

BODY/CHASSIS

Separate X-frame with steel two-door coupe body

SPECIAL FEATURES

Triple taillights distinguished Impalas from other 1958 Chevrolets.

An under-dash tissue dispenser was a popular item on Chevys during the 1950s.

RUNNING GEAR

Steering: Recirculating ball

Front suspension: Double A-arms with air springs, telescopic shock absorbers and anti-roll bar

Rear suspension: Live axle with four links, air springs and telescopic shock absorbers

Brakes: Hydraulically-operated drums, 11.5-in. dia.

Wheels: Pressed steel disc, 14-in. dia.

Tires: 8.00 x 14

DIMENSIONS

Length: 209.1 in. **Width:** 77.7 in.

Height: 56.4 in. **Wheelbase:** 117.5 in.

Track: 58.8 in. (front and rear)

Weight: 3,459 lbs.

Chevrolet MONTE CARLO SS 454

Super Sport™ is the meaning behind the SS designation, and the big-block Monte Carlo lives up to that name proudly. Grand-touring comfort is backed by a 360-horsepower, 454-cubic inch V8, making this one of the first executive-class luxury performance cars of all time.

"...unbelievable authority."

"Only a light touch of the throttle is needed to get a sneak preview to what lies ahead. When the big Quadrajet is running at wide open throttle, the stout 454-cubic inch big-block makes unbelievable mid-range power. As soon as the tires bite, the engine's 500 lb-ft. of torque will pin you deeply into the back of the seat with unbelievable authority. Yet the ride remains comfortably smooth and the big Monte will cruise happily at 100 mph all day long."

Plenty of room and plenty of comfort. The Monte SS is the ultimate highway cruiser.

Milestones

1970 Chevrolet

enters the personal luxury field with the Monte Carlo—a two-door coupe based on the Chevelle chassis. It boasts the longest hood ever fitted to a Chevrolet. In SS form it is available with the monster 454 V8. The moderate LS-5 makes 360 bhp and the bone-crushing LS-6 puts out 450 bhp.

The big 454 V8 in SS tune was also offered in the Chevelle.

1971 Having proved

to be a great success, the Monte Carlo returns for another season with a revised grill. The muscular SS 454 also returns, but with rising insurance premiums and lower octane fuel it is not popular with just 1,919 built.

A 'new' Monte Carlo SS arrived for 1983. This is a 1986 model.

1972 The Monte

Carlo enters its last season with the original body. The SS 454 is no longer available, but Monte Carlo sales remain strong with 180,819 built.

UNDER THE SKIN

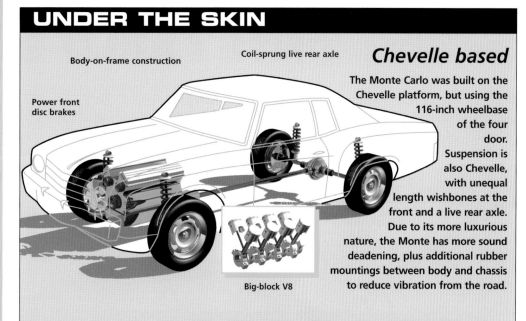

Body-on-frame construction

Coil-sprung live rear axle

Power front disc brakes

Big-block V8

Chevelle based

The Monte Carlo was built on the Chevelle platform, but using the 116-inch wheelbase of the four door. Suspension is also Chevelle, with unequal length wishbones at the front and a live rear axle. Due to its more luxurious nature, the Monte has more sound deadening, plus additional rubber mountings between body and chassis to reduce vibration from the road.

THE POWER PACK

Biggest stock Rat

Arriving in 1970, the big-block 454 was part of the Mk IV V8 series which were first introduced in Chevrolet passenger cars in 1965. It has a cast-iron block and cylinder heads, plus a forged-steel crankshaft and connecting rods. The LS-5 has a 10.25:1 compression ratio, hydraulic lifters and a single Rochester Quadrajet four-barrel carburetor. It thumps out an impressive 360 bhp at a low 4,400 rpm and a hefty 500 lb-ft of torque. If fitted with the infamous LS-6 it makes 450 bhp in 1970 and 425 bhp in 1971.

Rochester Quadrajet four-barrel carburetor

Hydraulic valve lifters

Cast-iron block and cylinder heads

Forged-steel crankshaft and connecting rods

Good buy

SS 454 Montes were only built for two years and production totalled just 5,742. Although rare, they are often overlooked. Excellent examples can be picked up for as little as $8,000, making the Monte Carlo 454 one of the best big-block muscle buys.

Few muscle cars could match the performance and luxury of the SS 45.

Chevrolet MONTE CARLO SS 454

To order an SS 454 you had to check RPO Z20 on the options list. Considering the added performance, this option was a bargain at $420.25. Surprisingly, less than 4,000 buyers chose the option in 1970.

Rally wheels

To go with its high-performance image, all SS 454s had G70-15 wide oval white stripe tires fitted on 7x15-inch Rally wheels.

Big-block muscle

The long 4-inch stroke in Chevrolet's famous cast-iron LS-5 big-block V8 is the reason why this 454-cubic inch Rat motor produces 500 lb-ft. of torque at a very usable 3,200 rpm. Its forged crankshaft is nitride and cross-drilled, making the bottom end virtually bullet proof. Big-valve cast-iron cylinder heads and a Rochester Quadrajet carburetor complete the package.

Front-end style

The bold front end sports a pair of single headlights surrounded by wide chrome bezels. The handsome grill has chrome trim and features a special badge in the center.

Vinyl top

To increase appeal for the luxury car buyer, a special vinyl top was made available as an option. For only $126.40, there was a choice of five distinct colors: black, blue, dark gold, green or white.

Distinctive styling

Built only as a two-door hardtop, the Monte Carlo's exterior styling is very European-looking with its long hood and short deck design. The pronounced fender profile that runs front to back is vaguely reminiscent of the old Jaguar XK models.

Special suspension

In addition to GM's normal practice of using unequal length A-arms up front and a solid, live axle at the rear, all SS 454s contained a unique Automatic Level Control system with built-in air compressor.

Optional interior

An optional console could be fitted between a pair of comfortable bucket seats upholstered in soft vinyl. Simulated burred-elm wood inlays were applied to the instrument panel.

Specifications

1970 Chevrolet Monte Carlo SS 454

ENGINE
Type: V8

Construction: Cast-iron block and heads

Valve gear: Two valves per cylinder operated by a single camshaft, pushrods and rocker arms

Bore and stroke: 4.25 in. x 4.00 in.

Displacement: 454 c.i.

Compression ratio: 10.25:1

Induction system: Rochester Quadrajet four-barrel carburetor

Maximum power: 360 bhp at 4,400 rpm

Maximum torque: 500 lb-ft at 3,200 rpm

TRANSMISSION
GM TurboHydramatic 400 automatic

BODY/CHASSIS
Separate steel body and frame

SPECIAL FEATURES

Discreet badges on the rocker panel are the only giveaway of the 454.

All production 1970 SS Monte Carlos were powered by the LS-5 454-cubic inch V8.

RUNNING GEAR
Steering: Recirculating ball

Front suspension: Unequal length A-arms, telescopic shock absorbers, coil springs and anti-roll bar

Rear suspension: Live solid axle with telescopic shock absorbers and coil springs

Brakes: Discs (front), drums (rear)

Wheels: Rally, 7 x 15 in.

Tires: Goodyear Polyglas, G70-15

DIMENSIONS
Length: 206.0 in.   **Width:** 76.0 in.

Height: 52.0 in   **Wheelbase:** 116.0 in

Track: 61.9 in. (front), 61.1 in. (rear)

Weight: 3,860 lbs.

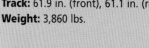

Chevrolet NOVA SS396

Redesigned and larger for 1968, Chevy's compact now had room for big-block engines. The 396-cubic inch rat motor was officially offered in 350-bhp tune, but those who lived by the phrase 'excess is best' selected the L78 engine option and got the 375-bhp 396 turning the plain-looking Nova into a street terror.

"...Dr. Jekyll and Mr. Hyde aura."

"Traditionally, the Nova has been stereotyped as a timid base-model with zero performance potential. This 396 V8 version proves this to be a blatant misconception. True, inside and out, it is plain and unadorned, but upon start up, you soon realize that this so- called 'grocery-getter' has a real Dr. Jekyll and Mr. Hyde aura. Grab the four-speed shifter, hit the gas and listen to the tires spin effortlessly. Its quick-ratio steering and stiff suspension give a fun-to-drive feel that is missing from other muscle cars.

Nova SSs are ideal racers because they're kept light with a minimum of interior embellishments.

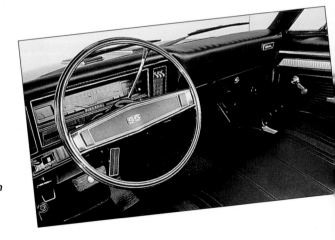

Milestones

1968 The Chevy II™ **is redesigned** and now rides on a 111-inch wheelbase. Hardtop coupes are dropped, leaving just two-door, pillared coupes and four-door sedans. The SS option returns, and for the first time a 396-cubic inch, big-block V8 is available.

The Nova Super Sport finally got a 327-cubic inch V8 in 1965.

1969 Thanks to a strong advertising campaign, sales are high. Of the 106,200 Novas built, only 7,209 are ordered as SS™ models.

The most powerful engine available in 1971 was a four-barrel 270-bhp, 350-cubic inch V8.

1970 Nova is now the official name, ousting the original Chevy II title. Despite an auto workers' strike early in the year, production is up. The number of SS models that are sold are doubled from the previous year. This is the final season for the 396-cubic inch V8 in Novas.

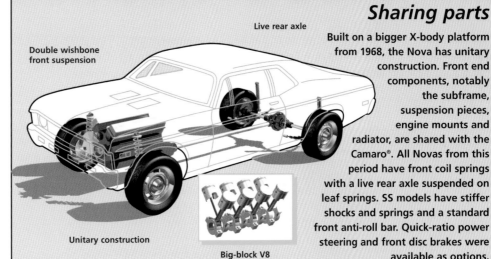

Double wishbone front suspension

Live rear axle

Unitary construction

Big-block V8

Sharing parts

Built on a bigger X-body platform from 1968, the Nova has unitary construction. Front end components, notably the subframe, suspension pieces, engine mounts and radiator, are shared with the Camaro®. All Novas from this period have front coil springs with a live rear axle suspended on leaf springs. SS models have stiffer shocks and springs and a standard front anti-roll bar. Quick-ratio power steering and front disc brakes were available as options.

THE POWER PACK

Mark IV monster

Introduced in 1965 as a replacement for the 409, the 396 was the smallest of the Mark IV series of big-block Chevrolet V8s. First made available in big Chevrolets and the Corvette®, the 396 became a Nova option partway through 1968. In L78 trim, it has a cast-iron block but features an aluminum dual-plane intake manifold and heads borrowed from the 427 with larger valves. Other high performance features include solid lifters and an 800-cfm Holley four-barrel carburetor. Horsepower is rated at 375 bhp at 5,600 rpm, while torque is a substantial 415 lb-ft. With this engine, the 3,400-lb. Nova could run the ¼-mile in 14.5 seconds bone stock.

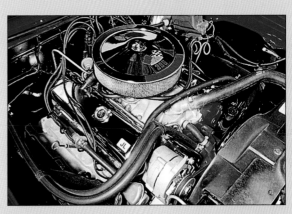

Speed king

With a very favorable weight distribution, the Nova SS396 was one of the most surprising and quickest muscle cars of the late 1960s. Those equipped with the 375-bhp, solid-lifter, L78 engine are especially sought after by collectors today.

Those who wanted lots of power in a light car were drawn to the Nova SS396.

93

Chevrolet **NOVA SS396**

Serious racers saw the Nova as the perfect street brawler. For just $280 they could transform their bare-bones coupe into a machine that could nearly outrun just about every GTO, Mustang and Road Runner in town.

Rat motor

The key to the Nova's surprising performance is the 396-cubic inch, big-block V8. Although not highlighted in factory brochures, the L78 version of this engine with its solid cam could be ordered by those who wanted a serious performance machine.

Pillared coupe styling

When the Chevy II was enlarged in 1968, the hardtop bodystyle was dropped, leaving the pillared coupe and sedan as the only choices. Even with SS badging, the 1969 Chevy II Nova is still demure in appearance.

Four-speed transmission

Back in the late 1960s, most racers still wanted a manual transmission. The Muncie M21, close-ratio four-speed was an ideal companion to the torquey 396 engine.

Side marker lights

From 1969, all cars sold in the U.S. required side marker lights (amber) front and (red) rear.

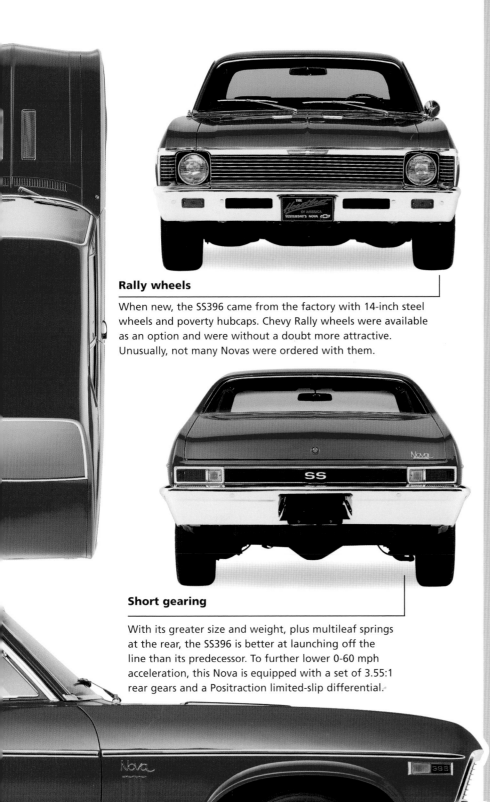

Rally wheels

When new, the SS396 came from the factory with 14-inch steel wheels and poverty hubcaps. Chevy Rally wheels were available as an option and were without a doubt more attractive. Unusually, not many Novas were ordered with them.

Short gearing

With its greater size and weight, plus multileaf springs at the rear, the SS396 is better at launching off the line than its predecessor. To further lower 0-60 mph acceleration, this Nova is equipped with a set of 3.55:1 rear gears and a Positraction limited-slip differential.

Specifications

1969 Chevrolet Nova SS396

ENGINE

Type: V8

Construction: Cast-iron block and heads

Valve gear: Two valves per cylinder operated by a single centrally-mounted camshaft with pushrods and rockers

Bore and stroke: 4.09 in. x 3.76 in.

Displacement: 396 c.i.

Compression ratio: 10.0:1

Induction system: Holley 800-cfm four-barrel downdraft carburetor

Maximum power: 375 bhp at 5,600 rpm

Maximum torque: 415 lb-ft at 3,600 rpm

TRANSMISSION

Muncie M21 four-speed manual

BODY/CHASSIS

Unitary steel chassis with two-door coupe body

SPECIAL FEATURES

These non-functional hood vents are part of the SS package.

'SS396' front fender badges give a clue to what lies under the hood.

RUNNING GEAR

Steering: Recirculating ball

Front suspension: Unequal length A-arms with coil springs, telescopic shock absorbers and anti-roll bar

Rear suspension: Live axle with semi-elliptic leaf springs and telescopic shock absorbers

Brakes: Discs (front), drums (rear)

Wheels: Rally, 7 x 14 in.

Tires: E70 14

DIMENSIONS

Length: 189.4 in.   **Width:** 70.4 in.

Height: 52.4 in.   **Wheelbase:** 111.0 in.

Track: 59.0 in. (front), 58.9 in. (rear)

Weight: 3,400 lbs.

Chrysler **AIRFLOW**

The Airflow was one of the most revolutionary and adventurous American cars of the 1930s, an extraordinary study of aerodynamic lines and novel packaging. It was a brilliant car, but too revolutionary for the masses of mainstream buyers.

"...inspires confidence."

"Press the gas pedal and the straight-eight rumbles willingly ahead of you. There is power to take it above 80 mph if you want, but it's better to enjoy the unbelievable amount of torque at your disposal and sit back at a gentle cruise of around 72 mph. In traffic it is tractable, and the view from the high driving position inspires confidence. The hydraulic brakes are surprisingly good and the worm-and-roller steering is remarkably accurate."

The Airflow has comfortable bench seats and an unusual instrument panel.

Milestones

1934 The wind tunnel-tested Airflow range receives straight-eight power, a choice of four wheelbases and various bodystyles. There are three lines—Standard, Imperial and Imperial Custom. It sets speed records and wins the Monte Carlo Concours d'Elegance for design.

Chrysler Airflows are all powered by straight-eight engines.

1935 The 298-cubic inch engine is dropped. The famous waterfall grill is replaced by a curious 'skyscraper' design.

Chrysler also offered a more conventional Airstream model.

1936 The flowing rear end is toned down with the addition of a built-in trunk. Only one engine (a 323-cubic inch) is now offered.

1937 In the final year of production the range is reduced to just two models, and sales dwindle to 4,600 cars.

UNDER THE SKIN

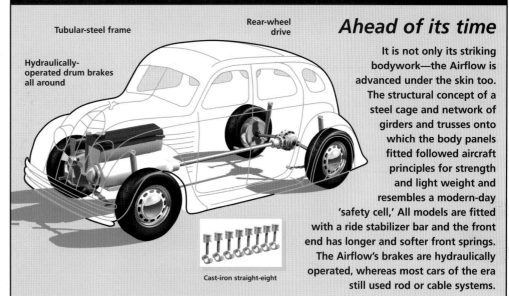

Tubular-steel frame

Rear-wheel drive

Hydraulically-operated drum brakes all around

Cast-iron straight-eight

Ahead of its time

It is not only its striking bodywork—the Airflow is advanced under the skin too. The structural concept of a steel cage and network of girders and trusses onto which the body panels fitted followed aircraft principles for strength and light weight and resembles a modern-day 'safety cell,' All models are fitted with a ride stabilizer bar and the front end has longer and softer front springs. The Airflow's brakes are hydraulically operated, whereas most cars of the era still used rod or cable systems.

THE POWER PACK

Straight-eight power

Chrysler used its range of straight-eight engines in the Airflow series. Carburetion was by Ball & Ball or dual Stromberg downdrafts with automatic choke and an integral air cleaner. During its first year of production there were three engine sizes—298-, 323- and 384-cubic inches—but the 298 was dropped after the first year and the 384 was not available after 1935. Airflows sold under the De Soto badge are fitted with straight-six engines instead of eights.

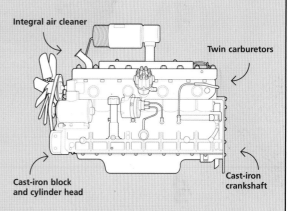

Integral air cleaner

Twin carburetors

Cast-iron block and cylinder head

Cast-iron crankshaft

1934 Imperial

The most stylish Airflow is the imposing long-wheelbase Imperial Custom —the 145-inch wheelbase best suits the car's aerodynamic lines. The most desirable model is the first year 1934, with its classic waterfall grill and sloping tail.

Airflow Custom Imperials from 1934 are highly sought after today.

Chrysler **AIRFLOW**

The Airflow was supposed to represent the future, but like so many advanced ideas the public was skeptical of this strange-looking new car, even though it offered new levels of comfort, space and driveability.

Straight-eight power

The straight-eight engine has a healthy power output and masses of torque. In addition, the unit is positioned directly over the front axle, making the hood quite short for a car of this period and allowing more room for passengers.

Aircraft-type construction

The method of construction was inspired by aviation principles. The body is mounted on steel beams and trusses, in a similar way to contemporary aircraft's.

Advanced transmission

The three-speed manual transmission is renowned for its silent operation. It is fitted with helical gears and later examples gained a hypoid rear axle. Above 45 mph, when you lift your foot off the accelerator, overdrive is automatically engaged.

Wind-tunnel-honed body

The Airflow was one of the first cars to be tested in a wind tunnel. The aerodynamic lines helped a 1934 Imperial coupe to complete the flying mile at the Bonneville Salt Flats at 95.6 mph.

Bold nose

The front end of the 1934 model features an amazing 'waterfall' grill, 'shaped by the wind' badging and triple bumper strips. The faired in headlights look curiously like bug eyes, especially on later cars.

A glazing world first

Although most Airflows, like this one, have split windshields, some later-model Imperials boasted a new curved glass design

Puncture-proof tires

By 1936 all Airflows were fitted with new Lifeguard tires with special heavy-duty tubes and a second 'floating' tube inside.

Specifications
1934 Chrysler Airflow Sedan

ENGINE

Type: In-line eight-cylinder
Construction: Cast-iron block and head
Valve gear: Two sidevalves per cylinder
Bore and stroke: 3.25 in. x 4.50 in.
Displacement: 298 c.i.
Compression ratio: Not quoted
Induction system: Two carburetors
Maximum power: 122 bhp at 3,400 rpm
Maximum torque: Not quoted
Top speed: 88 mph
0–60 mph: 19.5 sec.

TRANSMISSION

Three-speed manual

BODY/CHASSIS

Steel girder chassis with four-door steel sedan body

SPECIAL FEATURES

The rear wheel skirts are evocative of the 1930s art deco era.

The rigorously curved surfaces of the Airflow, shaped by Oliver Clark, were unique for 1930s design.

RUNNING GEAR

Steering: worm-and-roller
Front suspension: Beam axle with leaf springs and shock absorbers
Rear suspension: Rigid axle with leaf springs and shock absorbers
Brakes: Drums (front and rear)
Wheels: Steel, 16-in. dia.
Tires: Crossply, 16-in. dia.

DIMENSIONS

Length: 235.0 in.   **Width:** 77.9 in.
Height: 68.9 in.   **Wheelbase:** 146.5 in.
Track: 63.0 in. (front), 61.1 in. (rear)
Weight: 4,166 lbs.

Chrysler C-300

The Chrysler 300 is widely recognized as one of America's first muscle cars. However, the 300 wasn't about brute power; it also was a refined, full-size sportster with an abundance of luxury features.

"...immensely powerful."

"The immensely powerful 331-cubic inch Hemi engine produces superb performance by 1950s standards. It pushes the 4,005-lbs. Chrysler to 60 mph in less than 9 seconds, and cruising at over 120 mph is easily possible. Despite its considerable size, the big C-300 remains rock-steady at speed, and although it leans through corners, it manages to hold the line better than any of its contemporaries. It truly deserves its legendary status."

Power windows and a 150-mph speedometer are standard in the C-300.

Milestones

1951 Chrysler introduces its first mass-produced, widely available overhead-valve V8—the 331-cubic inch firepower Hemi. Although a late entry in the OHV V8 race, Chrysler's engine gains a fine reputation for its rugged, powerful and technically well-engineered design.

1958 was the last year for the original Hemi in Chrysler cars, here a DeSoto Adventurer.

1955 Chrysler installs a tuned 300-bhp Hemi into a two-door Windsor coupe and adds heavy-duty suspension and an Imperial grill. The result is the potent C-300.

The last of the tailfinned 300s was the 1961 300G.

1956 More power (340 bhp) and integrated fins mark the second-season 300B, which also starts the letter legacy, culminating in the square-rigged 300L of 1965.

UNDER THE SKIN

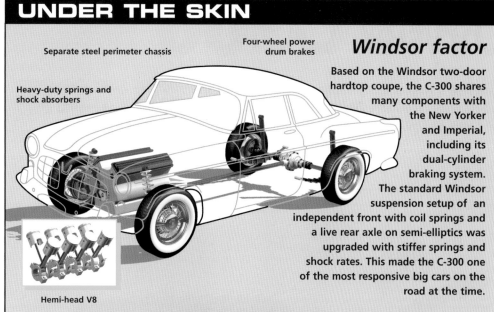

Separate steel perimeter chassis

Four-wheel power drum brakes

Heavy-duty springs and shock absorbers

Hemi-head V8

Windsor factor

Based on the Windsor two-door hardtop coupe, the C-300 shares many components with the New Yorker and Imperial, including its dual-cylinder braking system. The standard Windsor suspension setup of an independent front with coil springs and a live rear axle on semi-elliptics was upgraded with stiffer springs and shock rates. This made the C-300 one of the most responsive big cars on the road at the time.

THE POWER PACK

Hemi Legacy

Chrysler gained a lead on its competition when it launched its new overhead-valve V8 in 1951. This 331-cubic inch cast-iron engine featured hemispherical combustion chambers, which enabled it to produce more power than rival V8s at a lower compression ratio. In initial form, it was rated at 180 bhp, but more power was easily possible. For 1955, engineers fitted a tuned version into a two-door Windsor hardtop and christened it the 300. This engine featured bigger valves, a higher-lift camshaft, and a slightly higher compression. The result was nearly 1 bhp per cubic inch and staggering performance.

Bargain Blaze

Competing in the great American horsepower race, the C-300 packed a fearsome punch. It was faster than nearly every other car on sale in the U.S. in 1955, and although it cost a towering $4,110, this early muscle car was a bargain.

Back-up lights and external mirrors were not available on the C-300.

Chrysler **C-300**

America's first mass-produced car to break the 300-bhp ceiling, the C-300 was also incredibly stylish and dominated NASCAR, winning 37 races in the hands of drivers like Buck Baker and Tim Flock.

Stiffened suspension

While the front coil springs of the New Yorker are rated at 480 lbs./in., those on the C-300 are rated at 800 lbs./in. Likewise, the New Yorker's rear leaf springs are rated at 100 lbs./in., whereas the C-300's are 160 lbs./in.

Solid lifters

Chrysler engineers replaced the hydraulic lifters with solid lifters for the 300. Revving up to 5,200 rpm, the heat generated by the engine could 'pump up' hydraulic lifters as they expand and hold the valves open.

Automatics only

All C-300s came with two-speed PowerFlite automatic transmissions. However, experts agree that there was one car (number 1206) that was built with a three-speed manual transmission.

Unique wheels

Chrysler C-300 buyers had a choice of two wheel styles. The standard ones are steel with Imperial wheel covers and unique 300 center caps; or, for an extra $617, buyers could opt for a set of chrome, 48-spoke wheels by Motor Wheel.

Axle ratios

The standard rear axle ratio for the C-300 is a 3.54:1 ring-and-pinion, but steeper cogs were available.

Specifications

1955 Chrysler C-300

ENGINE

Type: V8

Construction: Cast-iron block and heads

Valve gear: Two valves per cylinder operated by a single camshaft with pushrods and rockers

Bore and stroke: 3.81 in. x 3.63 in.

Displacement: 331.1 c.i.

Compression ratio: 8.5:1

Induction system: Two Carter four-barrel carburetors

Maximum power: 300 bhp at 5,200 rpm

Maximum torque: 345 lb-ft at 3,200 rpm

Top speed: 130 mph

0-60 mph: 8.9 sec.

TRANSMISSION

PowerFlite two-speed automatic

BODY/CHASSIS

Separate chassis with steel two-door body

SPECIAL FEATURES

The protruding stalk shifter was only found on 1955 300s.

Fins on the C-300 were little more than extra chrome pieces grafted on.

RUNNING GEAR

Steering: Recirculating-ball

Front suspension: A-arms with coil springs and telescopic shock absorbers

Rear suspension: Live axle with semi-elliptic multileaf springs and telescopic shock absorbers

Brakes: Drums (front and rear)

Wheels: Wire, 15 x 5 in.

Tires: Goodyear Super Cushion Nylon Special tubeless white sidewalls 6-ply, 8.00 x 15

DIMENSIONS

Length: 218.8 in.   **Width:** 79.1 in.

Height: 60.1 in.   **Wheelbase:** 126.0 in.

Track: 60.2 in. (front) 59.6 in. (rear)

Weight: 4,005 lbs.

Chrysler TOWN & COUNTRY

Introduced as Chrysler's first woody station wagon in 1941, the Town & Country returned after World War II as a top-level series of sedans, convertibles and coupes built on the New Yorker chassis. The most elegant variant in the post-war years was the convertible.

"...unique driving experience."

"You can tell that a lot of effort went into building this car. The doors shut with vault-like firmness and everything feels rock solid. The huge steering wheel adds an air of authority. Once on the move, it's fun to watch others gaze as you glide by. While the Town & Country with its thick padded bench seat was designed for cruising, it has more than ample power, a satisfyingly smooth ride and comfortable seating—it's a unique driving experience."

Town & Countrys could be well equipped—this one has a cigarette lighter and clock.

Milestones

1941 Created under the direction of Dave Wallace, the Town & Country is Chrysler's first station wagon. It has clamshell doors and can seat six or nine. Based on the Windsor chassis, 997 are built.

Ford and Mercury were Chrysler's only rivals in 1946-1948. This is a Mercury Sportsman.

1942 The Town & Country becomes a Windsor, but production of all models ceases in February due to World War II.

1950 was the last year of sale for the T&C convertible.

1946 Automobile production resumes. The Town & Country is now an entire series instead of just a wagon. A Brougham, sedan, convertible and coupe are offered.

1947 Only the Town & Country sedan and convertible are offered this year.

UNDER THE SKIN

Separate steel chassis

Four-wheel drum brakes

Independent front suspension

Dependable eight

Playing it safe

Chrysler fielded restyled cars for 1942, but although sheet metal was new, mechanicals were essentially carried over. Town & Countrys rode two different wheelbases for 1947. The chassis is a separate steel affair with independent front suspension and solid axle attached to the rear. Springs are coils at the front, with semi-elliptics at the rear. Braking is courtesy of four-wheel drums.

THE POWER PACK

Proven eight

When relaunched for the 1946 model year, the Town & Country was available with either straight-six or straight-eight engines. Eights were first introduced for 1931, spanning 240 to 385 cubic inches and producing from 82 to 125 bhp. By 1947, only a single straight eight was still available—a 324-cubic inch unit. By then, the basic design was slightly dated, but the cast-iron unit, with a low 6.7:1 compression ratio and a five-main-bearing crankshaft, was very reliable and was used until 1951.

Rare woody

Town & Countrys, convertibles in particular, have long been coveted collectibles. They were little short of handmade cars and production was always low—only 8,368 convertibles were built. This makes them exceedingly rare today.

All T&C convertibles were powered by straight-eight engines.

Chrysler TOWN & COUNTRY

The name Town & Country came from Mr. Boyertown—the man who built the bodies for these special cars. He said the front of the car 'looked town, while the rear looked country,' and the name stuck.

Exclusively straight eight

Production 1946-1948 Town & Countrys are powered by Chrysler's venerable straight-eight engine sized at 324-cubic inches. With two Ball and Ball carburetors, it produces 135 bhp.

Semi-automatic transmission

Chrysler's fluid-drive transmission was standard on the Town & Country. This semi-automatic unit has two high and two low gears. The fluid drive means acceleration is slightly on the leisurely side.

Structural wood

Besides looking great, the wood is structural on the Town & Country. The door, quarter panel and trunk-lid framing are made from white ash, and the inserts are real Honduras mahogany, changed to DI-NOC decals in late 1947.

Fender skirts

Available as a dealer-installed accessory, rear fender wheel well skirts gave the car a more streamlined appearance.

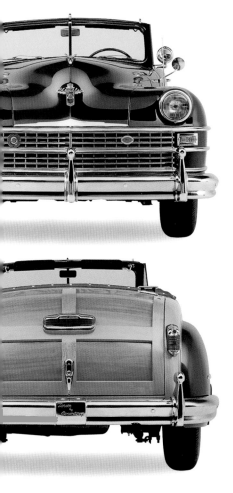

Specifications

1947 Chrysler Town & Country

ENGINE
Type: Inline eight-cylinder

Construction: Cast-iron block and head

Valve gear: Two side valves per cylinder operated by a single block-mounted cam

Bore and stroke: 3.25 in. x 4.88 in.

Displacement: 324 c.i.

Compression ratio: 6.7:1

Induction system: Twin Ball and Ball E7A1 carburetors

Maximum power: 135 bhp at 3,400 rpm

Maximum torque: Not quoted

TRANSMISSION
Fluid-drive four-speed semi-automatic

BODY/CHASSIS
Steel chassis with steel and wood two-door convertible body

SPECIAL FEATURES

Chrysler's fluid-drive semi-automatic transmission is fitted on this car.

Its body and door frames were made from ash with mahogany inserts.

RUNNING GEAR
Steering: Recirculating ball

Front suspension: Unequal-length wishbones with coil springs and telescopic shock absorbers

Rear suspension: Live axle with semi-elliptic leaf springs and telescopic shock absorbers

Brakes: Drums (front and rear)

Wheels: Pressed steel, 15-in. dia.

Tires: 8.20 x 15

DIMENSIONS
Length: 202.9 in. **Width:** 84.2 in.

Height: 66.8 in.   **Wheelbase:** 127.5 in.

Track: 64.7 in. (front), 65.7 in. (rear)

Weight: 4,332 lbs.

Long wheelbase

In 1947, the Town & Country was available either as a sedan or convertible. The six-cylinder powered sedans had a 121.5-inch wheelbase, while the eight-cylinder convertibles had 127.5 inches between the wheel centers.

Chrysler **TURBINE**

The 1963 Turbine was an experimental vehicle supplied to 45 families across the U.S., with each having a three-month trial. Although it had potential, there were too many problems for it to gain any commercial application.

"...makes a heat haze."

"When you start up the engine, there is an extraordinary whining sound. Look down at the tachometer and you will see that the engine idles at an incredible 20,000 rpm. The hot air from the tail pipes makes a heat haze behind the car. Despite its bulk, acceleration is good, although you need to get used to the curious sensation of the delay between pressing the throttle and feeling the power. In most other respects you could be driving any 1960s Detroit sedan."

The attractive interior is color-keyed to match the paintwork.

Milestones

1955 Chrysler fits
a gas turbine to a stock Plymouth Belvedere as an experiment.

The more conventional 1963 Lincoln Continental had the same designer as the Turbine.

1963 As an exercise
in evaluation and publicity, Chrysler releases 45 gas-turbine cars to members of the public for testing.

1964 One turbine
car is sent around the world to test public reaction.

The GM EV-1 is the latest attempt at mass-marketing an alternative-fuel car.

1977 Chrysler
pursues its turbine experiments throughout the 1960s and 1970s, culminating in a seventh-generation turbine in a 1977 Dodge Aspen.

UNDER THE SKIN

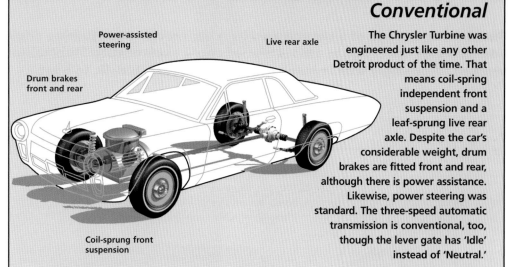

Power-assisted steering

Live rear axle

Drum brakes front and rear

Coil-sprung front suspension

Conventional

The Chrysler Turbine was engineered just like any other Detroit product of the time. That means coil-spring independent front suspension and a leaf-sprung live rear axle. Despite the car's considerable weight, drum brakes are fitted front and rear, although there is power assistance. Likewise, power steering was standard. The three-speed automatic transmission is conventional, too, though the lever gate has 'Idle' instead of 'Neutral.'

THE POWER PACK

Gas Turbine

Chrysler may not have been the first to produce a gas-turbine engine, but it was the world's greatest turbine exponent. The pistonless gas turbine engine has some very strong advantages: it can run on all sorts of fuel (from diesel and kerosene to aircraft fuel), it can rev to very high speeds (as much as 44,600 rpm) very quietly, it warms up instantaneously and boasts a huge amount of torque. However, the disadvantages outweigh the benefits. In pure horsepower terms the engine is quite feeble (only 130 bhp). It's heavy, and worst of all, it has appalling gas mileage figures, at around 12 mpg.

Museum piece

When Chrysler canned its Turbine experiment, 46 of the 55 examples were destroyed simply to avoid paying import duty on the Italian-built cars. The remaining 9 machines were dispatched to car museums and private collections across America.

The Chrysler's styling is particularly outlandish from the rear.

Chrysler TURBINE

The sight and sound of a car powered by a high-revving gas-turbine engine sounded very space-age in 1963. Chrysler's bold experimental Turbine car worked surprisingly well in many areas and looked futuristic to boot.

Turbine engine

Central to the Chrysler is its gas-turbine powerplant, a neat installation under the hood. Able to spin up to 44,600 rpm, its power is available right across the rev band, as is its torque. But it is too thirsty, even though it can run on a wide variety of fuels.

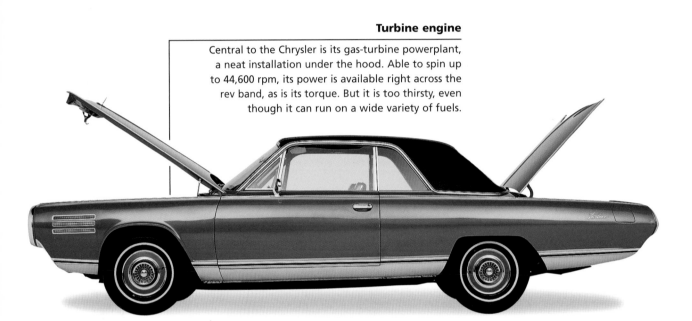

Designed by Mr. Thunderbird

The cigar-shaped Turbine body was designed by Elwood Engle, the father of the 1961 Ford Thunderbird. Many similarities exist in the profile of the two designs.

Orange paintwork

All 55 cars were built to basically the same specifications, including orange metallic paint and orange leather upholstery. Most, but not all, also had a black vinyl roof.

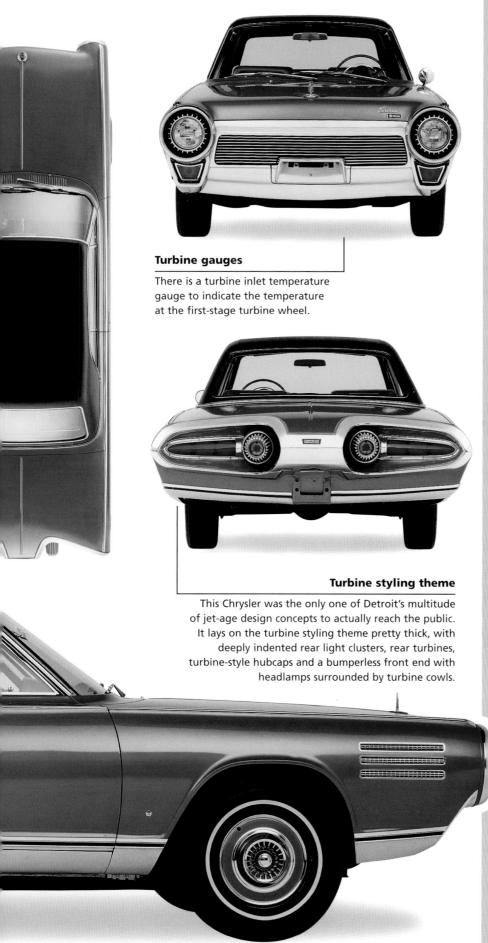

Turbine gauges

There is a turbine inlet temperature gauge to indicate the temperature at the first-stage turbine wheel.

Turbine styling theme

This Chrysler was the only one of Detroit's multitude of jet-age design concepts to actually reach the public. It lays on the turbine styling theme pretty thick, with deeply indented rear light clusters, rear turbines, turbine-style hubcaps and a bumperless front end with headlamps surrounded by turbine cowls.

Specifications

1963 Chrysler Turbine

ENGINE
Type: Gas turbine

Construction: Centrifugal air compressor with vaned power turbine

Valve gear: Compressor turbine operating power turbine

Bore and stroke: N/A

Displacement: N/A

Compression ratio: N/A

Induction system: Pressurized air in flame tube

Maximum power: 130 bhp at 44,600 rpm

Maximum torque: 425 lb-ft at zero rpm output shift speed

TRANSMISSION
Three-speed automatic

BODY/CHASSIS
Separate chassis with steel two-door sedan body

SPECIAL FEATURES

The rear-end styling drew inspiration from Flash Gordon.

Spent gases exit from under the car, as in a conventional engine.

RUNNING GEAR
Steering: Recirculating-ball

Front suspension: Upper and lower wishbones, coil springs and shock absorbers

Rear suspension: Live axle with leaf springs and shock absorbers

Brakes: Drums (front and rear)

Wheels: Steel, 14-in. dia.

Tires: 7.50 x 14

DIMENSIONS
Length: 201.6 in. **Width:** 72.9 in.

Height: 53.5 in. **Wheelbase:** 110.0 in.

Track: 59.0 in. (front), 56.7 in. (rear)

Weight: 3,900 lbs.

Cord **810/812**

The original Cord 810 was a revolutionary design with an advanced front-wheel drive layout and V8 power. Its performance was transformed when a supercharger was added to form the 190-bhp Cord 812.

"...outstanding performance."

"The supercharged V8 produces huge torque and once you've adjusted to the vague gearshifter, the Cord's outstanding performance can really be exploited. With front-wheel drive, steering is heavy at low speeds, although it becomes lighter as the car gains momentum. Cornering is almost neutral compared to rear-drive equivalents. The unique suspension design gives a choppy ride but the result is very little body roll for such a big, heavy car."

An aluminum instrument panel and white- faced gauges are sporty for the 1930s.

Milestones

1935 Built in record time, the first Cord 810 is exhibited at the New York Motor Show and immediately attracts potential customers.

The 1937 812 evolved from the 1936 810.

1936 Cord 810 production

begins in sedan and convertible versions. It is not as fast as it looks, with 0–60 mph taking 20.0 seconds with a top speed of 90 mph.

The 812 body tooling was bought by Graham and used for its rear-drive 1940 Hollywood sedan.

1937 To increase sales, Cord

introduces the supercharged 812. It is basically the same as the 810 apart from the addition of a Schwitzer-Cummins supercharger that produces more power (170/190 bhp) and greater performance. More than 6 seconds are trimmed off of the non-supercharged version. The more expensive Custom Cordis also introduced this year.

UNDER THE SKIN

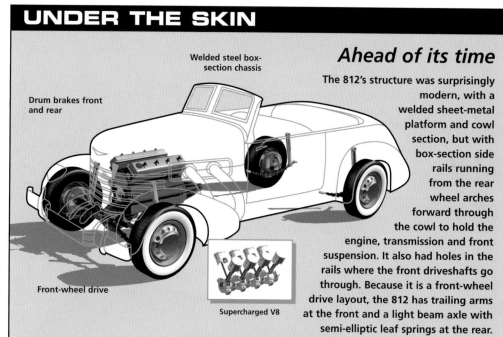

Welded steel box-section chassis

Drum brakes front and rear

Front-wheel drive

Supercharged V8

Ahead of its time

The 812's structure was surprisingly modern, with a welded sheet-metal platform and cowl section, but with box-section side rails running from the rear wheel arches forward through the cowl to hold the engine, transmission and front suspension. It also had holes in the rails where the front driveshafts go through. Because it is a front-wheel drive layout, the 812 has trailing arms at the front and a light beam axle with semi-elliptic leaf springs at the rear.

THE POWER PACK

Airplane inspiration

Engines for the Cord were made by another Auburn-Cord-Duesenberg subsidiary, the airplane engine manufacturer Lycoming. For the 812, a modified version of the 288.6-cubic inch V8 fitted in the 810 was used. Using an iron block and alloy head design with side valves in L-heads actuated by a single camshaft, the big V8 was fitted with a Schwitzer-Cummins centrifugal supercharger. It is driven by gears at the end of the camshaft, which also drives epicyclic gears at 24 times the cam speed inside the supercharger itself. Advertised power output was 170/190 bhp—more than 40 more bhp then the standard model.

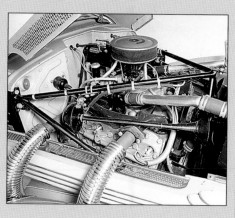

Open road

The sedan versions may be very stylish, but the most flamboyant and collectable Cord 812s are the convertible versions—the Phaeton and Sportsman. These look more stylish and sporty and, not surprisingly, command higher prices.

Externally, the Phaeton and Sportsman cabriolet are nearly identical.

Cord 810/812

The Cord 812 was styled by one of the great car designers, Gordon Buehrig. It was like no other car on the road, thanks to its coffin-like nose, unique radiator grill and pop-up headlights.

V8 engine

Lycoming's V8 is very strong yet relatively light thanks to its alloy cylinder heads. The valve-train is a unique design with upright rockers pivoted below the camshaft actuating the valves mounted in the block and angled at 35 degrees.

Independent front suspension

Helping to give the 812 its superb road holding independent front suspension with trailing arms and a single transverse leaf spring.

Four-speed transmission

An advanced feature of the 812 is the four-speed manual transmission (unusual for the time). Fourth gear is very tall with over 28 mph per thousand revs, making the Cord ideal for high-speed touring.

Electro-vacuum gear shifter

The Cord uses a Bendix 'Electric Hand' pre-selector gear shifter. This miniature gear linkage relies on the vacuum inside the intake manifold to suck the pistons controlling the movements of the selector rods. It only works with the clutch depressed and the driver's foot off the accelerator.

Drum brakes

Massive 12-inch, hydraulic, centrifuse drums are used on all four wheels.

Pop-up lights

Ordinary round headlights would have spoiled the Cord's bold styling and obstructed airflow, so they were designed to be concealed. In fact, the lights are basically landing light units from Stinson aircraft (also owned by Auburn-Cord-Duesenberg).

Specifications
1937 Cord 812 Supercharged

ENGINE

Type: V8

Construction: Cast-iron block and alloy cylinder heads

Valve gear: Two in-line side valves per cylinder operated by a single block-mounted camshaft with rocker arms and rollers

Bore and stroke: 3.50 in. x 3.75 in.

Displacement: 288.6 c.i.

Compression ratio: 6.3:1

Induction system: Single carburetor with mechanically driven Schwitzer-Cummins supercharger

Maximum power: 190 bhp at 4,200 rpm

Maximum torque: 272 lb-ft at 3,000 rpm

Top speed: 111 mph

0–60 mph: 13.8 sec.

TRANSMISSION

Four-speed manual

BODY/CHASSIS

Welded steel floorpan and side rails with two-door convertible body

SPECIAL FEATURES

Phaetons only differ stylistically from cabriolets by having a rear seat and quarter windows.

A crank mounted on the passenger side of the dash is used to raise and lower the headlights.

RUNNING GEAR

Steering: Gemmer centerpoint

Front suspension: Independent with trailing arms, transverse semi-elliptic leaf spring and friction shock absorbers

Rear suspension: Beam axle with semi-elliptic leaf springs and friction shock absorbers

Brakes: Hydraulically operated drums, 12-in. dia.

Wheels: 16 in. Stamped Steel, 16-in. dia.

Tires: 6.50 x 16

DIMENSIONS AND WEIGHT

Length: 195.5 in.   **Width:** 71.0 in.

Height: 58.0 in.   **Wheelbase:** 132.0 in.

Track: 55.9 in. (front), 60.9 in. (rear)

Weight: 4,110 lbs.

DeLorean **DMC**

John DeLorean had a dream, to build a sports car that would never rust or corrode. It was finished in brushed stainless steel over a fiberglass body, but the dream quickly turned into a nightmare.

"...adequate, not exciting."

"You sit deep in the somber interior. It's claustrophobic, but it is comfortable enough, as is the ride. Is it quick and sharp enough for a sports car? Not really; there just isn't enough power from the V6 to give either impressive acceleration or top speed. The DMC was intended to provide a futuristic look with its full electronic gadgetry, stainless steel body, and gullwing doors. Unfortunately, its performance isn't as impressive as the car's look suggests."

Lotus-inspired backbone chassis means there's a deep spine through the cockpit. Note the small opening section of the windows.

Milestones

1963 Pontiac's chief engineer John DeLorean becomes famous when he creates the GTO which becomes the first true 1960s American 'musclecar.'

Giugiaro's design proposals included a four-door sedan.

1974 After leaving General Motors, DeLorean founds the John Z. DeLorean Company, the first step on the way to developing his own car.

1976 First prototype, the Giugiaro-styled DMC12, is assembled.

1978 British Government loans money to help create a factory in Northern Ireland to manufacture the DeLorean.

1981 Production begins at the Dumurray factory near Belfast.

1982 Lack of sales forces the factory into a three-day week. DeLorean goes into receivership in February. By the end of the year there are more than 2,000 cars still unsold.

UNDER THE SKIN

Lotus influence

The Lotus influence is enormous; the backbone chassis is unmistakably a Lotus design very similar to the Esprit's. It looks like a very elongated X, with the V6 engine mounted between the chassis arms at the rear. That is balanced by putting the fuel tank and radiator at the other end of the chassis. There is more Lotus influence in the suspension, which is more compliant than other sports cars, using long semi-trailing arms at the rear.

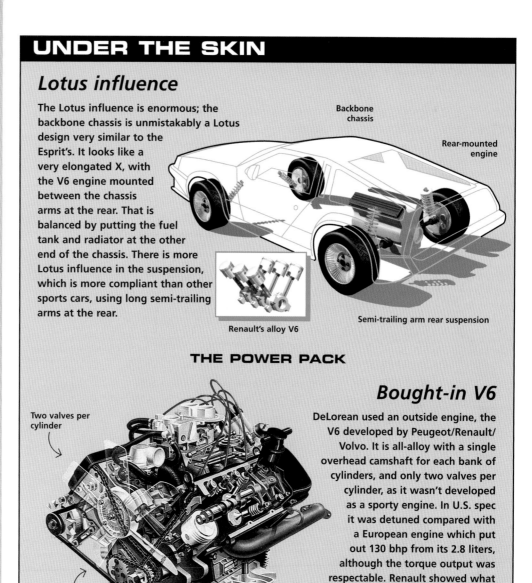

Backbone chassis

Rear-mounted engine

Renault's alloy V6

Semi-trailing arm rear suspension

THE POWER PACK

Two valves per cylinder

All-alloy construction

Single camshaft per bank

Bought-in V6

DeLorean used an outside engine, the V6 developed by Peugeot/Renault/Volvo. It is all-alloy with a single overhead camshaft for each bank of cylinders, and only two valves per cylinder, as it wasn't developed as a sporty engine. In U.S. spec it was detuned compared with a European engine which put out 130 bhp from its 2.8 liters, although the torque output was respectable. Renault showed what could be achieved with the engine in the Alpine A310 and the A610, particularly when it was turbocharged.

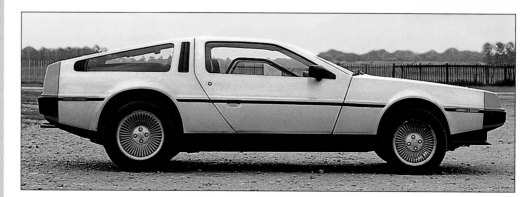

...Blown away

DeLorean was well aware he needed more power and so had Legend Industries build a prototype turbocharged DeLorean using two small Japanese IHI turbos. It worked extremely well, giving the car the performance it lacked.

Turbocharging would have given the DeLorean the performance it needed.

DeLorean DMC

The official name 'Sports Car' was hardly ever used. It showed a lack of imagination, which the design itself did not. With more development and power it could have been a great success.

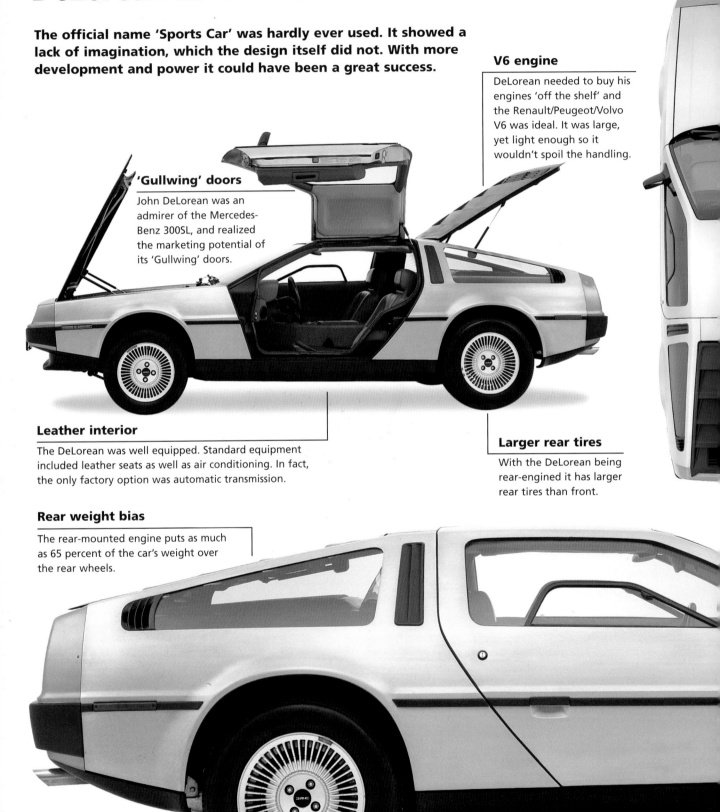

V6 engine

DeLorean needed to buy his engines 'off the shelf' and the Renault/Peugeot/Volvo V6 was ideal. It was large, yet light enough so it wouldn't spoil the handling.

'Gullwing' doors

John DeLorean was an admirer of the Mercedes-Benz 300SL, and realized the marketing potential of its 'Gullwing' doors.

Leather interior

The DeLorean was well equipped. Standard equipment included leather seats as well as air conditioning. In fact, the only factory option was automatic transmission.

Larger rear tires

With the DeLorean being rear-engined it has larger rear tires than front.

Rear weight bias

The rear-mounted engine puts as much as 65 percent of the car's weight over the rear wheels.

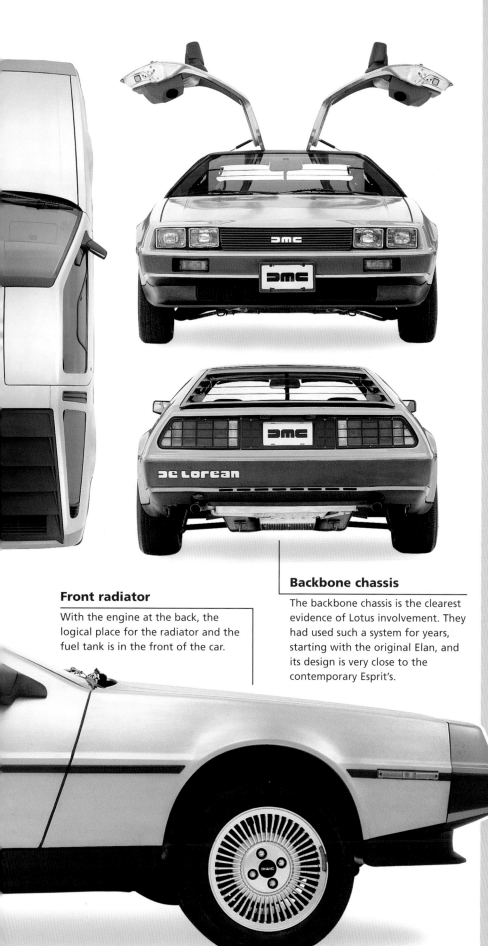

Specifications
1981 DeLorean Sports Car

ENGINE

Type: V6

Construction: Alloy block and heads

Valve gear: Two inclined valves per cylinder operated by single chain-driven overhead cam per bank of cylinders

Bore and stroke: 3.58 in. x 2.87 in.

Displacement: 2,849 cc

Compression ratio: 8.8:1

Induction system: Bosch K-Jetronic fuel injection

Maximum power: 145 bhp at 5,500 rpm

Maximum torque: 162 lb-ft at 2,750 rpm

TRANSMISSION

Renault five-speed manual

BODY/CHASSIS

Sheet-steel backbone chassis with fiberglass coupe body covered with stainless steel

SPECIAL FEATURES

To get some fresh air on the road, there are small opening electric windows set in the door.

Relatively low power and low weight means that the rear-mounted engine does not cause poor handling traits.

RUNNING GEAR

Steering: Rack-and-pinion

Front suspension: Double wishbones with coil springs, telescopic shocks, and anti-roll bar

Rear suspension: Semi-trailing arms, coil springs, and telescopic shocks

Brakes: Discs all around, 10.5 in. dia. (front), 10 in. dia. (rear)

Wheels: Alloy 6 in. x 14 in. (front), 8 in. x 15 in. (rear)

Tires: Goodyear NCT 195/60HR14 (front), 235/60HR15 (rear)

DIMENSIONS

Length: 168 in.   **Width:** 78.3 in.

Height: 44.9 in.   **Wheelbase:** 94.89 in.

Track: 62.6 in. (front), 62.5 in. (rear)

Weight: 2,840 lbs.

Front radiator

With the engine at the back, the logical place for the radiator and the fuel tank is in the front of the car.

Backbone chassis

The backbone chassis is the clearest evidence of Lotus involvement. They had used such a system for years, starting with the original Elan, and its design is very close to the contemporary Esprit's.

DeSoto **PACESETTER**

Arriving midway through 1956 was a new top-of-the line DeSoto—the Adventurer. Packing a bigger 341-cubic inch version of the Hemi engine, it was distinguished by gold anodized trim. A convertible version, which was the Indianapolis 500 pace car that year, was aptly named the Pacesetter.

"...majestic interior design."

"*The majestic interior design in the Pacesetter really strikes a chord. Sitting on sofa-like seats, you grasp a huge, narrow-rimmed steering wheel with push button shift controls to the left of the wheel. The wonderful-sounding Hemi V8 sings enthusiastically, combining seamlessly with the PowerFlite transmission. Despite its bulk, the DeSoto was quick for its day and will keep pulling past 100 mph long after its competition has reached its terminal top speed.*"

Anodized gold on the dash and door panels was an Adventurer/Pacesetter exclusive.

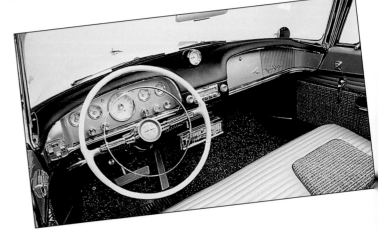

Milestones

1956 DeSoto launches a limited-production hardtop, the Adventurer. A convertible version, the Pacesetter, is also built in very small numbers.

1957 As part of an all-new Chrysler range, a new DeSoto lineup debuts, with the Adventurer coupe and convertible (replacing the Pacesetter) at the top of the range. The Hemi is bored out to 345 cubic inches and has 345 bhp.

1951 saw the arrival of the Hemi V8 in DeSotos.

1958 With a larger bore, the engine size grows to 361 cubic inches. There are minor changes to the grill and trim.

For 1958, the Pacesetter and Adventurer gained a 361-cubic inch engine.

1959 The size of the V8 increases again, to 383 cubic inches.

UNDER THE SKIN

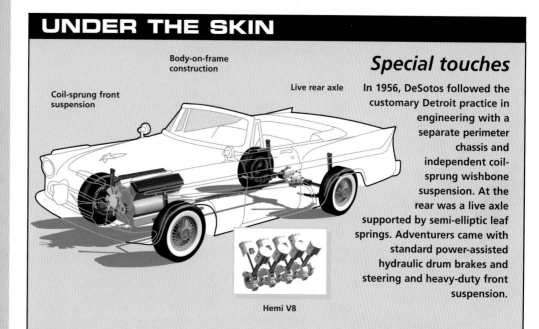

Body-on-frame construction

Coil-sprung front suspension

Live rear axle

Hemi V8

Special touches

In 1956, DeSotos followed the customary Detroit practice in engineering with a separate perimeter chassis and independent coil-sprung wishbone suspension. At the rear was a live axle supported by semi-elliptic leaf springs. Adventurers came with standard power-assisted hydraulic drum brakes and steering and heavy-duty front suspension.

Highland Park power

Regular Firedomes and Fireflites came with 330-cubic inch versions of Chrysler's superb hemi-head V8, rated at 230 and 255 bhp, respectively. In 1956, the Adventurer name first appeared and was the perfect limited-edition showcase for a larger, more powerful 341-cubic inch Hemi. With 320 bhp coupled to a PowerFlite automatic transmission, the new DeSoto flagship was a star performer with 0-60 mph acceleration in the 10- to 12-second range. This engine formed part of the so-called 'Highland Park' performance stable of that year, which included the legendary Chrysler 300B and Dodge D-500.

THE POWER PACK

Trendsetter

Although the 1956 Adventurer is an undisputed collectible, offering fine performance and style, its lesser known derivative, the Pacesetter, is worth a look. For 1956, its only year, just 100 were built compared to 996 hardtops.

Pacesetters are extremely rare these days.

DeSoto **PACESETTER**

DeSotos were always clean, stylish and classic. The Adventurer and Pacesetter, with their 320-bhp Hemi V8s and luxury trim, were flagships, and still look fresh and stylish today.

DeSoto Fireflite Eight

Chrysler's Hemi V8 was an engineering milestone of the 1950s. In the DeSoto Pacesetter it was known as the Fireflite Eight. It had smoother porting and manifold passages and better spark plug and valve location than rival V8s, which helped produce more power.

Coil-sprung suspension

Like rivals of the time, the Pacesetter has independent front suspension with upper and lower wishbones and telescopic shocks. Adventurers and Pacesetters have standard heavy-duty suspension, which slightly improves roadholding.

126-inch wheelbase

The Pacesetter is a full-size car riding a 126-inch wheelbase. In 1957, when Virgil Exner's 'Forward look' cars arrived, the entry-level Firesweep got a shorter 122-inch wheelbase; other DeSotos had a 126-inch wheelbase.

Single color scheme

In its debut year, the Adventurer and the Pacesetter were available only in two-tone white and gold. Special gold badging, interior paneling, grill and wheel covers completed the package. The result was one of the most striking Detroit cars in 1956.

Tailfins

1956 was a pivotal year for Chrysler products, which began sprouting true fins. Those on the Pacesetter were tasteful and mated well with the rest of the body. As the decade wore on, Desotos gained increasingly taller and more outlandish fins.

Convenience options

Pacesetters came with standard power steering, chrome exhaust tips and whitewall tires, which were optional on the Firedome and Fireflite. Air Temp air conditioning, power antenna and Solex safety glass were also available to Pacesetter buyers in 1956.

1956 DeSoto Pacesetter

ENGINE

Type: V8

Construction: Cast-iron block and heads

Valve gear: Two valves per cylinder operated by a single camshaft via pushrods and rockers

Bore and stroke: 3.78 in. x 3.80 in.

Displacement: 341 c.i.

Compression ratio: 9.5:1

Induction system: Two Carter four-barrel carburetors

Maximum power: 320 bhp at 5,200 rpm

Maximum torque: 365 lb-ft at 2,800 rpm

Top speed: 115 mph

0-60 mph: 10.2 sec.

TRANSMISSION

PowerFlite two-speed automatic

BODY/CHASSIS

Separate steel chassis with two-door convertible body

SPECIAL FEATURES

Fins were fashionable in 1956 and twin antennas were a popular option.

A dealer installed record player was just one of the DeSoto's unusual options.

RUNNING GEAR

Steering: Recirculating ball

Front suspension: Double wishbones with coil springs and telescopic shock absorbers

Rear suspension: Live axle with semi-elliptic leaf springs and telescopic shock absorbers

Brakes: Drums (front and rear)

Wheels: Pressed steel, 15-in. dia.

Tires: 7.60 x 15

DIMENSIONS

Length: 220.9 in.   **Width:** 76.5 in.

Height: 58.12 in.   **Wheelbase:** 126.0 in.

Track: 60.4 in. (front), 59.6 in. (rear)

Weight: 3,870 lbs.

Dodge CHALLENGER R/T SE

As the muscle car movement reached its peak in 1970, Dodge finally got a ponycar of its own. Aptly named Challenger, it offered a huge range of engines and options. Enthusiasts were drawn to the R/T model. In 440 Six Pack form, it could run with the best of them.

"...muscle at its finest."

"There is something really magical about E-body Mopars. The seats may offer little support and the light steering can make the Challenger feel a little unwieldy at times, but take the car for a blast and you cannot help but fall in love with it. The 440 Six Pack engine, coupled to a Pistol Grip four-speed enables the R/T to accelerate like a speeding bullet, accompanied by tremendous tire squealing and a thundering exhaust roar; it is muscle at its finest."

R/Ts got the Rallye Pack instrument cluster. This car has the rare Pistol-Grip shifter.

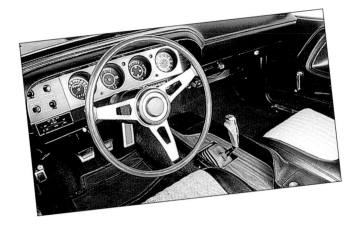

Milestones

1970 Dodge enters the ponycar war with its new Challenger. It is offered as a coupe or convertible with one of the longest option lists available, including nine engines. An R/T model caters to the performance crowd and was available with a 383, 440 or 426 Hemi engine.

The Challenger shares its firewall and front inner structure with B-bodies like this Charger.

1971 Due to rising insurance rates, safety issues and emissions regulations, the performance market enters its twilight years. The Challenger returns with just minor styling tweaks, but its sales figures drop by 60 percent—just 4,630 R/Ts are built this year.

The Cuda was Plymouth's version of the R/T. This is a 1971 model.

1972 High-horse-power engines, convertibles and the R/T package depart, leaving a Rallye 340 as the top performer.

UNDER THE SKIN

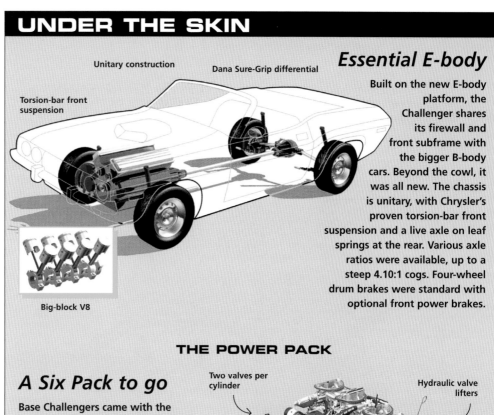

Unitary construction

Dana Sure-Grip differential

Torsion-bar front suspension

Big-block V8

Essential E-body

Built on the new E-body platform, the Challenger shares its firewall and front subframe with the bigger B-body cars. Beyond the cowl, it was all new. The chassis is unitary, with Chrysler's proven torsion-bar front suspension and a live axle on leaf springs at the rear. Various axle ratios were available, up to a steep 4.10:1 cogs. Four-wheel drum brakes were standard with optional front power brakes.

THE POWER PACK

A Six Pack to go

Base Challengers came with the bulletproof but hardly exciting 225-cubic inch Slant-Six, but eight V8s were optional. R/T models got a standard 335-bhp, 383-cubic inch mill, though the mighty Hemi and 440 were available. The 440 is an immensely robust and torquey engine, which cranks out a whopping 480 lb-ft at 3,200 rpm. In Six Pack form, with a trio of Holley two-barrel carburetors, the 440 gets an additional 10 lb-ft of torque.

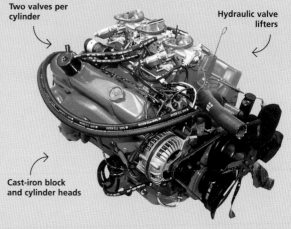

Two valves per cylinder

Hydraulic valve lifters

Cast-iron block and cylinder heads

SE Comfort

As with most Chrysler products, owners were free to order virtually any option on their Challenger R/T. If ordered in the sporty SE guise, these hot Dodges came with soft leather seats, a sporty vinyl top and smaller rear window.

1970 R/T-SEs are very rare: only 3,979 were built.

Dodge **CHALLENGER R/T SE**

Smoothly styled and an able performer in R/T guise, the Challenger was well received when new, and remains today as one of the most sought-after early muscle cars.

Mopar Power

Although the 383 was standard fare, the big 440 Magnum was an ideal choice for those into serious racing. Adding the Six-Pack option with three two-barrel carburetors resulted in 390 bhp and 490 lb-ft of torque. A good running Six Pack was a threat to just about anything with wheels.

Special Edition

An SE, or Special Edition, package was basically a luxury trim package on the Challenger. It added a vinyl roof with a smaller rear window, upgraded interior appointments and exterior trim. It could be ordered on both base and R/T models.

Manual transmission

Although the standard Challenger transmission was a three-speed manual, R/Ts ordered with the 440 or Hemi got the robust TorqueFlite automatic transmission. A handful were, however, fitted with four-speed manuals, complete with Hurst shifters with a wood-grain Pistol-Grip shift handle.

Standard R/T hood

Most Challenger R/Ts left the factory with a performance hood, which included dual scoops and a raised center section. For $97.30, however, buyers could order a Shaker hood scoop that attached directly to the air cleaner.

Dana Sure-Grip differential

A good way to reduce quarter-mile ETs was to order the Per-formance Axle Package with a 3.55:1 ring and pinion with a Sure-Grip limited-slip differential. Steeper 4.10:1 cogs could be specified as part of the Super Track Pak.

Heavy-duty suspension

s the R/T was the standard performance model, it has a heavy-duty suspension with thicker front torsion bars and stiffer rear leaf springs, plus a beefy front anti-roll bar.

Wide wheels

For the early 1970s, 6-inch-wide wheels were considered large. The Rallye rims fitted to the R/T are only 14 inches in diameter, shod in F-70 14 Goodyear Polyglas tires. Bigger G-60 15 tires and 15-inch Rallyes could be ordered resulting in slightly improved grip.

Specifications

1970 Dodge Challenger R/T-SE 440

ENGINE

Type: V8

Valve gear: Two valves per cylinder operated by a single V-mounted camshaft via pushrods, rockers and hydraulic lifters

Bore and stroke: 4.32 in. x 3.75 in.

Displacement: 440 c.i.

Compression ratio: 10.1:1

Induction system: Three Holley two-barrel carburetors

Maximum power: 390 bhp at 4,700 rpm

Maximum torque: 490 lb-ft at 3,200 rpm

TRANSMISSION

Four-speed manual

BODY/CHASSIS

Unitary steel chassis with steel body panels

SPECIAL FEATURES

All Challengers came with a racing-style fuel filler cap, which is also found on the bigger intermediate Charger.

As it was the performance model, the R/T got a full set of gauges.

RUNNING GEAR

Steering: Recirculating ball

Front suspension: A arms with longitudinal torsion bars, telescopic shock absorbers and anti-roll bar

Rear suspension: Live axle with semi-elliptic leaf springs, telescopic shock absorbers and anti-roll bar

Brakes: Drums, 11.0-in. dia. (front and rear)

Wheels: Stamped steel, 14x6 in.

Tires: Fiberglass belted, F-70 14

DIMENSIONS

Length: 192 in.   **Width:** 76.1 in.

Height: 50.9 in.   **Wheelbase:** 110.0 in.

Track: 59.7 in. (front), 60.7 in. (rear)

Weight: 3,437 lbs.

Dodge CHARGER DAYTONA

There was a street version of the Charger Daytona because Dodge had to build a certain number to qualify for NASCAR racing. With its Hemi-engined 200-mph missile, Dodge went on to win 22 races in 1969.

"...shattering performance."

"You do not notice the aerodynamic aids until you are well past 120 mph, but they really came into play on superspeedways, helping to keep the cars stable as they passed each other at around 200 mph.
It is unlikely you will reach that speed in a street-spec Hemi V8 since it only has 425 bhp; but that is still enough for earth shattering performance and acceleration. Low gearing and light steering do not give an immediate sense of confidence, but it is fairly accurate."

The interior of the street Charger is much more civilized than that of its NASCAR sibling.

Milestones

1969 Race goers at Alabama's Talledega track get the first sight of the racing Charger Daytona. Charlie Glotzbach laps the track at just under 200 mph. Charger driver Richard Brickhouse wins the race, and the Charger Daytona goes on to take another 22 checkers this season.

Plymouth's version of the Charger was the Superbird.

1970 Plymouth builds a sister to the Charger Daytona in the shape of the almost-identical Superbird.

Chargers and Superbirds often went head to head on the track.

1971 Both the Charger Daytona and the Plymouth Superbird are effectively outlawed from racing when NASCAR insists on a reduction in engine size by 25 percent. To prove a point, Dodge organizes a run at Bonneville on the Salt Flats, where Daytona 500 winner Bobby Isaacs reaches over 217 mph.

UNDER THE SKIN

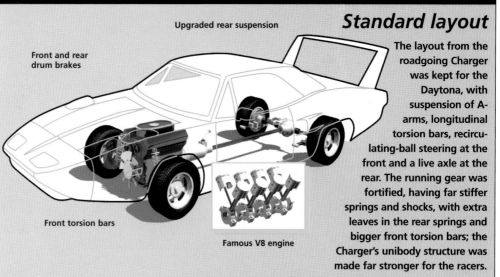

Upgraded rear suspension

Front and rear drum brakes

Front torsion bars

Famous V8 engine

Standard layout

The layout from the roadgoing Charger was kept for the Daytona, with suspension of A-arms, longitudinal torsion bars, recirculating-ball steering at the front and a live axle at the rear. The running gear was fortified, having far stiffer springs and shocks, with extra leaves in the rear springs and bigger front torsion bars; the Charger's unibody structure was made far stronger for the racers.

THE POWER PACK

MOPAR Muscle

The immortal Hemi engine first appeared in 1964, when Chrysler seriously decided to take on Ford in NASCAR. It is an all-cast-iron unit with a single camshaft in the V operating canted valves in highly efficient hemispherical combustion chambers through a combination of pushrods, solid lifters and rockers. It is oversquare with a large bore to allow room for the large valves. With its shorter stroke, it is designed to rev high, up to 7,200 rpm. The 426-c.i. alloy-headed, high-compression race engines gave over 650 bhp when fitted into the front of the Charger Daytona.

Special

The distinctive looks of the Charger Daytona have ensured its status as a cult classic. All cars are supremely powerful, but Keith Black (builder of MOPAR performance engines) prepared a promotional version with hair-raising performance.

The Daytona has one of the most outrageous wings ever seen on a stock car.

Dodge **CHARGER DAYTONA**

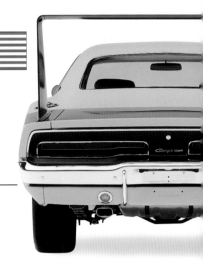

The Charger Daytona's outrageous look was no styling gimmick; the sharp extended nose and huge rear wing really did make the car far more aerodynamic and quicker around the track.

426-c.i. Hemi
The street version of the Hemi gave less power than the higher tuned race engines, with their outputs between 575 and 700 bhp. Also, they ran with iron heads, lower compression ratios, and later hydraulic rather than solid tappets which kept the potential engine speeds lower.

Four-speed transmission
Street versions of the Charger Daytona came with a standard three-speed manual, but the racers were equipped with a close-ratio, four-speed with a Hurst shifter. Customers could specify a four-speed as a no-cost option or opt for the TorqueFlite three-speed auto.

Two four-barrel carburetors
For the street Hemi engine there were two Carter four-barrel carburetors, arranged to open progressively. Just two barrels of the rear carb open at low throttle.

Extended nose

The new nose was made of Fiberglass and was some 17 inches long. It made the car more aerodynamically efficient. The poor fit, that is a feature of all Charger Daytonas and Plymouth Superbirds, clearly had no effect on the aerodynamics of this 200-mph car.

Unitary construction

Although it looks like a classic example of a traditional body-on-frame piece of American design, the Charger Daytona is a unitary vehicle, with the bodywork acting as the chassis.

Pop-up lights

With the addition of the sharp extended nose, the standard headlights were covered and had to be replaced by a new arrangement of pop-up light pods, with each having two headlights.

Rear wing

That distinctive rear wing is mounted more than two feet above the trunk lid, so there is room for the trunk to open. But its real benefit is to allow it to operate in clean air.

Specifications

1969 Dodge Charger Daytona

ENGINE

Type: V8

Construction: Cast-iron block and heads

Valve gear: Two valves per cylinder operating in hemispherical combustion chambers opened by a single V-mounted camshaft with pushrods, rockers and solid lifters

Bore and stroke: 4.25 in. x 3.75 in.

Displacement: 426 c.i.

Compression ratio: 10.25:1

Induction system: Two Carter AFB 3084S carburetors

Maximum power: 425 bhp at 5,600 rpm

Maximum torque: 490 lb-ft at 4,000 rpm

TRANSMISSION

Four-speed manual

BODY/CHASSIS

Unitary monocoque construction with steel body panels and fiberglass nose section

SPECIAL FEATURES

The aerodynamic fiberglass nose houses the unique pop-up headlights.

The black rear wing distinguishes the Charger from the Plymouth Superbird.

RUNNING GEAR

Steering: Recirculating-ball

Front suspension: A-arms with longitudinal torsion bars, telescopic shock absorbers and anti-roll bar

Rear suspension: Live axle with asymmetrical leaf springs and telescopic shock absorbers

Brakes: Drums, 11.0-in. dia. (front), 11.0-in. dia. (rear)

Wheels: Stamped steel, 14 in. x 6 in.

Tires: F70 x 14

DIMENSIONS

Length: 208.5 in.   **Width:** 76.6 in.

Height: 53.0 in.   **Wheelbase:** 117.0 in.

Track: 59.7 in. (front), 59.2 in. (rear)

Weight: 3,671 lbs.

Dodge CORONET R/T

The Coronet R/T was the first mid-size Dodge muscle machine to feature all the performance and luxury features in a single package. With a powerful 440-cubic inch V8, it didn't disappoint.

"...it just keeps on going."

"Unlike previous mid-size Chrysler muscle cars, the Coronet R/T has a more sporty feel. With a distinctive start-up sound, the giant Magnum V8 roars into life. Smooth and refined, the big V8 has plenty of torque. Dropping the pedal launches the car forward and it just keeps on going, daring you to go faster. Watch out for the corners though; the nose-heavy R/T doesn't handle very well and its 480 lb-ft of torque will surely result in oversteer."

The Coronet R/T has standard bucket seats, a center console and full instrumentation.

Milestones

1967 Dodge introduces its Coronet R/T (Road and Track). It is a complete high-performance package and is fitted with a standard 440-cubic inch V8, although the Hemi engine is also available. This year sales figures total 10,181.

The Coronet R/T debuted in both hardtop and convertible forms.

1968 The R/T returns with handsome new sheet-metal on an unchanged wheelbase.

1969 After a major facelift in 1968, changes this year are minor, with a new grill and rear tail panel. Engine choices remain the same.

The race-ready Super Bee was the Coronet's high performance stablemate.

1970 Greater competition in a heavily crowded market takes its toll on the Coronet R/T and sales fall to just 2,615. Only 13 of these cars are fitted with the Hemi V8.

UNDER THE SKIN

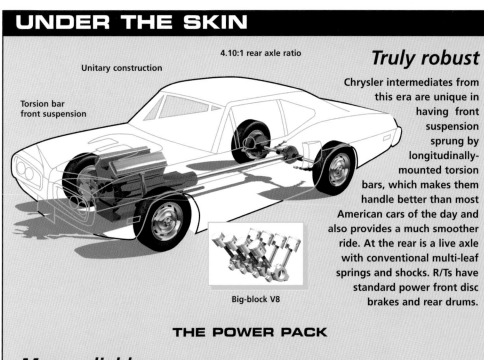

4.10:1 rear axle ratio

Unitary construction

Torsion bar front suspension

Big-block V8

Truly robust

Chrysler intermediates from this era are unique in having front suspension sprung by longitudinally-mounted torsion bars, which makes them handle better than most American cars of the day and also provides a much smoother ride. At the rear is a live axle with conventional multi-leaf springs and shocks. R/Ts have standard power front disc brakes and rear drums.

THE POWER PACK

More reliable

Only two engines were available with the R/T package: the more common 440-cubic inch Magnum and the street-lethal 426-cubic inch Hemi. The Magnum was lifted from the full-size Chrysler line, but in the R/T it has a longer duration camshaft profile, bigger exhaust valves, a dual snorkel intake, a four-barrel Carter carburetor, and free-flowing exhaust manifolds. It produces 375 bhp and 480 lb-ft of torque. By including the 'Six Pack,' the 440 received 3x2 carburetors for 490 bhp.

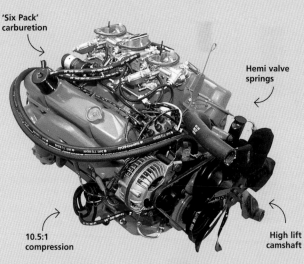

'Six Pack' carburetion

Hemi valve springs

10.5:1 compression

High lift camshaft

Short life

When the Coronet was launched in 1967, its styling was boxy and upright. A new, smoother body was introduced the following year, which was carried over to 1969 with few changes. 1970 models feature an aggressive twin 'horse collar'-type grill.

1970 was the last year for the convertible Coronet.

Dodge CORONET R/T

This peppermint green 1970 Coronet 440 is one of just 2,615 R/Ts built that year. With so much competition in the muscle car arena, sales plummeted in 1970, making this a desirable muscle car today.

Torsion bar suspension

Chrysler was unique in employing torsion bars for the front suspension. Mounted lengthways, they are extremely simple and robust.

Street racer's powerplant

Easier to maintain, more flexible and less temperamental than the Hemi, the 440 delivers plenty of torque and is perfect for drag racing. It is nicknamed the 'Wedge' because of the shape of its combustion chambers.

Bulletproof TorqueFlite

The V8 in this R/T is backed up by the optional 727 TorqueFlite three-speed automatic. This transmission is extremely reliable and has been used in countless Mopars over the years.

Bigger wheels

For 1970 handsome 15-inch Rallye wheels became available on the Coronet R/T. They feature chrome beauty rings and center caps.

Bumble bee stripe

A tail end stripe, usually in black, white or red, was available at no extra cost.

Specifications

1970 Dodge Coronet R/T

ENGINE

Type: V8

Construction: Cast-iron block and heads

Valve gear: Two valves per cylinder operated by pushrods and rockers

Bore and stroke: 4.32 in. x 3.75 in.

Displacement: 440 c.i.

Compression ratio: 10.5:1

Induction system: Single Carter AFB downdraft four-barrel carburetor

Maximum power: 375 bhp at 4,600 rpm

Maximum torque: 480 lb-ft at 3,200 rpm

TRANSMISSION

TorqueFlite 727 three-speed automatic

BODY/CHASSIS

Steel monocoque with two-door body

SPECIAL FEATURES

Side-mounted scoops are only fitted to 1970 Coronet R/Ts and are purely decorative features.

Though the engine in this Coronet R/T makes 375 bhp, it is the base engine. Also available was a 390 bhp version with three two-barrel carbs, and a 426 Hemi that made 425 bhp.

RUNNING GEAR

Steering: Recirculating ball

Front suspension: Longitudinally-mounted torsion bars with wishbones and telescopic shocks

Rear suspension: Live rear axle with semi-elliptic leaf springs and telescopic shocks

Brakes: Discs (front), drums (rear)

Wheels: Steel disc, 15-in. dia.

Tires: Goodyear Polyglas GT F60 15

DIMENSIONS

Length: 207.7 in.   **Width:** 80.6 in.

Height: 52.5 in.   **Wheelbase:** 117 in.

Track: 58.9 in. (front and rear)

Weight: 3,546 lbs.

Aggressive front

Twin 'horse collar'-type grills are unique to 1970 Coronets and give the car an aggressive appearance. The hood scoops are an R/T-only feature and are non-functional.

Dodge VIPER GTS-R

The Viper GTS had such a good platform that it cried out to be turned into a racing car. And in GT2 racing, the GTS-R, with its 650-bhp V10, has consistently beaten the best and won its class at the 24 Hours of Le Mans.

"...a raging animal."

"Climb in this raging animal and prepare for the ride of your life. Nail the throttle and dump the clutch and feel yourself catapult to 60 mph in a staggering 3.1 seconds. The thrill doesn't stop there though. This scorching Dodge continues to pull hard through all perfectly matched gears until it reaches its terminal velocity at just over 200 mph. Jam on the massive brakes and you will find that the GTS-R's stopping performance matches its astounding acceleration. "

With five-point harnesses and white-faced gauges this Viper is ready to bite.

Milestones

1995 Chrysler startles
viewers in Pebble Beach, California by unveiling its proposed racing version of the hardtop Dodge Viper GTS.

Dodge launched the Viper in 1991, with the RT/10.

1996 Dodge actually
takes the GTS-R racing as promised.

1997 Sensibly, Chrysler
focuses on the GT2 category in world sportscar racing. It finishes 1-2 in class at the Le Mans 24 Hours. The GTS-R takes the World GT2 championship overall, a first for an American production model. English GTS-R driver Justin Bell takes the driver's championship.

Viper driver Justin Bell (right) celebrates after winning the 1998 24 Hours of Le Mans.

1998 To celebrate its
stunning achievements, Dodge offers the GTS-R on sale to the public, on a limited basis.

UNDER THE SKIN

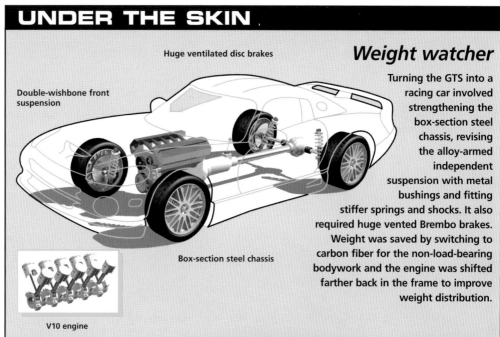

Huge ventilated disc brakes

Double-wishbone front suspension

Box-section steel chassis

V10 engine

Weight watcher

Turning the GTS into a racing car involved strengthening the box-section steel chassis, revising the alloy-armed independent suspension with metal bushings and fitting stiffer springs and shocks. It also required huge vented Brembo brakes. Weight was saved by switching to carbon fiber for the non-load-bearing bodywork and the engine was shifted farther back in the frame to improve weight distribution.

THE POWER PACK

Reworked V10

This engine is nothing like the standard Viper powerplant. For the racing GTS-R, Dodge seriously reworked the all-alloy 8-liter Ferrari eater V10 to give 650 bhp. It is still a single-cam, pushrod engine, but the fully balanced and blueprinted engine benefits from a 12.0:1 compression ratio and stronger forged steel connecting rods. Extensive work is done to both the intake and exhaust systems to extract maximum power. A dry sump oiling system prevents oil from surging when the car takes turns at high speeds. Maximum power is a massive 650 bhp at 6,500 rpm.

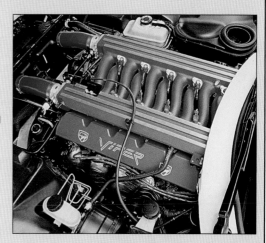

Track racer

The GTS-R is a rare model. It has outrageous power at 650 bhp, along with carbon-fiber bodywork, stripped racing interior with digital dashboard meter and a real racing suspension. Of course, a racetrack is needed to get the most out of it.

In GT2, the Vipers have proven almost unbeatable.

Dodge VIPER GTS-R

Dodge stunned the world when it decided to produce the RT/10 in 1991. It then went on to impress hard-core endurance racing enthusiasts when it took the FIA championship in the GT2 class in its fully outfitted GTS-R race car.

V10 engine

The roadgoing versions of the GTS-R, now known as the ACR, do get more power from their V10s, but nowhere near the 650 bhp of the racers. However, 460 bhp at 5,200 rpm is more than respectable.

Composite body

Composite paneling is used for the street GTS-R, just as it is in the usual GTS, but for the serious racing cars the bodywork was made from lightweight carbon fiber.

Front airdam

The GT2 rules allow some bodywork revision in aid of improved aerodynamics. This explains the GTS-R's different, deeper nose and rocker panel extensions. These modifications keep air away from the underside of the car, where it can generate drag and lift.

Adjustable pedals

The ideal driving position is vital in any performance car such as the GTS-R. To help achieve this, electronically controlled foot pedals let the driver get the right relationship between the pedals and steering wheel.

Multilink rear suspension

Rear suspension design is an SLA design with adjustable toe link. Similar to the front suspension the rubber bushings are replaced by spherical bearings and the springs and shocks are all stiffened.

Specifications

1997 Dodge Viper GTS-R

ENGINE

Type: V10

Construction: Alloy block and heads

Valve gear: Two valves per cylinder operated by a single V-mounted camshaft with pushrods and rockers

Bore and stroke: 4.00 in. x 3.88 in.

Displacement: 8.0 Liter

Compression ratio: 12.0:1

Induction system: Electronic fuel injection

Maximum power: 650 bhp at 6,000 rpm

Maximum torque: 650 lb-ft at 5,000 rpm

Top speed: 203 mph

0–60 mph: 3.1 sec

TRANSMISSION

Borg-Warner six-speed manual

BODY/CHASSIS

Separate steel box-section chassis with either carbon-fiber or glass-fiber two-door coupe body

SPECIAL FEATURES

With a sure-shifting six speed, it is easy to row through the gears in a Viper GTS-R.

The twin tailpipes help the GTS-R to produce a fantastic exhaust note.

RUNNING GEAR

Steering: Rack-and-pinion

Front suspension: SLA with coil springs, telescopic shock absorbers, spherical bearings and anti-roll bar

Rear suspension: SLA with extra toe-adjustment link, coil springs, telescopic shocks and anti-roll bar

Brakes: Ventilated discs, 13.0-in. dia.

Wheels: Alloy, 18 x 11(F), BB5 3-piece 18 x 13(rear)

Tires: Michelin Pilot SX Radial Slicks 27/65-18(front), 30/80-18(rear)

DIMENSIONS

Length: 176.7 in.   **Width:** 75.7 in.

Height: 45.1 in.   **Wheelbase:** 96.2 in.

Track: 59.8 in. (front), 60.9 in. (rear)

Weight: 2,750 lbs.

DUAL GHIA

Virgil Exner was a great styling talent for Chrysler for several decades. One of his show cars even made it to the road, thanks to the intervention of Eugene Casaroll, a longtime Chrysler consultant.

"...a cruising machine."

"Considering its extraordinarily high price, the Dual Ghia had to compete with some very fine imported machinery, though the driving experience is very definitely American, not European. When you start the V8 engine and engage the PowerFlite floorshift transmission, the feel is distinctly 1950s and distinctly Dodge. The short wheelbase and low center of gravity make it stable, but this is still a cruising machine, not a sports car."

Only the finest leather and trim were used on the ultra-exclusive Dual Ghia.

Milestones

1952 Virgil Exner's Dodge
Firearrow show car breaks new ground.

The Dual Ghia uses a Dodge D-500 chassis and running gear.

1953 A more practical,
restyled show car called the Firebomb impresses a certain Mr. Eugene Casaroll.

1956 Production of the Dual
Ghia gets underway. For the greatest prestige possible, only select people may purchase them.

Among Virgil Exner's later lavish creations was the Stutz.

1958 Warranty claims
force the Dual Ghia out of production after only 117 have been built. Eugene Casaroll returns in 1960 with another design based on Chrysler parts. Named the Ghia L-610, it boasts unitary construction and a 335-bhp, 383-cubic inch V8. It is unsuccessful and production ends after 26 cars are built.

UNDER THE SKIN

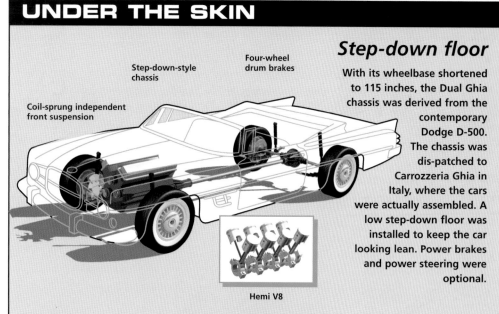

Step-down-style chassis

Four-wheel drum brakes

Coil-sprung independent front suspension

Hemi V8

Step-down floor

With its wheelbase shortened to 115 inches, the Dual Ghia chassis was derived from the contemporary Dodge D-500. The chassis was dis-patched to Carrozzeria Ghia in Italy, where the cars were actually assembled. A low step-down floor was installed to keep the car looking lean. Power brakes and power steering were optional.

THE POWER PACK

Mighty Red Ram

Dual Motors took one of the most powerful engines from Chrysler's lineup, the Dodge Red Ram V8. This featured hemispherical combustion chambers, enabling it to produce more power on a lower compression engine than its V8 rivals. This massive engine was offered in three power levels starting with a 315-cubic inch Dodge V8 out of the D-500. It had an 8.0:1 compression ratio and 230 bhp on tap. Next up was the larger 325-cubic inch D-500-1 motor. This $100 offer had an 8.5:1 compression ratio and 260 bhp. The top of the line was a 285-bhp version of the engine that was not far off Chrysler's '1-bhp-per-cubic-inch' dream.

Status symbol

In its day, the Dual Ghia was a Hollywood special. It may not have the same mystique today, but its status as a high-quality Italian-American hybrid will always ensure it has a high collector value. Especially if its former owner has celebrity status.

Opinions on it may be divided, but the Dual Ghia is a definite collector's piece.

DUAL GHIA

Virgil Exner's 1953 Firebomb styling prototype for Dodge impressed Eugene Casaroll so much that he ambitiously launched a modified version of the show car for an independent production run.

Ghia-built bodywork

Chassis were shipped from the U.S. for the new bodywork to be fitted and trimmed by Ghia in Turin, Italy. They were then shipped back for final assembly and sale.

Hardtop or convertible

Almost all Dual Ghias were convertibles, but a hardtop was available. This was made from fiberglass rather than steel. However, only two hardtops are known to have been built.

Modified Dodge chassis

The Dual Ghia body sat on what was essentially a Dodge D-500 chassis. It was shipped to Ghia in Italy, and its wheelbase was shortened seven inches for a total length of 115 inches. Ghia's Giovanni Savonuzzi designed the new step-down floor for the car.

Luxury interior

At over $7,500, the Dual Ghia ranked as one of the most expensive cars on sale in 1956. Some justification was provided by the luxury specification, including hand-finished English leather upholstery for the four seats, a radio and a heater.

Questionable build quality

Because it was handbuilt by Italian craftsmen who used a lot of body filler to get the smooth lines right, the Dual Ghia was not the most durable. This resulted in an overwhelming number of warranty claims, which led to the company's demise.

Hollywood style

The Dual Ghia was brashly advertised with the line: 'Rolls-Royce is the car of those who cannot afford a Dual Ghia.' Casaroll himself decided who would be permitted to buy one of his cars. Frank Sinatra was one such owner.

Exner styling

Chrysler's chief of styling, Virgil Exner, created the Firebomb's shape. It was translated into the pro-duction Dual Ghia with very few changes. The front and rear bumpers were, however, stock Dodge pieces.

Specifications

1956 Dual Ghia

ENGINE

Type: V8

Construction: Cast-iron block and heads

Valve gear: Two valves per cylinder operated by a single camshaft with pushrods and rocker arms

Bore and stroke: 3.63 in. x 3.80 in.

Displacement: 315 c.i.

Compression ratio: 8.0:1

Induction system: Single Carter four-barrel carburetor

Maximum power: 230 bhp at 4,300 rpm

Maximum torque: Not quoted

TRANSMISSION

Two-speed automatic

BODY/CHASSIS

Separate chassis with steel two-door convertible body

SPECIAL FEATURES

Sharp, blade-like fins were typical styling features in the 1950s.

Spinner wheel covers represent the Dual Ghia's exotic image.

RUNNING GEAR

Steering: Recirculating ball

Front suspension: Double wishbone with coil springs and telescopic shock absorbers

Rear suspension: Live axle with semi-elliptic leaf springs and telescopic shock absorbers

Brakes: Drums (front and rear)

Wheels: Steel, 15-in. dia.

Tires: 6.70 x 15

DIMENSIONS

Length: 203.5 in. **Width:** 79.0 in.

Height: 51.0 in. **Wheelbase:** 115.0 in.

Track: 58.9 in. (front), 59.2 in. (rear)

Weight: Not quoted

Duesenberg SJ

The Duesenberg J was one of the world's finest motor cars, but the SJ was even more powerful and opulent. The addition of a supercharger turned it into a phenomenal performer.

"...sense of superiority."

"When you enter the SJ, a sense of superiority pervades in terms of both design function and quality. It is not an obtrusive, heavy beast like so many of its contemporaries: indeed, the steering is light, accurate and full of feel. Open the throttle up and the gutsy noise from the engine and supercharger is almost overwhelming, as is the sheer speed—it is possible to top 100 mph in second gear! However, the antiquated chassis is not the equal of the engine."

The Duesenberg has an aura of quality that was only equaled by few of its peers.

Milestones

1926 Duesenberg brothers sell their car-manufacturing business to Cord.

Duesenberg was taken over by Cord when faced with the prospect of bankruptcy.

1928 An all-new Model J was announced, complete with the presupposed title of 'the world's finest car.'

The SJ uses the same engine as the J but has a supercharger.

1932 With a supercharger, the mighty SJ becomes one of the fastest road cars available. Fred Duesenburg is tragically killed behind the wheel of a SJ.

1935 A.B. Jenkins averages 135 mph on a 24-hour Bonneville run and clocks a 160-mph lap.

1937 Along with Cord and Auburn, Duesenberg is dragged down amid severe economic hardship.

UNDER THE SKIN

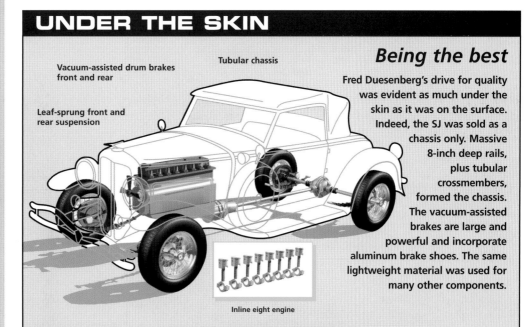

Vacuum-assisted drum brakes front and rear

Tubular chassis

Leaf-sprung front and rear suspension

Inline eight engine

Being the best

Fred Duesenberg's drive for quality was evident as much under the skin as it was on the surface. Indeed, the SJ was sold as a chassis only. Massive 8-inch deep rails, plus tubular crossmembers, formed the chassis. The vacuum-assisted brakes are large and powerful and incorporate aluminum brake shoes. The same lightweight material was used for many other components.

THE POWER PACK

Supercharged superlative

A centrifugal supercharger gives the straight-eight Duesenberg engine awesome power. Even in the naturally aspirated J model, the 420-cubic inch twin-overhead camshaft engine delivers an advertised 265 bhp. The addition of a blower, with 5 psi of boost at 4,000 rpm, rockets that to an incredible 320 bhp at 4,200 rpm in stock form, with an equally impressive 425 lb-ft of torque at 2,400 rpm. Modifications required for this power output included tubular-steel con rods. With different exhaust manifolds, one engine was dyno-tested at an incredible 400 bhp, way above other engines of the 1930s.

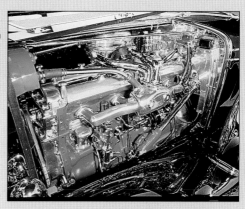

SSJ

Duesenbergs guarantee exclusivity, none more so than the two SSJ's that were specially made for Gary Cooper and Clark Gable. The 125-inch short-wheelbase cars had shattering performance. Both cars still exist as museum pieces.

Bigger and stronger than other cars, the SJ has real road presence.

Duesenberg **SJ**

With a stiffened-up engine and a blower fitted, Duesenberg's supremely accomplished Model J was transformed into the exclusive and powerful SJ. Only the extraordinarily wealthy could afford one.

Aircraft-quality engine

The undoubted centerpiece of any Duesenberg is its engine. The fabulous straight eight was extremely advanced, boasting twin overhead camshafts and four valves per cylinder. The basic engine was built by Lycoming to Fred Duesenberg's specifications.

Power brakes

The brakes were as advanced as the rest of the car's specification. With oversized shoes, braking power was impressive and was made easier by standard vacuum assistance.

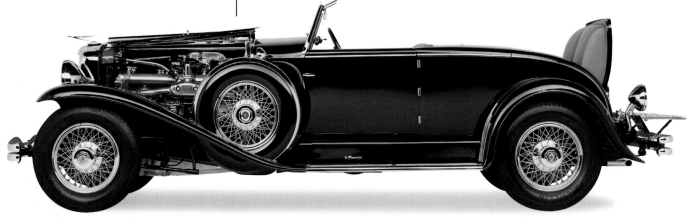

Custom bodywork

In the best coachbuilt traditions, Duesenberg supplied only the chassis. Customers were expected to patronize independent coachbuilders to create whatever body-work struck their fancy. With its sporty bias, the SJ's performance suited a roadster or convertible body.

ch use of aluminum

As many production SJs measured more than 20 feet long, there was naturally some concern to keep weight down. Therefore, many parts were made from aluminum, including some of the engine, dash, crankcase, water pump, intake manifold, brake shoes and gas tank.

Snaking pipes

One of the hallmarks of the SJ is its dramatic and beautifully plated exhaust headers emerging from the side of the engine. However, elaborate pipework like this does not necessarily mean the car is an SJ—the ordinary Model J was often fitted with such plumbing, even if there wasn't a supercharger.

Supercharger

A centrifugal blower was added to the straight eight to deliver crushing performance on a mildly higher compression ratio. Power shot up to 320 bhp, making it easily the most powerful auto production engine in the world.

Specifications
Duesenberg SJ

ENGINE

Type: Inline eight

Construction: Cast-iron cylinder block and head

Valve gear: Four valves per cylinder operated by double chain-driven camshafts

Bore and stroke: 3.70 in. x 4.50 in.

Displacement: 420 c.i.

Compression ratio: 5.7:1

Induction system: Single Schebler carburetor plus supercharger

Maximum power: 320 bhp at 4,200 rpm

Maximum torque: 425 lb-ft at 2,400 rpm

Top speed: 130 mph

0–60 mph: 8.5 sec.

TRANSMISSION

Three-speed manual

BODY/CHASSIS

Separate chassis with convertible bodywork

SPECIAL FEATURES

A fold out rumble is available to fit two additional passengers.

As part of the effort to reduce weight, even the dashboard is aluminum.

RUNNING GEAR

Steering: Cam-and-lever

Front suspension: Beam axle with leaf springs and shock absorbers

Rear suspension: Live axle with leaf springs and shock absorbers

Brakes: Drums (front and rear)

Wheels: Wire, 19-in. dia.

Tires: Crossply, 9 in. x 16 in.

DIMENSIONS

Length: 222.5 in.

Width: 72.0 in.

Height: 70.0 in.

Wheelbase: 142.5 in.

Track: 37.5 in. (front), 58.0 (rear)

Weight: 5,000 lbs.

Edsel **CITATION**

Recognized as one of the biggest flops of all time, the Edsel, in all honesty, was not really a bad car. The 1958 Citation convertible, in particular, was fast and well equipped, and had fairly restrained looks for its time.

"...cruises happily."

"Sitting on the big, padded bench seat, the Citation feels similar to most 1958 Detroit cars. Give her a little gas, however, and the picture begins to change. It has noticeably more urge off the line than many of its contemporaries, and on the highway, it cruises happily at speeds around 70 mph. Throw the Edsel into a sharp corner and it leans alarmingly, but then again, so does any other car built during the 1950s."

Citation was the top-of-the-line Edsel in 1958 and was loaded to the gills.

Milestones

1954 With Ford returning to prosperity after near collapse, chairman Ernest R. Breech lays plans to match GM with a five-make hierarchy.

Rarest of all the 1958 Edsels is the 9-seater Bermuda wagon—just 779 were built.

1958 After various delays, Ford launches its new medium-priced car—the Edsel—into a depressed market. Four series are offered (Ranger, Pacer, Corsair and Citation).

Citations and Corsairs shared their chassis with Mercurys.

1959 As a result of sluggish sales, the Edsel lineup is pared back to just Corsair, Ranger and station wagons, on a single 118-in. wheelbase. Less than 45,000 cars are built for the 1959 model year.

1960 Edsel production ends.

UNDER THE SKIN

Separate steel chassis with X-bracing

Four-wheel drum brakes

Live rear axle

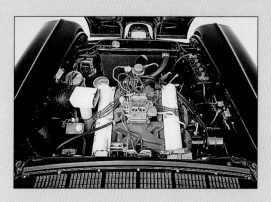

Big-block V8

Mercury chassis

Citations used the 124-inch wheelbase Mercury chassis. It was a substantial affair with long side members kicking up at the rear to go over the live axle. On the convertible, a center cruciform X-bracing helped to increase overall stiffness. Suspension was straight-forward, with double wishbones and coils at the front and a live axle on semi-elliptic leaf springs at the rear. Like the vast majority of U.S. cars in the late 1950s, the Citation had four-wheel drum brakes.

Continental power

For the larger Edsels, Ford used basically the same engine as in the Lincoln Continental, but with a smaller (4.20 inch) bore, resulting in a displacement of 410 cubic inches instead of 430. Construction was typical for its time with a cast-iron block and cylinder heads, single cam, pushrods, rockers and hydraulic lifters. One different feature was having flat cylinder heads, with the wedge-shaped combustion chambers set in the block. With 345 bhp and 475 lb-ft of torque, the engine made the Edsel quite a performance-oriented car for its time.

THE POWER PACK

Collectible

With only 930 built, the 1958 Citation was rare.

Considered a disaster when new, the Edsel—especially convertible models—has gained strong collector interest in recent years. The big 401-powered Citation, of which only 25 are believed to exist today, is sought after, and often sells for over $30,000.

Edsel CITATION

There are many reasons the Edsel failed in the marketplace, but perhaps the greatest was poor quality control. This factor alone sent buyers scurrying almost immediately to other makes.

V8 engine

The Citation V8 was tuned for torque, as the output of 475 lb-ft at only 2,900 rpm indicates. Even the smaller 361 engine used in the Ranger and Pacer put out an impressive 303 bhp and 400 lb-ft of torque. That engine had its combustion chambers in the head, unlike the bigger 401 unit.

Convertible top

There was a choice of four colors available for the vinyl-covered convertible top on the Citation: black (seen here), white, turquoise and copper. The top folded down flush with the rear deck and was power-operated like most convertibles of the era. It had a flexible plastic rear window.

Mercury chassis

There were three different wheelbase lengths for 1958 Edsels: 116 inches for wagons; 118 inches for Pacer and Ranger coupes, sedans and convertibles; and 124 inches for Corsairs and Citations. The latter two actually rode on a Mercury chassis and were built on the same assembly line as the slightly plusher Mercurys.

Recirculating-ball steering

The recirculating-ball steering could be ordered with or without power assistance (an $85 option). If you went without, the steering ratio was altered accordingly to make the wheel easier to turn. There were 5.25 turns lock to lock, compared with 4.25 when power was added.

Power seats

An Edsel Citation convertible was a luxury vehicle and there was the $76 option of four-way power adjustable front seats which were formed by a 30/70 divided front bench seat.

1958 Edsel Citation

ENGINE
Type: V8
Construction: Cast-iron block and heads
Valve gear: Two valves per cylinder operated by single V-mounted camshaft
Bore and stroke: 4.20 in. x 3.70 in.
Displacement: 410 c.i.
Compression ratio: 10.5:1
Induction system: Single four-barrel carburetor
Maximum power: 345 bhp at 4,600 rpm
Maximum torque: 475 lb-ft at 2,900 rpm
Top speed: 105 mph
0-60 mph: 9.7 sec

TRANSMISSION
Three-speed automatic

BODY/CHASSIS
Separate curbed-perimeter chassis frame with center X-brace and convertible body

SPECIAL FEATURES

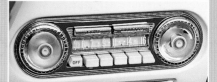

A station seeking radio with an electric antenna was an expensive ($143.90) option.

One interesting gimmick on 1958 Edsels was the Cyclops Eye rotating-drum speedometer.

RUNNING GEAR
Steering: Recirculating-ball
Front suspension: Double wishbones with coil springs, telescopic dampers and anti-roll bar
Rear suspension: Live axle with semi-elliptic leaf springs and telescopic shock absorbers
Brakes: Drums, 11.0-in. dia. front, 11.0-in. dia. rear
Wheels: Pressed steel disc, 14 in. dia.
Tires: 8.50 -14

DIMENSIONS
Length: 218.8 in. **Width:** 79.8 in.
Height: 57.0 in. **Wheelbase:** 124.0 in.
Track: 59.4 in front, 59.0 in rear
Weight: 4,311 lbs.

Ford DELUXE V-8

The 1939-1940 Ford V8 is regarded by many collectors as the best of the famous pre-war V8 Ford line. With up-to-the-minute styling and plenty of power, it was immensely popular with buyers, too.

"...ride in total comfort."

"Open up the door and climb in. After you take your position behind the Deluxe's wide steering wheel and start up its flat-head V8, some of the embellishments that make this a Deluxe model become evident—namely the wood-grain dash and large-faced clock. Like all upgraded models, this Deluxe has the optional 85 bhp engine. Its firm body construction and advanced (for its time) suspension give a better than average ride in total comfort."

The stylish sprung steering wheel and beautiful dash make for a classic interior.

Milestones

1932 America's first bargain-priced

V8 appears as Henry Ford boldly launches a range of eight-cylinder cars.

Fords gained fender-mounted headlights for 1938.

1933 New and widely admired airflow

designs are now on a longer 112-inch wheelbase.

1935 More engine changes

and a fuller body style enhance the V8's attractiveness.

A new grill and minor refinements distinguish the 1939 from the 1940 model.

1939 Distinctive styling

changes are made, notably to the front grill.

1942 As Ford turns over

its factories exclusively to war-time production, the V8 line is shut down.

UNDER THE SKIN

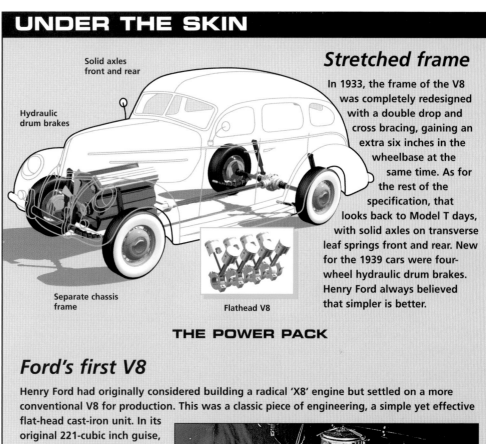

Solid axles front and rear

Hydraulic drum brakes

Separate chassis frame

Flathead V8

Stretched frame

In 1933, the frame of the V8 was completely redesigned with a double drop and cross bracing, gaining an extra six inches in the wheelbase at the same time. As for the rest of the specification, that looks back to Model T days, with solid axles on transverse leaf springs front and rear. New for the 1939 cars were four-wheel hydraulic drum brakes. Henry Ford always believed that simpler is better.

THE POWER PACK

Ford's first V8

Henry Ford had originally considered building a radical 'X8' engine but settled on a more conventional V8 for production. This was a classic piece of engineering, a simple yet effective flat-head cast-iron unit. In its original 221-cubic inch guise, it put out 65 bhp, rising to 85 bhp in 1934 thanks to a new carburetor and intake manifold. Initial reliability problems were soon cured, and the V8 gained a reputation as one of the most durable engines around, particularly with hot rodders. After the war, the V8 would return with a larger 239-cubic inch displacement.

V8 Deluxe

The V8 has a strong and enduring reputation and will always be regarded as one of the all-time greats. The 1940 Deluxes are among the most coveted pre-war Fords, due in part to their neat Bob Gregorie styling, rugged engineering and unabashed charm. Hydraulic brakes make stopping easier, too.

1940 Deluxes have long been collectors' favorites.

Ford **DELUXE V-8**

Durability and affordability were the hallmarks that established Ford, and though the V-8 boasted both of those qualities, its performance was the most impressive feature.

V8 engine

Crucial to Ford's success in the 1930s was its V8 powerplant. When other car makers had only fours and sixes, Ford could justly claim superiority with not one but two different V8 engines.

V-grill

The distinctive V-shaped grill arrived in 1935 and developed into the streamlined profile seen on this 1939 Deluxe four-door sedan. The 1939 has vertical grill bars in place of the horizontal bars of the 1940 Deluxe.

Steel roof

Early V8 models had a fabric roof insert, but in 1937 Ford began using a full steel roof panel.

Deluxe interiors

All Deluxe models came with a woodgrain dashboard and a centrally mounted clock.

Faired-in headlights

The popular airflow look arrived for the Ford range in 1937. Apart from the chiseled front end styling, this took the form of fully faired-in, ellipsoid headlights.

Optional taillight

Only the Deluxe models came with two taillights as standard. The base models only came with one taillight. However, certain states at this time required cars to have two taillights. So some standard models had the extra taillight installed at the dealership.

Specifications

1939 Ford Deluxe V8

ENGINE
Type: V8
Construction: Cast-iron cylinder block and heads
Valve gear: Two side-mounted valves per cylinder operated by a single camshaft
Bore and stroke: 3.06 in. x 3.75 in.
Displacement: 221 c.i.
Compression ratio: 6.2:1
Induction system: Single carburetor
Maximum power: 85 bhp at 3,800 rpm
Maximum torque: 155 lb-ft at 2,200 rpm

TRANSMISSION
Three-speed manual

BODY/CHASSIS
Separate chassis with steel two-door or four-door sedan, coupe or convertible body

SPECIAL FEATURES

Suicide-type rear doors were offered on four-door sedans in 1939.

Ellipsoid headlights were faired into the front fenders.

RUNNING GEAR
Steering: Worm-and-roller
Front suspension: Beam axle with transverse leaf spring and shocks
Rear suspension: Live axle with transverse leaf spring and shocks
Brakes: Drums (front and rear)
Wheels: Steel, 17-in dia.
Tires: 6 x 16 in.

DIMENSIONS
Length: 179.5 in. **Width:** 67.0 in.
Height: 68.6 in. **Wheelbase:** 112.0 in.
Track: 55.5 in. (front), 58.3 in. (rear)
Weight: 2,898 lbs.

Ford FAIRLANE 427

To fight its opposition on the street Ford built the Fairlane 427, which had widened shock towers and larger front coil springs to fit a detuned 427 V8. Unfortunately, the Fairlane 427 was costly to build so only 70 units were made in 1966 and 200 in 1967. Most went to pro racers for NHRA Super Stock competition.

"...uses a detuned race engine."

"Only a Borg-Warner 'Top-Loader' four-speed transmission was able to handle the 480 lb-ft of torque that the massive engine was capable of making. Though it uses a detuned version of its race engine, the brutal 427, if equipped with dual four-barrel carbs, it 'only' makes 425 bhp. On the street, the Fairlane 427 was very competitive. Only a handful were made and at $5,100 were very pricey, thus giving a slight edge to the competition.

The only indication of power from the vinyl-clad interior was a 9,000 rpm tachometer.

Milestones

1964 After minimal success

on the drag strips with the larger Galaxies, Ford creates the Thunderbolt—a specially prepared 427-powered lightweight Fairlane sedan. These factory-built race cars helped Ford secure the NHRA manufacturers' championship.

The first Fairlanes to be equipped with the 427 were the competition-only Thunderbolts.

1966 A new, bigger Fairlane

is released, which has plenty of room for 427 FE V8 engines. Only 70 white hardtops and coupes are built to qualify for Super Stock drag racing.

The 1966 Fairlane has similar styling to the 1966-67 Galaxie.

1967 The 427 returns

as a regular production option for its second and final season. Only 200 Fairlanes are equipped with the side-oiler 427 and are available in a variety of colors and optional trim packages.

UNDER THE SKIN

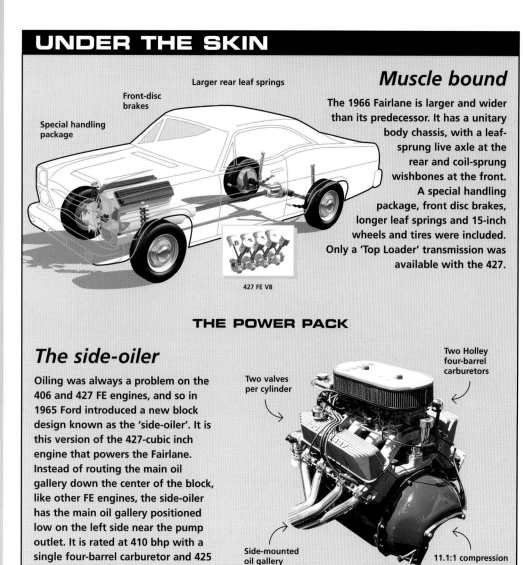

Special handling package

Front-disc brakes

Larger rear leaf springs

427 FE V8

Muscle bound

The 1966 Fairlane is larger and wider than its predecessor. It has a unitary body chassis, with a leaf-sprung live axle at the rear and coil-sprung wishbones at the front. A special handling package, front disc brakes, longer leaf springs and 15-inch wheels and tires were included. Only a 'Top Loader' transmission was available with the 427.

THE POWER PACK

The side-oiler

Oiling was always a problem on the 406 and 427 FE engines, and so in 1965 Ford introduced a new block design known as the 'side-oiler'. It is this version of the 427-cubic inch engine that powers the Fairlane. Instead of routing the main oil gallery down the center of the block, like other FE engines, the side-oiler has the main oil gallery positioned low on the left side near the pump outlet. It is rated at 410 bhp with a single four-barrel carburetor and 425 bhp with a dual carburetor set up.

Two valves per cylinder

Two Holley four-barrel carburetors

Side-mounted oil gallery

11.1:1 compression

Rare beast

Although the 1966 models are very rare, this no frills homologation special isn't very refined. For 1967, Ford offered the Fairlane 427 in a variety of colors and exterior trim. The cars still had the potent 427 V8 and also carried the equally potent price tag.

The 1967 Fairlane 427s were a serious threat on the streets and at the track.

Ford **FAIRLANE 427**

Although it was one of the quickest muscle cars around in 1966, the rarity of the Fairlane 427 prevented it from having the same impact among street racers as a Chevelle SS396 or a tri-power GTO.

Heavy-duty suspension

To cope with the weight and power of the 427 engine, the standard Fairlane suspension was reworked with stiffer spring rates and larger front coil springs. This unit also took up considerable space, which necessitated relocating the front shock towers.

Race-derived engine

The 427-cubic inch engine was only available with the base model trim and was never used in the plusher GT/GTA model. After all, it was a thinly-disguised race car and potential purchasers were carefully screened by dealers.

Four-speed transmission

Unlike the Fairlane GT/GTA, the 427 was only available with one transmission: a Borg-Warner 'Top Loader' T-10 four-speed.

Handling package

A special handling package, consisting of manual front disc brakes, longer rear leaf springs and larger blackwall tires, was available. This particular car is one of the very few to be fitted with these items.

Smooth styling

For 1966, the Fairlane hardtop received similar styling to the Pontiac GTO, with stacked headlights and smooth-flowing contours.

Specifications
1967 Ford
Fairlane 427

ENGINE
Type: V8
Construction: Cast-iron block and heads
Valve gear: Two valves per cylinder actuated by a single camshaft via pushrods, rockers and solid lifters
Bore and stroke: 4.23 in. x 3.78 in.
Displacement: 427 c.i.
Compression ratio: 11.1:1
Induction system: Two Holley four-barrel downdraft carburetors with aluminum intake manifold
Maximum power: 425 bhp at 6,000 rpm
Maximum torque: 480 lb-ft at 3,700 rpm
Top speed: 121 mph
0-60 mph: 6.0 sec

TRANSMISSION
Borg-Warner 'Top Loader' T-10 four-speed

BODY/CHASSIS
Steel unitary chassis with two-door body

SPECIAL FEATURES

Stacked headlights are a feature of 1966-1967 Fairlanes. The lower units are the high beams.

Dual 652 cfm Holley four barrel carburetors are housed beneath an open element aircleaner

RUNNING GEAR
Steering: Recirculating ball
Front suspension: Double wishbones with heavy duty coil springs, telescopic shock absorbers, anti-sway bar
Rear suspension: Live axle with long semi-elliptic leaf springs and telescopic shock absorbers
Brakes: Discs front, drums rear
Wheels: 14 x 5.5-in.
Tires: 7.75 x 14

DIMENSIONS
Length: 197.0 in.	**Width:** 74.7 in.
Height: 54.3 in.	**Wheelbase:** 116.0 in.
Track: 58.0 in.	**Weight:** 4,100 lbs.

Fiberglass hood
In 1966 all 427 Fairlanes were built with a fiberglass lift-off hood with four tie-down pins. For 1967 a steel hood was available alongside the fiberglass unit.

Ford FAIRLANE CROWN VICTORIA

Dearborn first pioneered the use of a transparent roof on its 1954 Skyliner. When Fords were extensively restyled for 1955, the Plexiglas roof was retained for the new Crown Victoria. This novel idea is considered to be the forerunner of the modern 'moon' roof.

"...feather-light steering."

"Driving the Crown Victoria is like piloting any other mainstream Detroiter of the time. It has feather-light steering with a huge steering wheel as well as four-wheel, power-assisted, drum brakes. Although riding on big 15-inch wheels, the Ford is no handling champ, but it does ride smoothly. With Thunderbird power under the hood and lots of lowdown torque, acceleration is swift and instant once you step on the gas pedal."

Smart black and white, two-tone upholstery marks out the fairly restrained interior.

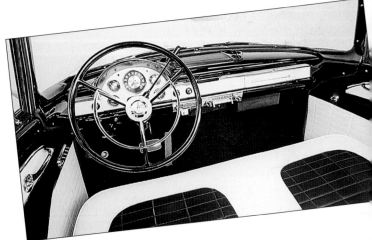

Milestones

1954 A longtime show car
feature, a transparent Plexiglas roof finally makes production. It is offered on the Skyliner, a Crestliner hardtop coupe. Although a 223-cubic inch six is standard, the new 239-cubic inch, Y-block V8 is optional. Only 13,344 Skyliners are built this year.

The 312 V8 was also offered in the 1957 retractable top Skyliner.

1955 Restyled Fords are longer
and lower with a more streamlined profile. Replacing the Skyliner is the glass-roof Crown Victoria. It does not prove popular, however, with fewer than 2,000 built compared to 33,165 steel-roof coupes.

Thunderbirds shared drivetrain choices with standard Fords.

1956 The Crown Victoria
glass top returns, although very poor sales make it too costly to sustain and the model is banished for 1957.

UNDER THE SKIN

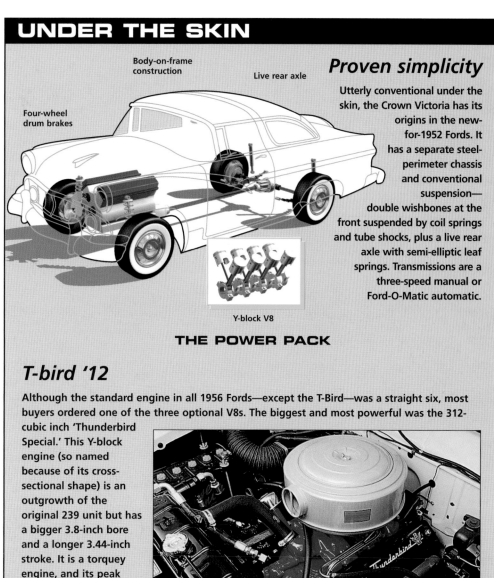

Body-on-frame construction

Four-wheel drum brakes

Live rear axle

Y-block V8

THE POWER PACK

Proven simplicity

Utterly conventional under the skin, the Crown Victoria has its origins in the new-for-1952 Fords. It has a separate steel-perimeter chassis and conventional suspension—double wishbones at the front suspended by coil springs and tube shocks, plus a live rear axle with semi-elliptic leaf springs. Transmissions are a three-speed manual or Ford-O-Matic automatic.

T-bird '12

Although the standard engine in all 1956 Fords—except the T-Bird—was a straight six, most buyers ordered one of the three optional V8s. The biggest and most powerful was the 312-cubic inch 'Thunderbird Special.' This Y-block engine (so named because of its cross-sectional shape) is an outgrowth of the original 239 unit but has a bigger 3.8-inch bore and a longer 3.44-inch stroke. It is a torquey engine, and its peak power of 225 bhp gives the Crown Victoria considerable grunt.

Fully loaded

Not popular when new, the 1955-1956 Fairlane Crown Victoria is a collectible automobile today. Many owners loaded these cars with dealer-installed options, which cost a lot of money. One of these cars with period extras is a real find.

Only 603 glass-topped Crown Victorias were built during the car's final season.

161

FAIRLANE CROWN VICTORIA

Dramatic-looking in its day, the Crown Victoria was not a great commercial success, and this, coupled with the new maximum-volume policy instigated by Ford, sounded the death knell for the bubbletop.

Lifeguard luxuries

Ford began touting safety in the mid-1950s, and the Crown Victoria boasted such features as a padded dashboard and sun visors, a deep-dish steering wheel, a breakaway rearview mirror and factory-installed seatbelts. All these items were grouped under the Lifeguard package.

Y-block power

Three versions, displacing 272, 292 and 312 cubic inches, of the new-for-1952 Y-block were available in the Crown Victoria. The top 312 unit, shared with the Thunderbird, put out 225 bhp with a four-barrel carburetor if teamed with the Ford-O-Matic automatic transmission.

Automatic transmission

The three-speed, Ford-O-Matic unit was a popular option and was smoother and more refined than arch rival Chevrolet's two-speed Powerglide.

Roof band

The Crown Victoria has a wraparound chromed roof band, which gives a tiara effect. The band adds no structural strength to the body, but gives the car a very 1950s, luxurious look.

Bubbletop roof

Costing an extra $70, the optional glass roof panel was heavily tinted, but on hot days it acted like a greenhouse, making the inside of the cabin unbearably hot. A zip-out headliner helped to reduce the problem.

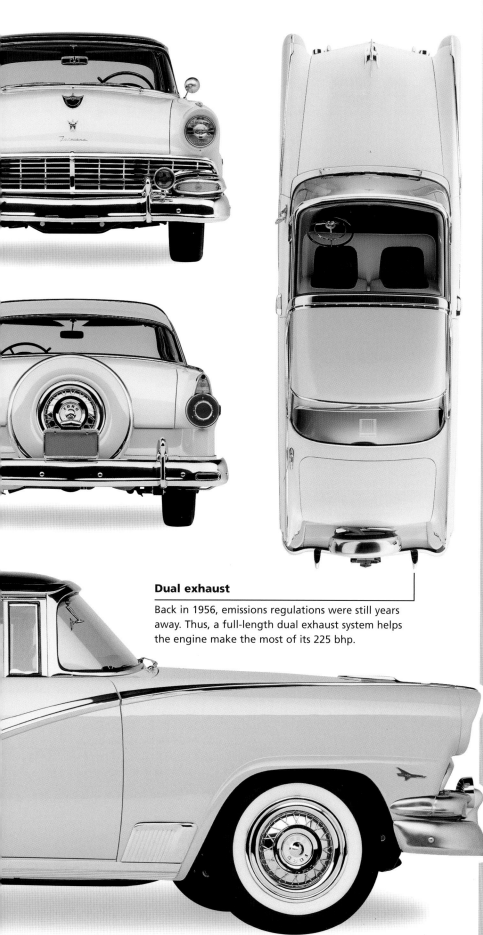

Dual exhaust

Back in 1956, emissions regulations were still years away. Thus, a full-length dual exhaust system helps the engine make the most of its 225 bhp.

Specifications

1956 Ford Crown Victoria

ENGINE
Type: V8

Construction: Cast-iron block and heads

Valve gear: Two valves per cylinder operated by a single camshaft with pushrods and rockers

Bore and stroke: 3.8 in. x 3.44 in.

Displacement: 312 c.i.

Compression ratio: 8.4:1

Induction system: Holley four-barrel carburetor

Maximum power: 225 bhp at 4,600 rpm

Maximum torque: 317 lb-ft at 2,600 rpm

TRANSMISSION
Ford-O-Matic three-speed automatic

BODY/CHASSIS
Separate steel chassis with two-door hardtop body

SPECIAL FEATURES

The Continental kit hinges to the left to gain access to the trunk.

A rear-mounted antenna was a dealer-installed option.

RUNNING GEAR
Steering: Recirculating ball

Front suspension: Double wishbones with coil springs and telescopic shock absorbers

Rear suspension: Live axle with semi-elliptic leaf springs and telescopic shock absorbers

Brakes: Drums (front and rear)

Wheels: Pressed steel, 15-in. dia.

Tires: 7.10 x 15

DIMENSIONS
Length: 198.5 in. **Width:** 75.9 in.

Height: 52.5 in.   **Wheelbase:** 155.0 in.

Track: 58.0 in. (front), 56.0 in. (rear)

Weight: 3,299 lbs.

Ford FAIRLANE SKYLINER

For the 1950s, the Skyliner was a technological miracle. At the touch of a button the car, which looks like a standard two-door hardtop coupe, lifts up its steel roof and tucks it neatly into the trunk. The idea has been revived by Mercedes-Benz for the SLK sports car.

"...retractable hardtop"

"The most dynamic feature of the Skyliner is its retractable roof. Just press the button under the dash and enjoy the show. The trunk opens to about 80 degrees and the roof emerges with the forward flap hanging down. It then moves forward and lowers and locks in place. As for performance, the Skyliner is quick and powerful, but rolls a bit through turns. It is an unstressed and comfortable car with a retractable hardtop."

By late-1950s standards, the interior is tastefully restrained.

Milestones

1957 Fords are totally restyled

and the new Fairlane range is far lower and much longer than the 1956 models. The Skyliner, with its amazing electrically-powered, fully-retractable metal roof is launched; 20,766 are sold.

The Skyliner retractable appeared halfway through 1957.

1958 Minor styling changes

are made, including four headlights and a fake hood scoop, and more power is available with the Interceptor Special V8 option. Ford V8 engines have an improved cylinder head, valve design, bearings and crankshafts. The roof is also strengthened.

The Skyliner proved unprofitable and was duly axed in 1959.

1959 Despite a complete restyle,

sales fall to 12,915. A totally restyled range is scheduled for 1960 and production of the Skyliner comes to an end.

UNDER THE SKIN

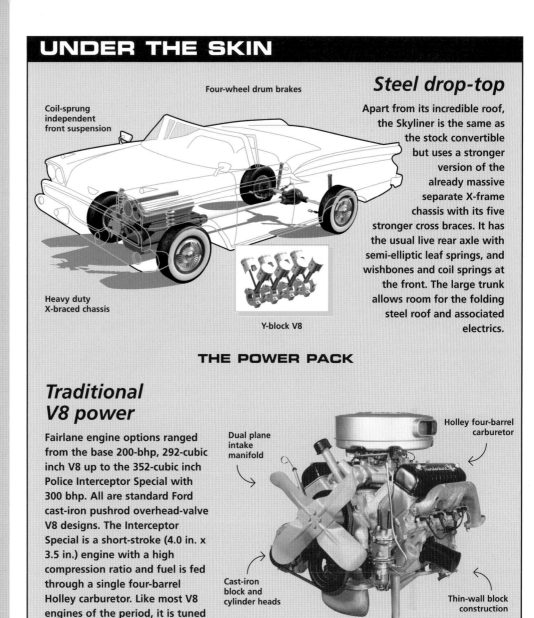

Four-wheel drum brakes

Coil-sprung independent front suspension

Heavy duty X-braced chassis

Y-block V8

Steel drop-top

Apart from its incredible roof, the Skyliner is the same as the stock convertible but uses a stronger version of the already massive separate X-frame chassis with its five stronger cross braces. It has the usual live rear axle with semi-elliptic leaf springs, and wishbones and coil springs at the front. The large trunk allows room for the folding steel roof and associated electrics.

THE POWER PACK

Traditional V8 power

Fairlane engine options ranged from the base 200-bhp, 292-cubic inch V8 up to the 352-cubic inch Police Interceptor Special with 300 bhp. All are standard Ford cast-iron pushrod overhead-valve V8 designs. The Interceptor Special is a short-stroke (4.0 in. x 3.5 in.) engine with a high compression ratio and fuel is fed through a single four-barrel Holley carburetor. Like most V8 engines of the period, it is tuned to produce maximum power and torque at low rpm.

Dual plane intake manifold

Holley four-barrel carburetor

Cast-iron block and cylinder heads

Thin-wall block construction

Vintage year

1959 Fords were regarded as the most attractive full-size cars the company had built up to that time. As far as Skyliners are concerned, the 1959 models are also the rarest—only 12,915 were produced. This makes them the most sought-after of all 1959 Fords.

The 1959 models are far more collectable than earlier Skyliners.

Ford **FAIRLANE SKYLINER**

For three years Ford was the only car company brave enough to make a true mass-production car with a foldaway steel roof. It cost millions to develop, and is a real treat to see today.

Folding rear deck

When the roof is folded away in the trunk, the deck is fully extended. When the roof is up, however, the end of the deck lid folds away. The end section of the deck is moved by an electric motor.

Powerful V8

In 1959 the Skyliner came with a standard 292-cubic inch Mercury V8. With gas selling for around 20 cents a gallon at the time, big-blocks were popular. This car is fitted with a 352-cubic inch unit producing 300 bhp.

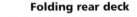

Automatic transmission

The standard transmission was a three-speed manual, but by 1958 the three-speed Cruise-O-Matic automatic could be ordered. There was also a manual transmission with automatic overdrive, but this was not popular.

Seven electric motors

To operate the roof, seven electric motors are required. The biggest is in the trunk and operates the two very long screw jacks that raise and lower the roof. Thirteen switches, 10 solenoids, eight circuit breakers and over 600 feet of wiring serve the electric motors.

Optional power brakes

To get the best from the four-wheel drum brakes, they are power-assisted. Brake fade is common after repeated hard use.

Specifications

1959 Ford Skyliner

ENGINE

Type: V8

Construction: Cast-iron block and heads

Valve gear: Two valves per cylinder operated by a single V-mounted camshaft via pushrods and rockers

Bore and stroke: 4.00 in. x 3.50 in.

Displacement: 352 c.i.

Compression ratio: 9.6:1

Induction system: Four-barrel Holley carburetor

Maximum power: 300 bhp at 4,600 rpm

Maximum torque: 381 lb-ft at 2,800 rpm

TRANSMISSION

Three-speed Cruise-O-Matic automatic

BODY/CHASSIS

Steel X-frame chassis with steel two-door convertible body

SPECIAL FEATURES

When the roof is up, the trunk is quite spacious.

With the top up the Skyliner looks like a normal hardtop car.

RUNNING GEAR

Steering: Recirculating ball

Front suspension: Double wishbones with coil springs and telescopic shock absorbers

Rear suspension: Live axle with semi-elliptic leaf springs and telescopic shock absorbers

Brakes: Drums (front and rear)

Wheels: Steel discs, 14-in. dia

Tires: 6.00 x 14

DIMENSIONS

Length: 208.1 in. **Width:** 76.6 in.

Height: 56.5 in.   **Wheelbase:** 118.0 in.

Track: 59.0 in. (front), 56.5 in. (rear)

Weight: 4,064 lbs.

Round tail lights

One of the best styling changes made to 1959 Fords was to replace the four protruding taillights in the rectangular housings by single, large round lights. These became a trademark on early-1960s Fords.

Two-tone paintwork

The side trim of the 1957 model lent itself to a two-tone finish, and the 1958 model, with a long chrome-edged side panel, was ideal for a three-tone treatment. This panel became almost a stripe on the 1959 model.

Ford FAIRLANE THUNDERBOLT

In 1963 Ford campaigned race-prepped Galaxies in Super Stock drag racing. Because they were too heavy, the Max Wedge Mopars and Super Duty Pontiacs beat Ford's finest every time. In 1964 Ford modified its smaller Fairlane, added a full race suspension, and a high-strung 427 V8. It slaughtered the competition.

"...specialized racing machine."

Let it be known that this is not a car for the faint hearted. The stripped-out interior, light weight and 13:1 compression engine were designed to win NHRA's highly competitive Super Stock drag racing class. The fiberglass body panels, tuned racing suspension and trunk-mounted battery give the T-bolt a traction advantage over the competition. Six out of seven NHRA divisional championships were won by these specialized racing machines.

In the interest of light weight, the sun visors, sound-deadening and mirrors were removed.

Milestones

1963 With its Total Performance campaign underway Ford launches a new 427 engine. It enables the big Galaxies to run 12.07 ETs. Unfortunately, the cars fail to win an NHRA championship. Rhode Island Ford dealer Bob Tasca stuffs a 427 in a Fairlane and goes to the NHRA Nationals, but fails to win a race.

50 1963 lightweight Galaxies were the first 427 race cars.

1964 In order to combat the Mopar threat, Ford puts the 427 engine into 100 lightweight Fairlanes. They give Ford the manufacturer's trophy and racer Gas Ronda wins the NHRA driver's championship.

In the 1990s, Ford rereleased its potent 427 for specialized racing.

1966 A 427-powered Fairlane intended for the street is offered, although it proves more successful at the drag strip than on the road.

UNDER THE SKIN

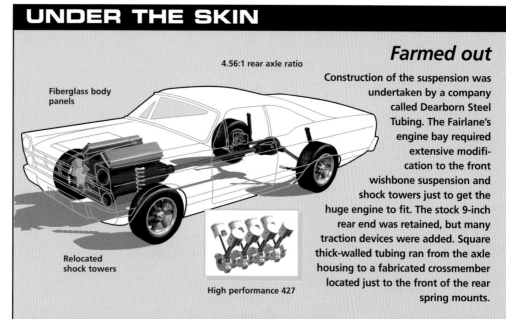

4.56:1 rear axle ratio

Fiberglass body panels

Relocated shock towers

High performance 427

Farmed out

Construction of the suspension was undertaken by a company called Dearborn Steel Tubing. The Fairlane's engine bay required extensive modification to the front wishbone suspension and shock towers just to get the huge engine to fit. The stock 9-inch rear end was retained, but many traction devices were added. Square thick-walled tubing ran from the axle housing to a fabricated crossmember located just to the front of the rear spring mounts.

THE POWER PACK

King of the drags

For the Thunderbolt, the 427 engine used in the 1963 lightweight Galaxie was the weapon of choice. The bottom end consists of a cast-iron block, forged steel crankshaft and cross-bolt main bearing caps. Fortified with 13:1 compression domed pistons, a long duration camshaft, high rpm valve springs and dual Holley four barrels, the engine makes a factory rated 425 bhp (actual figures are closer to 550 bhp). Cool air induction runs from the in-board headlight housings to the dual carbs, while special tubular headers release the exhaust.

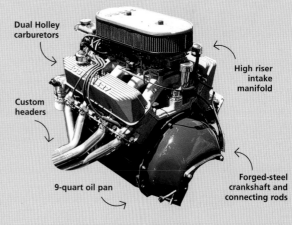

Dual Holley carburetors

Custom headers

High riser intake manifold

9-quart oil pan

Forged-steel crankshaft and connecting rods

High prices

Because of their rarity, Thunderbolts are highly sought after today and prices reflect this. If you're interested in a weekend racer then one of these cars is ideal, since they are among the fastest in their class. They are unsuitable for street driving, however.

Only approximately 100 Thunderbolts were built in 1964.

Ford FAIRLANE THUNDERBOLT

Although the Thunderbolt was street legal and anyone could walk into a Ford dealer and buy their own factory drag car, it wasn't meant to be driven on the street. It was the most brutal ¼-mile race car that Ford has ever produced.

Teardrop hood

The aluminum air box sits too high on the engine to fit under a conventional flat hood. So a teardrop shaped hood bulge is molded into the fiberglass hood for adequate clearance. Two larger cut-outs in the rear section of the teardrop allow hot air in the engine compartment to escape.

427 engine

With its high compression ratio, long-duration cam and other heavy duty components. The 427 V8 was able to churn out much more than the factory rated 425 bhp.

Maximum traction

For maximum traction, the left rear is suspended by a two-leaf spring, while the right side has a three-leaf spring.

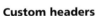

Custom headers

Tubular headers replace the cast iron exhaust manifolds. They were used not only for their tremendous performance gain, but also because the engine bay was too tight for the stock units.

Stripped-out interior

All non-essentials were removed from the interior including the sun visors, heater, radio, armrests and sound deadening. In addition, the stock front seats were replaced with lightweight buckets, the window cranks for the rear windows were removed and an unpadded rubber mat covers the floor pan.

Severe duty rear suspension

Square-tubed radius arms are welded from the crossmember directly to the rear axle housing. This design prevents the chassis from rolling above the axle unless something bends or breaks.

Body modifications

All Thunderbolts were built with fiberglass front fenders, hoods and trunk lids. While the front windshield is standard safety glass, all other windows have been replaced with lightweight Plexiglas.

Air intakes

All T-bolts had their high beams removed and replaced by screen-covered ram-air intakes which feed the carburetors cool air through twin 6-inch diameter flexible ducts.

Modified front suspension

Many modifications had to be made to the Thunderbolt's front suspension to get the 427 to fit. The shock towers were trimmed and a flat steel plate welded in place to retain body strength. The upper A-arms were shortened and their pivot points moved out 1 inch.

Specifications

1964 Ford Fairlane Thunderbolt

ENGINE

Type: V8

Construction: Cast-iron block and heads

Valve gear: Two valves per cylinder operated by pushrods and rockers

Bore and stroke: 4.23 in. x 3.78 in.

Displacement: 427 c.i.

Compression ratio: 13:1

Induction system: Two Holley four-barrel carburetors

Maximum power: 425 bhp at 6,000 rpm

Maximum torque: 480 lb-ft at 3,700 rpm

TRANSMISSION

Borg-Warner T10 four-speed

BODY/CHASSIS

Steel unitary chassis with two-door sedan body

SPECIAL FEATURES

Twin air scoops replace the stock inner headlights to give the engine cool air.

A 125-lb. battery is located in the trunk for better traction off the line.

RUNNING GEAR

Steering: Recirculating ball

Front suspension: Modified shock towers, unequal length wishbones with coil springs and telescopic shocks

Rear suspension: Custom fabricated suspension, live axle with multi-leaf springs and telescopic shocks

Brakes: Drums (front and rear)

Wheels: Steel discs, 15-in. dia.

Tires: Goodyear bias ply (front), Mickey Thompson slicks (rear)

DIMENSIONS

Length: 190.3 in. **Width:** 73.6 in.

Height: 56.9 in. **Wheelbase:** 115.5 in

Track: 58.6 in. (front), 55.3 in. (rear)

Weight: 3,225 lbs.

Ford GALAXIE 500 7 LITRE

The Galaxie 500 7 Litre formula was a simple one. Tried-and-true mechanical components, luxury fittings, and a huge 428-cubic inch V8 came together in a single package that made for a powerful driving experience.

"...solidly built."

"Ford sought refinement with the Galaxie 500. It is solidly built, quiet, and very comfortable. Its soft suspension insulates passengers from severe road bumps. Because this is the sporty member of the Galaxie family, the steering is reasonably responsive and turn-in is good for such a large car. With 428-cubic inches under the hood, it is also a star performer; hit the gas pedal and this leviathan leaps forward. With front disc brakes, it stops well, too.

As it is a top-line model, the Galaxie 500 boasts leather-trimmed upholstery.

Milestones

1965 Like arch rival Chevy,

Ford fields new big cars. They have more linear styling, stacked headlights, and all-new suspensions. Models are divided into Custom and Galaxie ranges, the latter including a top-line XL coupe, convertible, and plush LTD coupe and sedan. Engines range from a 240-cubic inch six up to the 427 V8.

Halfway through 1963, Galaxies could be fitted with the 427 V8 as an option.

1966 Joining the LTDs as big,

upmarket Fords are the Galaxie 500 7 Litre coupes and convertibles, powered by 345-bhp 428 V8s. Only 11,073 7 Litres to 101,096 LTDs are built.

Big Fords were all restyled for 1965; this is a 427 Galaxie 500XL.

1967 More exaggerated

Coke-bottle contours mark the Galaxies this year. Due to poor sales, the 7 Litre models do not return.

Unitary construction

Independent front suspension

Live rear axle

Massive FE V8

Vast and fast

New from the ground up, the big Fords for 1965 received a stronger, unitary structure and an unequal length A-arm front suspension that proved to be so effective that it was used in NASCAR racing well into the 1970s. At the rear a live axle was retained, but coil springs and control arms replaced the leaf springs. The 1966 models differ only in detail. A front anti-roll bar was standard, as were four-wheel drum brakes, though front discs were available as an option.

THE POWER PACK

Torque monster

In 1965, the biggest engine offered in the Galaxie was the fearsome 427 unit. It had four-bolt main bearings, a forged-steel crank, and either a single four-barrel carburetor or two fours.

For 1966, a new 428-cubic inch engine joined the option list. Still a member of the FE-series family of big-blocks, the cast-iron 428 was tuned more for torque than power and had two-bolt main bearings, a cast-iron crankshaft, and cast-alloy pistons. It was more streetable than the 427 and with 345 bhp on tap it still had more than enough power to satisfy the vast majority of drivers.

Extra luxury

The Mid-1960 Galaxie has a large following. The most popular model is the rare 1965 427 car with a dual-quad intake. The 1966 7 Litre model is also worth considering. It is quite rare (11,073 built) and in convertible form makes the ideal summer cruiser.

Galaxie 7 Litres were offered only for 1966.

Ford GALAXIE 500 7 LITRE

As if to signify their departure from competition and the performance market, the 1965-1966 Fords were more formal-looking than their predecessors. The 7 Litres were among the most refined cars of their day.

V8 engines

Because it was the flagship of the Ford line, the 7 Litre had to have the largest Ford powerplant available: in this case the 345-bhp, 428-cubic inch V8 also found in that year's Thunderbird. This engine makes the Galaxie a 16.5-second ¼-mile runner—impressive considering its 4,000-lbs. curbweight.

Three-speed automatic

The standard transmission with the V8 Galaxie 7 Litre is the C6 Cruise-O-Matic three-speed automatic transmission. This unit can also be shifted between first and second manually for improved acceleration off the line.

Front discs

Standard brakes on the Galaxie were 11-inch diameter drums. The front pair were wider than the one in the rear. However, by this stage, front discs were available and were standard equipment on the Galaxie 500 7-liter.

Independent front suspension

Through the 1960s, Ford played around with its unequal length A-arm front suspension in an effort to get the greatest ride comfort. This was achieved by improving the bushings in the lower A-arms.

Power top

Unlike small sports cars, large convertibles had the space for proper power operation of the convertible top. In the Galaxie's case it folds down almost flush with the top of the car to give a smooth, uncluttered line.

Bucket seat interior

Galaxies could be ordered with a wide range of interior equipment including front power bucket seats with a power center console and power windows and door locks.

Coil-sprung rear

Although still retaining a live rear axle, from 1965 the big Fords got coil springs and semi-trailing arms. This was to improve the ride, which was said by some to be in the same league as a Rolls-Royce.

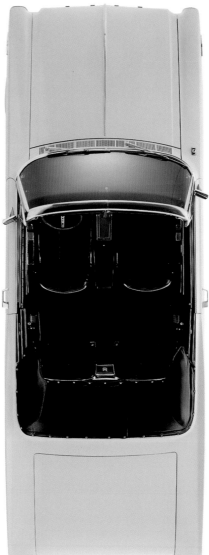

Specifications

1966 Ford Galaxie 500 7 Litre

ENGINE

Type: V8

Construction: Cast-iron block and heads

Valve gear: Two valves per cylinder operated by a single V-mounted camshaft via pushrods, rockers and hydraulic valve lifters

Bore and stroke: 4.13 in. x 3.98 in.

Displacement: 428 c.i.

Compression ratio: 10.5:1

Induction system: Autolite four barrel carburetor

Maximum power: 345 bhp at 4,600 rpm

Maximum torque: 462 lb-ft at 2,800 rpm

TRANSMISSION

C6 Cruise-O-Matic three-speed automatic

BODY/CHASSIS

Unitary steel construction, steel body panels and convertible top

SPECIAL FEATURES

One of the more noticeable changes for 1966 was using exposed turn signal lenses.

The "Galaxie 500" tag signifies Ford's involvement in NASCAR racing which it dominated in the mid 1960s.

RUNNING GEAR

Steering: Recirculating-ball

Front suspension: Unequal length A-arms with coil springs, telescopic shock absorbers and anti-roll bar

Rear suspension: Live axle with coil springs, control arms and telescopic shock absorbers

Brakes: Drums, 11 x 3 in. (front), 11 x 2.5 in. (rear)

Wheels: Stamped steel, 15-in. dia.

Tires: 8.45 x 15

DIMENSIONS

Length: 210.0 in.   **Width:** 78.0 in.

Height: 53.9 in.   **Wheelbase:** 119.0 in.

Track: 62.0 in. (front and rear)

Weight: 4,059 lbs.

Ford **GT40**

The GT40 showed that when a company the size of Ford decides to go into racing, their vast resources will ensure success. After some initial teething trouble, the mighty V8 Ford humiliated the Ferraris with a sweep at Le Mans in 1966.

"...V8 thumps you in the back."

"Even in the road car, with its milder engine and rubber-bushed suspension it's easy to get a realistic impression of what it was like to drive the GT40s through the June heat at Le Mans. The open road and wide, sweeping corners soon beckon; somewhere you can floor the throttle and feel the gutsy V8 thump you in the back as it tears to 100 mph in just 12 seconds. If it's this good on the road, it must have been fantastic on the Mulsanne Straight."

The cabin is small and claustrophobic. Tall drivers cannot even fit in and miss out on one of the greatest driving experiences available.

Milestones

1963 After failing to buy Ferrari, Ford joins forces with Lola to turn the Lola GT into the prototype Ford GT.

1964 Now known as the GT40, the Ford makes its racing debut at the Nurburgring 1000 km. It is forced to retire, as it does in every race this year.

GT40 was so named because its overall height was 40 inches.

1965 Production starts for homologation and a GT40 wins its first race: the 2000-km Daytona Continental.

1966 The big-block cars finish 1-2-3 at Le Mans and win the International Sports Car Championship for GTs.

GT40 won Le Mans in 1968 and '69 after Ford had withdrawn from sports car racing in '67.

1967 Once again the car wins both the International Sports Car Championship and the 24 Hours of Le Mans. Although Ford withdraws from racing at the end of '67, the GT40 races on in the hands of the Gulf team, winning Le Mans again in '68 and '69.

UNDER THE SKIN

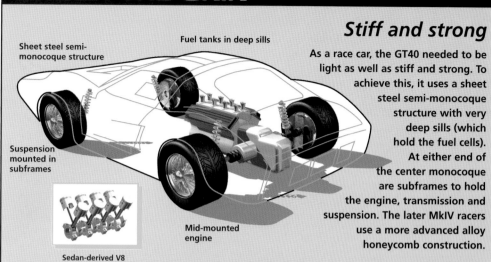

Sheet steel semi-monocoque structure

Fuel tanks in deep sills

Suspension mounted in subframes

Sedan-derived V8

Mid-mounted engine

Stiff and strong

As a race car, the GT40 needed to be light as well as stiff and strong. To achieve this, it uses a sheet steel semi-monocoque structure with very deep sills (which hold the fuel cells). At either end of the center monocoque are subframes to hold the engine, transmission and suspension. The later MkIV racers use a more advanced alloy honeycomb construction.

THE POWER PACK

Tuning potential

Most GT40s used the 289-cubic inch V8 also found in the Sunbeam Tiger, Ford Mustang and early AC Cobra. With a cast-iron block and cylinder heads, a single camshaft operating two valves per cylinder via pushrods and rockers, it is not a sophisticated engine. Its design dates back to the 1950s, but it has huge tuning potential. In full racing tune, it can produce around 400 bhp which was more than enough to blow past the more sophisticated, but often less reliable, Ferraris.

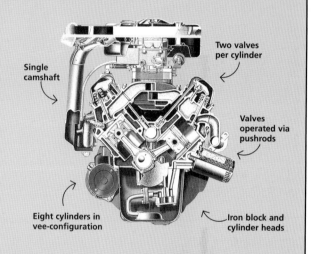

Single camshaft

Two valves per cylinder

Valves operated via pushrods

Eight cylinders in vee-configuration

Iron block and cylinder heads

Big blocks

Ford's first Le Mans-winning GT40 used the big-block 427-cubic inch engine; a unit that proved in the tough world of NASCAR racing it had the strength required for 24-hour racing. Only a few big-block cars were built.

Big-block cars had extra power and strength to compete in endurance racing.

Ford **GT40**

Fast and immensely strong, the GT40 showed what a production car company could do when it wanted to go racing, particularly with Carroll Shelby, father of the AC Cobra, running the racing program.

Final specification

Although this car first raced in 1965, it was later brought up to the final racing specs, those of the Le Mans-winning cars of 1968 and '69.

Mid-engined design

By the 1960s, it was obvious that a successful racing car had to be mid-engined and Ford followed suit. The engine is behind the driver, mounted lengthwise, and by 1968, the displacement of the small-block engine had risen to 302 cubic inches. With Gurney-Weslake-developed cylinder heads, as on this car, power output was up to 435 bhp.

Front-mounted radiator

Ford decided to keep the radiator in its conventional position rather than mounting it alongside or behind the engine as on some modern mid-engined designs.

Four-speed transmission

The first racers are equipped with a four-speed Colotti transmission with right-hand change. Road cars have a ZF five-speed box with conventional central shifter.

Opening side windows

GT40s get incredibly hot inside and although the main side windows do not open, there are small hinged windows to allow air to pass through the cockpit.

Fiberglass body

The GT40's body played no structural role, so it was made from fiberglass and consisted basically of two large hinged sections, which gave the best access during pit stops.

Radiator outlet

By 1968, the air passing through the radiator was exhausted through this one large vent. It has a small upturned lip on the leading edge to accelerate air flow through the radiator.

Competition record

This car was one of the first driven at Le Mans, in 1965 by Bob Bondurant, but it failed to finish after cylinder head gasket failure. Three years later, it came fourth in the 1000 km at Spa Francorchamps.

Magnesium suspension components

The GT40 is a heavyweight racing car, but some effort was still made to save weight—the magnesium suspension uprights, for example.

Halibrand wheels

The wide Halibrand wheels are made from magnesium, so they are very light. The design also provides good cooling for the disc brakes. They are a knock-off design for quick changes at pit stops.

Specifications
1967 Ford GT40 MkIII (road spec)

ENGINE
Type: V8
Construction: Cast-iron block and heads
Valve gear: Two valves per cylinder operated by single camshaft via pushrods and rockers
Bore and stroke: 4 in. x 2.87 in.
Displacement: 289 c.i.
Compression ratio: 10.5:1
Induction system: Single four-barrel Holley carburetor
Maximum power: 306 bhp at 6,000 rpm
Maximum torque: 328 lb-ft at 4,200 rpm
Top speed: 165 mph
0-60 mph: 5.5 sec.

TRANSMISSION
Five-speed ZF manual transaxle

BODY/CHASSIS
Sheet steel central semi-monocoque with front and rear subframes and fiberglass two-door, two-seat GT body

SPECIAL FEATURES

The GT40 was made as low as possible to help its aerodynamics. On this car, to help fit a driver with helmet into the cockpit, this bump was added onto the roof.

To help achieve a low overall height, the exhaust pipes run over the top of the transmission.

RUNNING GEAR
Steering: Rack-and-pinion
Front suspension: Double wishbones with coil springs, telescopic shocks and anti-roll bar
Rear suspension: Trailing arms and wishbones with coil springs, telescopic shocks and anti-roll bar
Brakes: Discs, 11.5 in. dia. (front), 11.2 in. dia. (rear)
Wheels: Halibrand magnesium 6.5 in. x 15 in. (front), 8.5 in. x 15 in. (rear)
Tires: 5.5 in. x 15 in. (front), 7 in. x 15 in. (rear)

DIMENSIONS
Length: 169 in. **Width:** 70 in.
Height: 40 in. **Wheelbase:** 95.3 in.
Track: 55 in. (front), 53.5 in. (rear)
Weight: 2,200 lbs.

COLVILL

Ford MODEL A

After 19 years and more than 15 million sales, the venerable 'Tin Lizzie' gave way to a new Ford, the Model A. It was more complex and boasted twice as much power and proved hugely succcessful with the public.

"...huge improvement from the T."

"Even today, the Model A is recognized as a huge improvement over its predecessor, the Model T; the big L-head four is much more torquey and smooth. Given a good road, it is possible to wind the car all the way up to 65 mph, though it takes time to get there. Greatly improved springing, bigger tires and four-wheel mechanical brakes also make the A feel much more stable and secure than the Tin Lizzie. Moreover, refinement is not far shy of contemporary luxury cars."

The basic interior design of the Model A lasted through the 1930s.

Milestones

1927 After a remarkable 19-year production run, the Ford Model T is phased out. Production stands at 15,007,033, a record which will remain unbroken until after World War II.

The Model A continued the legacy established by the versatile and popular 'Tin Lizzie.'

1927 Ford's Model A is introduced to much fanfare. Powered by a new 201 c.i. L-head four, 10 million people view the car during its first 36 hours on the market.

Replacing the A was the four-cylinder Model B.

1929 The two millionth Model A is built in July.

1931 Competition from Chevrolet and the Depression eat into sales. Production plumets amid rumors of a V8 Ford for 1932.

UNDER THE SKIN

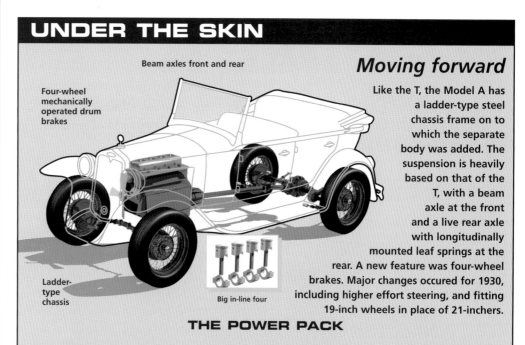

Beam axles front and rear

Four-wheel mechanically operated drum brakes

Ladder-type chassis

Big in-line four

Moving forward

Like the T, the Model A has a ladder-type steel chassis frame on to which the separate body was added. The suspension is heavily based on that of the T, with a beam axle at the front and a live rear axle with longitudinally mounted leaf springs at the rear. A new feature was four-wheel brakes. Major changes occured for 1930, including higher effort steering, and fitting 19-inch wheels in place of 21-inchers.

THE POWER PACK

All-new motor

An all-new car needs an all-new engine and that was exactly what Ford did with the Model A. A new 201-cubic inch four-cylinder L-head design, it had a cast-iron block and cylinder head. With two valves per cylinder and fuel drawn in through a single Holley carburetor, it produced 40 bhp with a 4.22:1 compression ratio—20 more than the previous Model T engine—and was far more torquey, due to a much longer 4.25 inch stroke. It was the first Ford engine to have a battery-fed ignition.

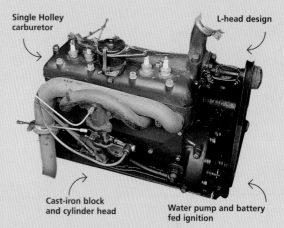

Single Holley carburetor

L-head design

Cast-iron block and cylinder head

Water pump and battery fed ignition

Open-top

During its four-year life, the Model A was an undisputed best seller, so there are still a sizeable number around. Although not the most popular when new, Roadsters and Cabriolets are the most collected of these due to their sportier looks.

Back in 1930, a Cabriolet would set you back the princely sum of $645.

Ford MODEL A

A huge gamble for the company, the Ford Model A nevertheless proved to be a hit, and its basic engineering was so sound that its legacy lived on in Ford cars built through 1948.

Big four-cylinder engine

Big displacement four-cylinder engines were common in the 1920s, offering good low end power. The Model A's 201-cubic inch 40 bhp enabled 0–60 mph times of just over 30 seconds.

Four-wheel brakes

More complex than the T, the Model A introduced a few features worthy of merit. One such was four-wheel brakes, still mechanically operated, while 19-inch wheels were used instead of 21-inch wheels from 1930, resulting in greater safety and an improved ride.

Adjustable windshield

Like Roadsters, Phaetons had a windshield that could be lowered by hinging it forward to rest on the hood. This feature lasted until 1937, when fixed pillars were standardized.

Phaeton body

Model As were offered with a variety of different bodies. The cheapest in 1930 was the two-seat roadster priced at $435 and followed by the four-door convertible phaeton at $440. The most popular Model A body style, however, was the Tudor sedan, of which 425,124 were built.

Improved interior

1930 brought a number of noticeable changes, both inside and out. Highlighting a roomier interior was an improved dash with centrally placed instruments, including a 'cyclops eye' speedometer.

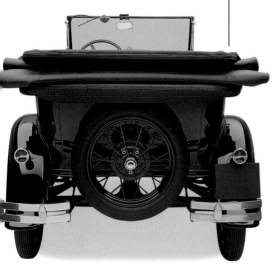

Ladder-type frame

In keeping with Henry Ford's ideas of standardization in manufacturing, all Model As rode the same 103.5-inch, fully boxed steel chassis. This also saved production time and enabled competitive pricing in an increasingly crowded automobile market.

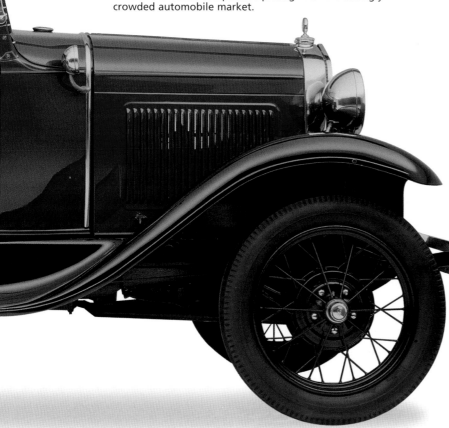

Specifications
1930 Model A Phaeton

ENGINE

Type: In-line four
Construction: Cast-iron block and head
Valve gear: Two valves per cylinder operated by a single camshaft via pushrods
Bore and stroke: 3.88 in. x 4.25 in.
Displacement: 201 c.i.
Compression ratio: 4.22:1
Induction system: Single Holley carburetor
Maximum power: 40 bhp at 2,200 rpm
Maximum torque: 128 lb-ft at 1,000 rpm
Top speed: 65 mph
0–60 mph: 32.0 sec

TRANSMISSION

Three-speed manual

BODY/CHASSIS

Steel ladder chassis with steel Phaeton body

SPECIAL FEATURES

Turn signals are a later addition to this otherwise stock Phaeton.

The engine could still be started by turning a handle off the crankshaft.

RUNNING GEAR

Steering: Worm-and-roller
Front suspension: Beam axle with transverse leaf spring and lever arm type shock absorbers
Rear suspension: Live axle with longitudinal leaf springs and lever-arm-type shock absorbers
Brakes: Drums, front and rear
Wheels: Steel, 19-in. dia.
Tires: 4.5 x 19 in.

DIMENSIONS

Length: 146.8 in. **Width:** 63.5 in.
Height: 71.6 in. **Wheelbase:** 103.5 in.
Track: 56.0 in. (front and rear)
Weight: 2,212 lbs.

Ford **MODEL T**

If ever a car helped the world get motoring it was the Ford Model T. Built in one piece, robust and reliable, Henry Ford's dream became a global reality. The Model T is rightly recognized by many as the world's most important car.

"...Living in the past..."

"The Model T is a vastly confusing place for anyone who drives a modern car to be. The pedal layout is baffling, you have to think constantly about which lever or pedal controls what, and even then you sometimes get it wrong. Even when you've mastered the controls, the Model T isn't a pleasant car to drive. The ride is atrocious, the steering heavy and vague and the brakes practically useless. But to decry the driving experience is missing the point. The Model T was never intended to be a good drive – it was intended to be a reliable and efficient means for as many people as possible to get from A to B."

Today it might look basic, but the simple appearance disguises a very complicated layout.

Milestones

1908 Ford's Model T

goes on sale on 1 October. By the end of the year, 305 examples have been built.

1914 The Model T is

famously offered by Henry Ford in "any colour as long as it's black", due to the low cost of lead-based black paint.

1915 Production

levels exceed one million. Electric windscreen wipers are fitted.

One of the prettiest body styles: a Doctor's Coupé.

1919 A wish is

answered: Model Ts get an electric starter. The original brass finished radiator is dropped and replaced by a black-painted nickel one.

Some Model Ts, such as this one, were built in Manchester, England.

1924 The different

bodywork styles on offer are standardized and finished in the factory. The same year, Ford builds its 10 millionth Model T – a four-seat roadster.

1927 With 15

million cars built, production of the Model T ceases and the all-new Model A goes on sale to replace it.

UNDER THE SKIN

Unbreakable

The running gear is of very simple construction, with a direct gear linkage and a single propshaft to the rear axle. The axles are attached to two subframes, which are bolted to the chassis. The engine is mounted in the middle of the front subframe and sits low in the body, with a side-hinged bonnet for easy access should it need repairs or maintenance. The front bulkhead is fixed in place, meaning that owners had to build the bodywork from the rear in whatever style they chose.

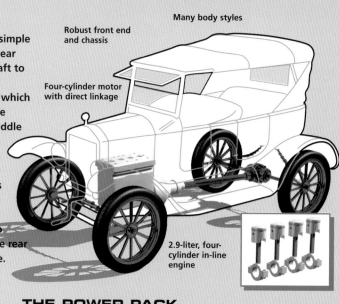

Many body styles

Robust front end and chassis

Four-cylinder motor with direct linkage

2.9-liter, four-cylinder in-line engine

THE POWER PACK

Slats in the bonnet allowed the engine to keep cool

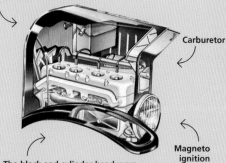

Carburetor

Magneto ignition

The block and cylinder head were made from cast iron

Built for longevity

With 2.9 liters displacement, the Model T's engine is quite big considering it's only a four-cylinder. On paper, the 20bhp sounds like a poor output for such a large capacity unit, but the engine was designed to operate at low speeds and provide effortless torque. Because the unit spins so lazily, it will go on for years without wearing out, but the inbuilt low compression means it can be very difficult to start up. Thanks to the wide torque spread, only two forward and one backward gear were considered necessary.

Sporty Speedster

In 1910, a sporty version of the Model T appeared called the Speedster. With stripped-down bodywork and seating for just one occupant, it was designed primarily with racing in mind. it wasn't fast by today's standards, but the lighter weight meant performance, handling and braking were much better than a car with a standard body.

More show than go: The Speedster was an early attempt at a sports car.

185

Ford **MODEL T**

Probably the single most important technical advance in motoring history, the Model T brought car ownership to the masses. Henry Ford's vision of an integrated production line is still used in automobile factories today.

Gearbox

The Model T was nothing like a modern car. You had two forward gears, which you selected by pulling an outside lever and then pressing a foot pedal, where the clutch is on a modern car, in order to change gear. Reverse gear was selected using the middle pedal.

Windscreen wipers

Model T drivers had to use a very rudimentary way of keeping their screens clear. Wipers didn't exist, but part of the screen could be lifted up so the driver could reach out and clean it with his hand.

Starting handle

Until an electric starter was introduced in 1919, Model T owners had to turn the engine by hand in order to get it to fire. The handle slotted in beneath the radiator grille and you had to turn on a tap to get fuel to the engine first.

Mudguards

This model features streamlined rear mudguards as it's a two-seater coupe. Saloon models had the guards integrated into the rear body, while van bodies sat over the axle to create a wheelarch. Basic and racing models had exposed wheels, but these were vulnerable to damage from road debris.

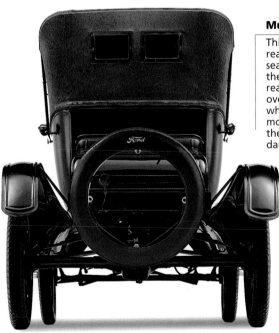

Hand throttle

The three foot pedals were for changing gear, engaging reverse and braking, with the brake where the gas pedal can be found on a modern car. To accelerate, drivers had to use a lever on the steering wheel to increase the amount of fuel entering the engine.

Quarter-elliptical leaf springs

Most contemporary cars came with semi-elliptic leaf springs as standard, but the Model T had smaller quarter-elliptic ones instead. This kept production costs to a minimum, but the trade-off was a harsh and bumpy ride quality.

Rear brakes

The right-hand foot pedal operated the cable brake, which applied itself to the front wheels only. It slowed the car down, but emergency stops were out of the question as it would heat up and fail completely. The rear brakes were more efficient and were operated with a hand lever.

Under the hood

The Model T engine was typical of its time. The 2.9-litre four-cylinder unit ran at low compression and had a realtively small output of just 20bhp, but it had enormous reserves of torque and could pull from very low speeds.

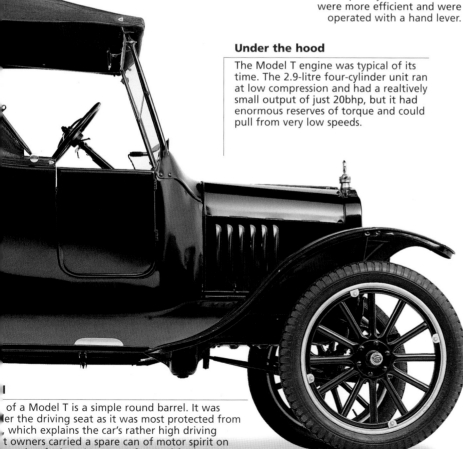

... of a Model T is a simple round barrel. It was ... er the driving seat as it was most protected from ... which explains the car's rather high driving ... t owners carried a spare can of motor spirit on ... ooard as fuel stations were few and far between..

Specifications

1908 Ford Model T

ENGINE
Engine: Four cylinder in-line
Construction: Cast iron block and cylinder head
Valve gear: Two valves per cylinder, mounted in block
Bore and stroke: 3.74 in. x 3.97 in.
Capacity: 2,895cc
Compression ratio: 4.5:1
Carburettor: One Holley direct unit
Power: 20bhp @ 1,800rpm
Top speed: 42mph
0–60mph: Not applicable

TRANSMISSION
Two-speed manual

BODY/CHASSIS
Chassis available in two lengths, wide range of bodies on offer.

SPECIAL FEATURES

Totally confusing: The left-hand pedal operates the forward gearbox, the middle pedal is used to select reverse and the right-hand pedal applies the brakes.

Front and rear, the Model T was equipped with quarter-elliptic leaf springs in order to cut production costs.

RUNNING GEAR
Steering: Direct linkage
Front suspension: Subframe, diagonal crosstubes, quarter-elliptic leaf springs
Rear suspension: Subframe, diagonal crosstubes, quarter-elliptic leaf springs
Brakes: Foot pedal operating cable to front, hand-operated cable linkage to rear
Wheels: Wooden, 30-spoke
Tires: 3.5 x 30 solid tyres

DIMENSIONS
Length: 140.0 in. **Width**: 66.0 in.
Height: Dependent on selected bodywork
Wheelbase: 100.5 in.
Track: 57.0 in. (front), 57.5 in. (rear)
Weight: 1475 lb. (applies to chassis and front bodywork only)

Ford MUSTANG 1966

Following its 1964 launch, the Mustang was a massive hit. Creating a place in the pony car market, its sales continued to increase. A modification of a 1966 car was the next step for this almost perfect package.

"...no ordinary Mustang."

"Do not be fooled by its looks; this is no ordinary Mustang. Underneath there have been a multitude of changes. The supercharged engine delivers considerable power, and the modified chassis gives more stability and poise than the original. Great attention has been paid to the interior, which blends well with the orange exterior. You would be hard-pressed to find a better example of a 1966 Mustang."

The carpet of this car is taken from Mercedes and it certainly looks elegant.

Milestones

1961 Inspirational
Ford President Lee Iacocca decides that the company should produce a sporty-looking car. Prototypes are built using a German four-cylinder engine.

1966 Mustangs came as convertibles as well as hardtops.

1964 Six months
ahead of the 1965 calendar year, Ford releases the Mustang. It is an instant hit, sparking a host of imitators from other manufacturers as the pony car war heats up.

The Mustang's first major design changes were introduced on the 1967 model, a bigger car.

1974 After a series
of styling changes, the original Mustang is replaced by the Mustang II. Initially a strong seller, it falls victim to the impending oil crisis and becomes a bloated, underpowered version of its previous self. Sales suffer as a result.

UNDER THE SKIN

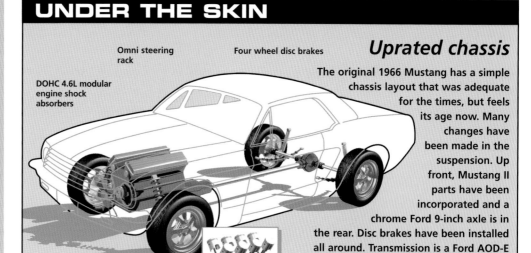

Omni steering rack

Four wheel disc brakes

DOHC 4.6L modular engine shock absorbers

All-alloy V8

Uprated chassis

The original 1966 Mustang has a simple chassis layout that was adequate for the times, but feels its age now. Many changes have been made in the suspension. Up front, Mustang II parts have been incorporated and a chrome Ford 9-inch axle is in the rear. Disc brakes have been installed all around. Transmission is a Ford AOD-E automatic with a Lokar shifter. The rack-and-pinion steering is taken from a Dodge Omni.

THE POWER PACK

4.6 Liter "modular" V8

In 1966, the Mustang was available with a 200-c.i. inline six or a 289-c.i V8, in either 200 bhp or 225/271 bhp state of tune. The venerable cast-iron motor was considered too heavy for this Mustang and has been replaced by a 32-valve, 4.6 liter modular Ford V8 unit with all-alloy construction. From its relatively small displacement, 281 c.i., it produces 392 bhp with the aid of a Kenne Bell twin-screw whipplecharger running at 6 pounds of boost. This is in combination with a multipoint electronic fuel-injection system and a modern engine layout of four valves per cylinder operated by four chain-driven overhead camshafts.

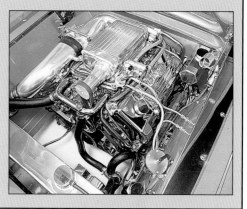

Dynamite

For some people, the pre-1967 Mustangs are the best of the breed. The lines are uncluttered and classic. When mated with a stiff chassis and powerful engine, excellence is created—exactly what this 1966 example is.

Tasteful modifications have not betrayed the Mustang's good looks.

Ford MUSTANG 1966

If you like the looks but not the performance, what can you do? Build your ideal car, of course. With nearly 400 bhp and a chassis that can handle the power, this Mustang would be your dream car.

Supercharged engine

To get phenomenal performance from the Mustang, a 32-valve, all-alloy 4.6 liter "modular" Ford V8 engine, from a late-model Mustang Cobra, has been fitted. The power has been upped to 392 bhp by the addition of a Kenne Bell supercharger running at 6 pounds of boost.

Tangerine dream

Completing the modified look is the tangerine pearl custom paint scheme. The side scallops are finished in a blend of gold pearl and candy root beer.

Billet grill

A lot of attention has been paid to the look of this car. This is illustrated by the six-bar chrome front grill and the five-bar rear fascia, which incorporates 900 LEDs.

Four-wheel disc brakes

To balance the enhanced performance, disc brakes have been installed. At the front these are 11 inches in diameter with 9-inch ones at the rear.

Custom interior

As much work has gone into customizing the interior as modifying the mechanics of this car. There are two shades of leather upholstery, cream and biscuit. There is also a wool carpet from a Mercedes, as well as modified 1965 T-Bird front seats.

Upgraded suspension

As with many modified first-generation Mustangs, this car uses the coil-sprung front suspension from the Mustang II. A chrome 9-inch rear axle combines with a Global West stage III suspension system out back.

Specifications

1966 Ford Mustang

ENGINE
Type: V8

Construction: Alloy block and heads

Valve gear: Four valves per cylinder operated by four chain-driven overhead cams.

Bore and stroke: 3.61 in. x 3.60 in.

Displacement: 281 c.i.

Compression ratio: 9.8:1

Induction system: Multipoint fuel injection with Kenne Bell twin-screw whipple supercharger

Maximum power: 392 bhp at 5,800 rpm

Maximum torque: 405 lb-ft at 4,500 rpm

Top speed: 141 mph

0-60 mph: 4.3 sec.

TRANSMISSION
Three-speed automatic

BODY/CHASSIS
Steel chassis with steel body

SPECIAL FEATURES

Even the trunk has been upholstered in matching fabrics.

Budnick alloy wheels are a fine addition to the car.

RUNNING GEAR
Steering: Rack-and-pinion

Front suspension: A-arms with coil springs and telescopic shock absorbers

Rear suspension: Live rear axle with leaf springs and telescopic shock absorbers

Brakes: Discs, 11-in. dia. (front), 9-in. dia. (rear)

Wheels: Alloy, 17 x 7 in. (front); 17 x 8 in. (rear)

Tires: Toyo 215/45ZR17 (front), 245/45ZR17 (rear)

DIMENSIONS
Length: 176.0 in.   **Width:** 71.0 in.

Height: 50.3 in.   **Wheelbase:** 108.0 in.

Track: 58.6 in. (front and rear)

Weight: 2,358 lbs.

Ford **MUSTANG MACH 1**

1973 was the final year of the big, original-style Mustang. The pick of the range was the Mach 1. It looked sporty, had special interior trim, competition suspension and standard V8 power. It was one of the most popular of Ford's ponycar range.

"*...sporty aspirations.*"

"*A standard 1973 Mustang is a long way from the original 1964 model. It became known as the Mustang that was bigger, heavier and plusher but not really as sporty as its forebearer. The Mach I, with its 302-cubic inch V8 changed that myth. It may not have a sense of urgency to it, but the Mach 1 offers adequate acceleration compared to other 1973 muscle missiles. The competition suspension virtually eliminates body roll, while ride comfort remains soft for a car with sporty aspirations.*"

The Mach 1's sporty theme extends to the cabin, with extra gauges and tach as standard.

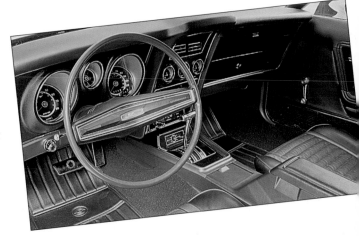

1969 The very first Mach 1 performance

SportsRoof model is launched by Ford in response to demand.

A matte-black hood section with an aggressive hood scoop were typical trademarks of the 1969 Mach 1.

1971 The Mustang grows in all dimensions,

addressing previous criticisms of cramped passenger space in early ponycars. There is extra space under the hood, too. Among other options, the 429 Cobra Jet V8 is offered, packing all of 375 bhp.

By 1974, in Mustang II guise, the Mach 1 was built for an environmentally conscious market.

1973 In its last year before it was replaced

by the slimmer, more economical Mustang II (fitting, given the approaching fuel crisis), the Mustang is offered in a range of five variations topped by the sporty Mach 1.

UNDER THE SKIN

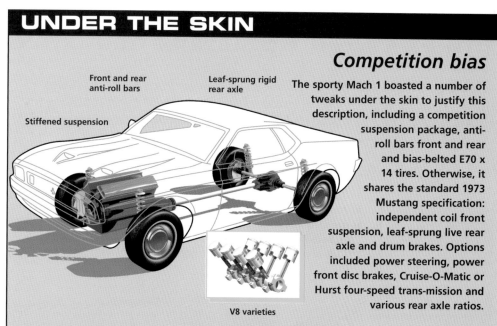

Front and rear anti-roll bars

Leaf-sprung rigid rear axle

Stiffened suspension

V8 varieties

Competition bias

The sporty Mach 1 boasted a number of tweaks under the skin to justify this description, including a competition suspension package, anti-roll bars front and rear and bias-belted E70 x 14 tires. Otherwise, it shares the standard 1973 Mustang specification: independent coil front suspension, leaf-sprung live rear axle and drum brakes. Options included power steering, power front disc brakes, Cruise-O-Matic or Hurst four-speed trans-mission and various rear axle ratios.

THE POWER PACK

Two-barrel terror

In the 1973 Mustang lineup, the Mach 1 was the only model to come with a standard V8. The base V8 was the 302-cubic inch overhead-valve unit, fitted with a Motorcraft two-barrel carburetor. It made 136 bhp. For an extra $128 you could choose the 351-cubic inch Windsor V8 with the two-barrel carb and 156 bhp, or the 351 Cleveland with a two-barrel carb and 154 bhp. Among further options was a four-barrel 351 V8. It made much more power and had large-port cylinder heads and a different intake manifold.

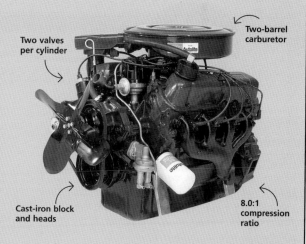

Two valves per cylinder

Two-barrel carburetor

Cast-iron block and heads

8.0:1 compression ratio

Best of breed

Although it was hardly recognizable as a first generation Mustang, the 1973 model, though restyled, was just that. While the Mach 1 isn't the most desirable of the early 1970 Mustangs—the earlier Boss 351 model takes the top honors here—it was still very fast and sporty.

Of all the 1973 Mustangs, the Mach 1 is the most collectable today.

Ford **MUSTANG MACH 1**

The Mach 1 line, which began in 1969, enhanced the sporty qualities of the Mustang, picking up on some of the themes of Carroll Shelby's modifications. The 1973 Mach 1 boasted a variety of enhancements.

Standard V8 power

All Mustangs for 1973 came with a six-cylinder engine as standard except the Mach 1, with its 302-cubic inch V8. Because it had an emissions-restricted output of 136 bhp, ordering one of the optional V8 engines was an attractive choice.

Competition suspension

Justifying its reputation as the sporty member of the Mustang group, the Mach 1 received a standard competition suspension, with heavy-duty front and rear springs and revalved shock absorbers.

SportsRoof style

The Mach 1 was offered in one body style only, a fastback coupe known as the SportsRoof. This is characterized by a near-horizontal rear roof line, in contrast to the cut-away style of the Mustang hardtop coupe. The rear window is tinted on the Mach 1 and a rear spoiler was optional.

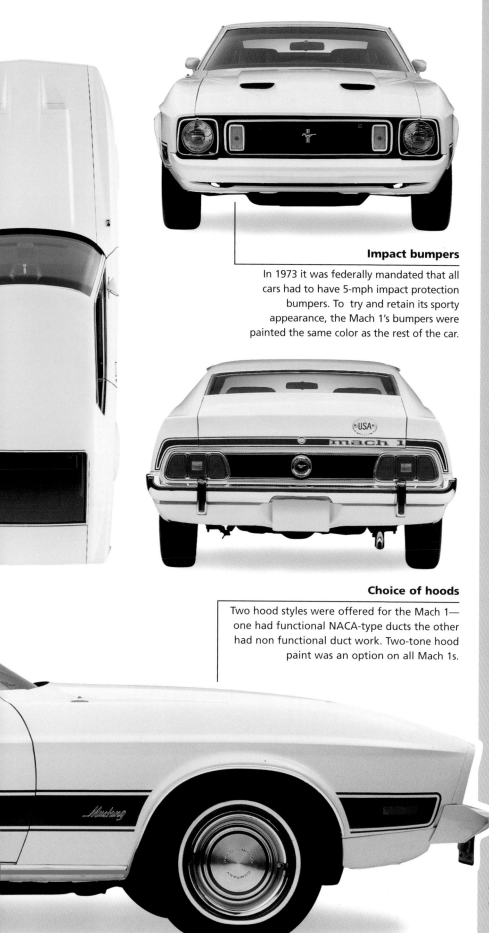

Impact bumpers

In 1973 it was federally mandated that all cars had to have 5-mph impact protection bumpers. To try and retain its sporty appearance, the Mach 1's bumpers were painted the same color as the rest of the car.

Choice of hoods

Two hood styles were offered for the Mach 1—one had functional NACA-type ducts the other had non functional duct work. Two-tone hood paint was an option on all Mach 1s.

Specifications

1973 Ford Mustang Mach 1

ENGINE

Type: V8

Construction: Cast-iron block and heads

Valve gear: Two valves per cylinder operated by a single camshaft with pushrods and rocker arms

Bore and stroke: 4.00 in. x 3.00 in.

Displacement: 302 c.i.

Compression ratio: 8.5:1

Induction system: Single Motorcraft two-barrel carburetor

Maximum power: 136 bhp at 4,200 rpm

Maximum torque: 232 lb-ft at 2,200 rpm

TRANSMISSION

Three-speed automatic

BODY/CHASSIS

Unitary monocoque construction with steel two-door coupe body

SPECIAL FEATURES

Fold-down rear seats allow access to the trunk from inside. It also permits more room to carry unusually long items.

The hood scoops took different forms on Mach 1s, but they were always present on all models from 1969 on.

RUNNING GEAR

Steering: Recirculating ball

Front suspension: Wishbones with lower trailing links, coil springs, shock absorbers and anti-roll bar

Rear suspension: Live axle with semi-elliptic leaf springs, shock absorbers and anti-roll bar

Brakes: Discs (front), drums (rear)

Wheels: Steel, 14-in. dia.

Tires: E70 x 14

DIMENSIONS

Length: 189.0 in.   **Width:** 74.1 in.

Height: 50.7 in.   **Wheelbase:** 109.0 in.

Track: 61.5 in. (front), 59.5 in. (rear)

Weight: 3,090 lbs.

Ford THUNDERBIRD '55

Although there's been a Thunderbird in the Ford lineup since 1955, the sporty two-seater convertible version only lasted until 1957. In those first three years, it had all the style—and almost the performance—to match the Chevrolet Corvette.

"...the real T-Bird."

"They're very rare now, so just seeing one of the original two-seat Thunderbirds is a treat. For true car enthusiasts, this is the only real T-Bird. Driving this 1956 model, one of the last off the line, instantly puts a smile on your face. Yes, it's a little loose and a little soft, but none of its faults matter: its looks and style make up for everything. With the V8 working hard, the T-Bird has the performance to match its style, easily exceeding 100 mph."

The Thunderbird's interior is typical of a 1950s American car—loud, brash and very stylized, a little like a jukebox of the period.

Milestones

1954 The T-Bird first appears at the Detroit Auto Show in February and goes on sale in October as a 1955 model. It's powered by a 292-cubic inch V8 with three-speed manual or three-speed automatic transmission.

After 1958 the Thunderbird became a four-seater.

1955 Changes for the 1956 model year are minor. Cooling flaps are added to the front fenders. To make more room in the trunk, the spare wheel is mounted vertically outside behind the body, making the whole car longer. A larger, 312-cubic inch V8 is also available with 215 or 225 bhp. Round 'porthole' windows are installed in the sides of the hardtop.

1956 Much more obvious changes are made for the 1957 model year with fins added at the rear. The car is also lengthened enough to allow the spare wheel back inside the trunk. The front grill and bumpers are also changed and smaller wheels added. Power increases to 270 bhp, but with a supercharger, the engine makes much more.

1957 The last 1957 model T-Birds are produced on December 13, replaced by a larger, four-seater car for 1958.

UNDER THE SKIN

Two-seater

The T-Bird has very simple construction, with a separate chassis and a live rear axle with leaf springs. Front suspension is independent wishbone and coil spring, with most parts coming from existing Ford sedans. The T-Bird had advanced features such as power brakes and steering.

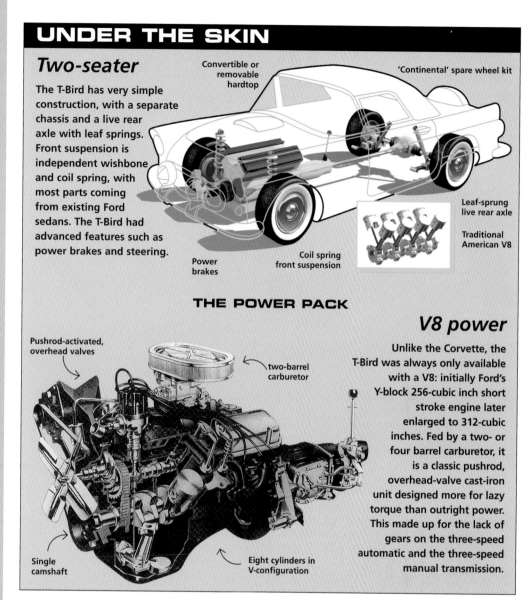

Convertible or removable hardtop

'Continental' spare wheel kit

Leaf-sprung live rear axle

Traditional American V8

Power brakes

Coil spring front suspension

THE POWER PACK

V8 power

Pushrod-activated, overhead valves

two-barrel carburetor

Single camshaft

Eight cylinders in V-configuration

Unlike the Corvette, the T-Bird was always only available with a V8: initially Ford's Y-block 256-cubic inch short stroke engine later enlarged to 312-cubic inches. Fed by a two- or four barrel carburetor, it is a classic pushrod, overhead-valve cast-iron unit designed more for lazy torque than outright power. This made up for the lack of gears on the three-speed automatic and the three-speed manual transmission.

Blown bird

The F-Bird, the Supercharged T-Bird, is the rarest, and now the most desirable, of all the early T-Birds. These are the supercharged 1957 models, with a Paxton-McCulloch supercharger added to a larger version (312 cubic inches) of the original V8 to give 300 bhp, or 340 bhp in race trim. Only 211 were sold.

Rare F-bird used 340-bhp, supercharged engine.

Ford THUNDERBIRD

The T-Bird was one of the smallest and most striking cars Ford built in the U.S. in many years. Ford called it a 'personal luxury' car rather than a sports car. It was never intended to be a serious rival to Jaguars or Ferraris.

Choice of transmissions

There was a choice of three different transmissions: a three-speed Fordomatic automatic or the three-speed manual; and perhaps the best option—a manual transmission with high overdrive ratios.

Cooling flaps

The 1955 models had poor ventilation, so Ford added a flap in the front fenders which could be opened to let cold air into the footwells.

Wrap-around windshield

Like the Chevy Corvette, which came out two years before it, the T-Bird has a wrap-around-type front windshield, a design which avoided the blind spot caused by conventional front windshield pillars.

V8 engine

From the beginning, the Thunderbird had a V8 engine. The prototype had only a 256-cubic inch engine with 160 bhp, but that was enlarged for production and became steadily more powerful year by year. By 1957, the most powerful engine—apart from the rare supercharged V8—was the 285-bhp, 312-cubic inch V8.

14/15-inch wheels

For its first two years, the Thunderbird ran on tall, 15-inch wheels. For the 1957 model year, they changed to 14-inch wheels which made the cars look sleeker.

Stretched rear

The original 1955 Thunderbird is very short, so the spare wheel had to be carried above the bumper. For 1957, Ford redesigned the back of the car to make the trunk longer so the spare wheel could be carried inside.

Open hardtop or convertible

As standard, the Thunderbird came with a bolt-on fiberglass hardtop. The car could also be ordered with a folding rayon convertible top instead of the hardtop, or in addition to it, for an extra $290.

Specifications

1957 Ford Thunderbird

ENGINE

Type: V8

Construction: Cast-iron block and heads

Valve gear: Two valves per cylinder operated via pushrods and rockers from a single block-mounted camshaft

Bore and stroke: 3.74 in. x 3.31 in.

Displacement: 292 c.i.

Compression ratio: 8.1:1

Induction system: two- or four-barrel carburetor

Maximum power: 212 bhp at 4,400 rpm

Maximum torque: 297 lb-ft at 2,700 rpm

TRANSMISSION

Three-speed manual with optional overdrive or three-speed Fordomatic automatic

BODY/CHASSIS

Separate cruciform steel chassis with steel two-door body: choice of removable hardtop or convertible roof

SPECIAL FEATURES

Exhausts exiting through holes in the bumper are a typical 1950s American styling feature.

From 1956, the hardtop was available with 'porthole' windows to improve rear three-quarter vision.

RUNNING GEAR

Steering: Power-assisted recirculating ball

Front suspension: Double wishbones, coil springs and telescopic shocks

Rear suspension: Live axle with semi-elliptic leaf springs and telescopic shocks

Brakes: Drums front and rear with optional power assistance

Wheels: Steel 14 in. dia.

Tires: Crossply, 7.5 in. x 14 in.

DIMENSIONS

Length: 181.4 in. **Width:** 70.3 in.

Height: 51.6 in. **Wheelbase:** 102 in.

Track: 56 in. (front and rear)

Weight: 3,050 lbs.

Rear fenders

Setting the 1957 T-Bird apart from the 1955 and 1956 cars was the introduction of tail fins. This was the start of the fin era in the U.S., but those on the Thunderbirds are a little more restrained than those on some other models of the period.

Ford **TORINO TALLADEGA**

In the late 1960s Ford and Chrysler were waging war in NASCAR. In 1969 Ford revealed its aero-styled Torinos, which cleaned up in the year's stock car racing by collecting 30 victories. To satisfy homologation rules at least 500 road-going versions had to be built. The result was the Ford Talladega.

"...the car was lethal."

"Though sedate looking, the Torino Talladega was the answer to watching the taillights of quicker Mopars and Chevrolets. Its nose was tapered and stretched five inches, and a flush mounted grill replaced the stock Torino piece. In street trim, the Talladega, named after NASCAR's fastest super-speedway, used a 335 bhp 428 Cobra Jet engine with a Drag Pack oil cooler. On the street the car was lethal, but in NASCAR trim it was deadly."

Talladegas have basic interiors, but they are equipped with full instrumentation.

Milestones

1968 Ford restyles

its Fairlane model with swoopier styling. A new top-of-the-line Torino, including a GT fastback and convertible, joins the line up. The latter can be ordered with a 390-or 428-cubic inch V8 big-block engine.

The Torino made its debut as a top-of-the-range Fairlane in 1968.

1969 In response to

the Dodge Charger 500 built for NASCAR racing, Ford releases the Talladega for NASCAR using the 427 engine at first, but switched to the semi-hemi Boss 429 engines after enough were homologated into the Mustang. Ford's aero-aces trounced the Charger 500 and the even more slippery winged Daytonas by winning 30 races that season.

Restyled 1970 Torinos had smoother styling.

1970 A redesigned

Talladega was disappointing in testing, so Ford retained the 1969 cars for NASCAR. Though successful the previous year, the Fords were no match to Plymouth's winged Superbirds.

UNDER THE SKIN

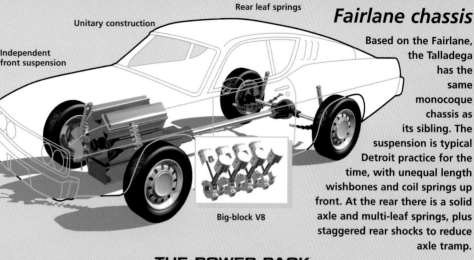

Rear leaf springs
Unitary construction
Independent front suspension
Big-block V8

Fairlane chassis

Based on the Fairlane, the Talladega has the same monocoque chassis as its sibling. The suspension is typical Detroit practice for the time, with unequal length wishbones and coil springs up front. At the rear there is a solid axle and multi-leaf springs, plus staggered rear shocks to reduce axle tramp.

THE POWER PACK

Motown muscle

All production Talladegas are powered by Ford's stout 428-cubic inch Cobra Jet big-block V8s. Underrated at 335 bhp, this engine was Ford's ace in the late 1960s horsepower race. The engines all had 10.6:1 compression, steel cranks, stronger con rods and received fuel from a Holley four-barrel 735-cfm carburetor. While this was the street engine, the NASCAR competition version used the sinister Boss 429 semi-hemi engine that was homologated the same year in the Boss 429 Mustang.

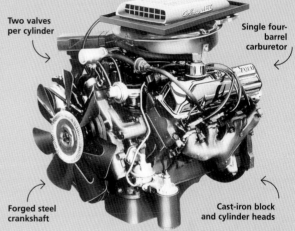

Two valves per cylinder
Single four-barrel carburetor
Forged steel crankshaft
Cast-iron block and cylinder heads

Two of a Kind

While Ford built only 745 Talladegas, its crosstown brother, Mercury, made similar modifications to 353 of its 1969 Cyclones and called it the Spoiler II. Its body was slightly longer and lower to the ground and included a rear spoiler and unique badging.

Cyclone IIs were offered with a 351 cubic inch V8 but a 428 was optional.

Ford TORINO TALLADEGA

Through the use of aerodynamics and the Boss 429 engine, the purpose-built Talladegas accomplished its mission—to take the 1969 NASCAR championship. Once again, Ford's 'Total Performance' campaign shines through.

Cobra Jet power

The standard engine is the monster 428-cubic inch Cobra Jet unit. It was factory rated at 335 bhp for insurance reasons, but the true output is probably somewhere in the region of 450 bhp. In race trim the engine of choice was the Boss 429 that was homologated for racing in the Mustang Boss 429.

Handling suspension

All Talladegas are equipped with a 'handling' suspension, which basically consists of stiffer springs and shocks plus a thick front anti-roll bar.

Rocker Panel Modifications

The rocker panels were raised over an inch so the NASCAR prepared cars could be lowered while being in full compliance with the ride height requirements.

Traction-Lok rear

Ford's Traction-Lok differential, with a 3.25:1 final-drive ratio, was the only rear gearing available. It makes the Talladega surprisingly capable at high-speed cruising, although all-out acceleration suffers as a result.

Lack of ornamentation

The exterior of the Talladega is very plain and does not have any nameplates. Instead, it carries 'T' motifs on the fuel cap and above the door handles.

Nose modifications

The Talladega was based on the Fairlane SportsRoof but with some aerodynamic advantages. The nose was stretched more than five inches and brought closer to the ground. It also features a flush mounted grill and a narrowed Fairlane bumper.

Staggered rear shocks

Like many Detroit cars of the era, the Talladega has a solid axle and rear leaf springs. Staggered shocks are used to prevent severe axle tramp during hard acceleration.

Lightweight interior

To keep weight to a minimum, the Talladega uses a base interior, with a standard vinyl front bench seat and column shifter for the C6 automatic transmission.

Specifications

1969 Ford Torino Talladega

ENGINE
Type: V8

Construction: Cast-iron block and heads

Valve gear: Two valves per cylinder operated by a single camshaft via pushrods and rockers

Bore and stroke: 4.13 in. x 3.98 in.

Displacement: 428 c.i.

Compression ratio: 10.6:1

Induction system: Single Holley four-barrel carburetor

Maximum power: 335 bhp at 5,200 rpm

Maximum torque: 440 lb-ft at 3,400 rpm

TRANSMISSION
Ford C-6 Cruise-O-Matic

BODY/CHASSIS
Steel monocoque with two-door fastback body design

SPECIAL FEATURES

'T' (for Talladega) emblems are carried in the coach stripe on each side.

All Talladegas left the factory with 428 Cobra Jet V8 engines. In NASCAR-prepped cars they ran the notorious Boss 429.

RUNNING GEAR
Steering: Recirculating ball

Front suspension: Unequal length wishbones with coil springs, telescopic shocks and anti-roll bar

Rear suspension: Live axle with semi-elliptical multi-leaf springs and staggered telescopic shocks

Brakes: Discs (front), drums (rear)

Wheels: Ford slotted chrome steel, 14-in. dia.

Tires: Goodyear Polyglas F70-14

DIMENSIONS
Length: 209.8 in.   **Width:** 84.4 in.

Height: 59.1 in.   **Wheelbase:** 116 in.

Track: 64.7 in. (front), 62 in. (rear)

Weight: 3,536 lbs.

Graham HOLLYWOOD

When Auburn-Cord-Duesenberg went out of business, two companies tried to save the incredible Cord. One was Graham-Paige, which transformed the front-wheel drive 810/812 into the rear-drive Hollywood.

"...in a class all its own."

"It may be based on the Cord 810, but the Hollywood behaves differently due to its rear-wheel drive chassis. Narrow tires and vague steering can be somewhat disconcerting at first, especially with so much power on command from the supercharged engine. The three-speed transmission is surprisingly smooth, and for cruising at high speed, the Graham is in a class all its own. A short wheelbase results in fair handling, though stopping needs care."

A stainless steel dashboard and split windshield give a typical 1940s look.

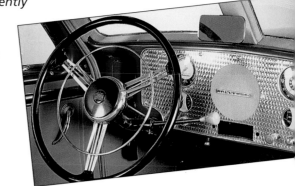

Milestones

1935 The Auburn Motor Co. introduces the Cord 810 at the New York Show. It has completely new styling and front-wheel drive.

Brothers Joe, Robert and Ray Graham started building cars in 1928 as Graham-Paige.

1936 Production gets underway with four bodystyles.

1937 The more powerful supercharged 812 is launched.

Graham production jumped in 1935, to 18,500 cars.

1939 Joe Graham approaches Norm de Vaux to build a version of the Cord 810 using a rear-drive chassis. De Vaux, owner of Cord tooling, agrees and the Holly-wood goes into production in 1940. It is expensive to produce and is a slow seller. Graham ends production in late 1940.

UNDER THE SKIN

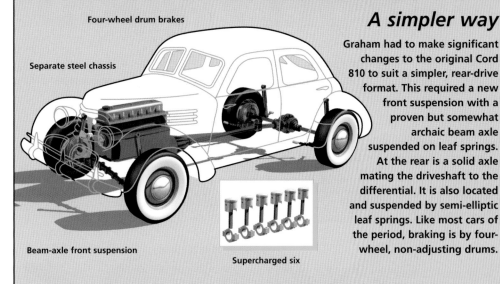

Four-wheel drum brakes

Separate steel chassis

Beam-axle front suspension

Supercharged six

A simpler way

Graham had to make significant changes to the original Cord 810 to suit a simpler, rear-drive format. This required a new front suspension with a proven but somewhat archaic beam axle suspended on leaf springs. At the rear is a solid axle mating the driveshaft to the differential. It is also located and suspended by semi-elliptic leaf springs. Like most cars of the period, braking is by four-wheel, non-adjusting drums.

THE POWER PACK

Continental engine

The original Cord 810/812 series relied on a Lycoming V8 engine, but the Graham brothers chose a different, less expensive route. In this case, it was Continental that supplied the 218-cubic inch, inline six-cylinder engine. This sidevalve design, with an iron block and alloy head, was available in normally aspirated form, producing 93 bhp (95 for 1941). Fitting Graham's own supercharger gave an extra 26 bhp (29 in 1941). Like most sidevalve engines, it had a long stroke (in this case 4.38 inches) and was designed for low-rpm torque. All the valves are on one side, operated by a single camshaft.

Hip Hup

Even rarer than the Graham Hollywood, with just 354 built, is the Hupmobile Skylark. Like the Hollywood, it was a way of keeping the look of the Cord 812 alive. It has a different engine and rear-wheel drive layout, as well as a restyled nose.

Hupmobile's Skylark looks almost identical to the Graham.

Graham **HOLLYWOOD**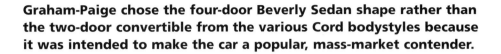

Graham-Paige chose the four-door Beverly Sedan shape rather than the two-door convertible from the various Cord bodystyles because it was intended to make the car a popular, mass-market contender.

Side-valve engine

The Graham-Paige company had used six-cylinder, side-valve engines supplied by Continental since the late 1920s when the three Graham brothers took over Paige-Detroit to form Graham-Paige. The 218-cubic inch six used for the Graham Hollywood was by no means the largest. Previous models featured a 287-cubic inch six.

Pod headlights

The idea behind the Graham Hollywood was to produce a simpler, and less expensive car than the Cord. One of the complicated items to be dispensed with was the pop-up headlights. The lights were replaced by free-standing units mounted in pods on top of the fenders.

Three-speed transmission

While the Cord has a complicated remote electromagnetic-vacuum gear shifter with its own miniature gate (a system that could also be used as a pre-selector transmission), the Graham Hollywood uses a much simpler conventional manual unit. Like many Detroit cars of the time, the transmission has a column shift.

Split windshield

Technology to produce compound curved glass had not been perfected in 1940. Even Cadillacs had split windshields, and the Cord and Graham Hollywood followed suit. The design is mirrored in the back window, which is also a two-piece split unit.

Live rear axle

With a switch from front to rear drive, the Cord beam rear axle was replaced by a live unit and differential, located and sprung on semi-elliptic leaf springs like most contemporary automobiles.

Specifications
1941 Graham Hollywood

ENGINE

Type: Inline six-cylinder

Construction: Cast-iron block and alloy head

Valve gear: Two inline sidevalves per cylinder operated by a single block-mounted camshaft and solid valve lifters

Bore and stroke: 3.25 in. x 4.38 in.

Displacement: 218 c.i.

Compression ratio: 7.1:1

Induction system: Single Carter carburetor with Graham supercharger

Maximum power: 124 bhp at 4,000 rpm

Maximum torque: 182 lb-ft at 2,400 rpm

Top speed: 89 mph

0–60 mph: 14.6 sec.

TRANSMISSION

Three-speed manual

BODY/CHASSIS

Separate box-section steel frame with four-door sedan body

SPECIAL FEATURES

A split rear window is standard on all Graham Hollywoods.

In addition to fixed headlights, the Graham also has a different grill.

RUNNING GEAR

Steering: Worm-and-roller

Front suspension: Beam axle with semi-elliptic leaf springs and telescopic shock absorbers

Rear suspension: Live axle with semi-elliptic leaf springs and telescopic shock absorbers

Brakes: Drums (front and rear)

Wheels: Pressed steel discs, 5 x 16 in. dia.

Tires: Bias-ply, 6.00 x 16

DIMENSIONS

Length: 190.5 in.   **Width:** 71.0 in.

Height: 60.5 in.   **Wheelbase:** 115.0 in.

Track: 57.5 in. (front), 61.0 in. (rear)

Weight: 3,240 lbs.

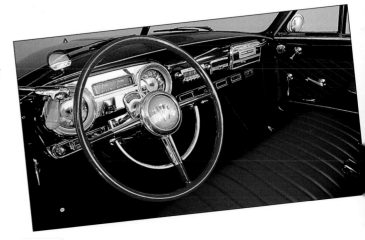

Hudson HORNET

The product of a relatively small-time Detroit maker, the 'Fabulous Hudson Hornets' were great to look at, not to mention drive and race. The Hornet was a true stand-out design among more adventurous sedans.

"...balanced and controllable."

"It may be an American car of the 1950s, but the Hornet really handles. Other Detroit iron of this period wallows, oversteers and screeches around corners, but the Hornet feels balanced and controllable. It will float into bends and drift on all four wheels rather than break away. The L-head straight-six engine may not have much top-end power, but low down it pulls like a truck. The cabin feel is great too, with comfortable seats."

The Hornet's cabin is awash with fine chrome detailing and has very comfortable seats.

Milestones

1947 Hudson first presents its revolutionary Step-Down range, so called because of its dropped floorpan. Production begins in 1948.

1951 The larger-engined Hornet gains in popularity and becomes available in two- and four-door forms.

Sales were buoyant by 1950 when semi-automatics arrived.

1952 Marshall Teague wins the AAA title in a Hornet. Herb Thomas, Tim Flock and Dick Rothman help the Hornet domination.

The 1948 Hudson Super Six was one of the safest cars of its time.

1953 The Hornet consolidates its position as a leading racer with 46 AAA and NASCAR wins.

1954 Hudson merges with Nash and, as a result of the merger and changing tastes, the old Step-Down range comes to an end.

UNDER THE SKIN

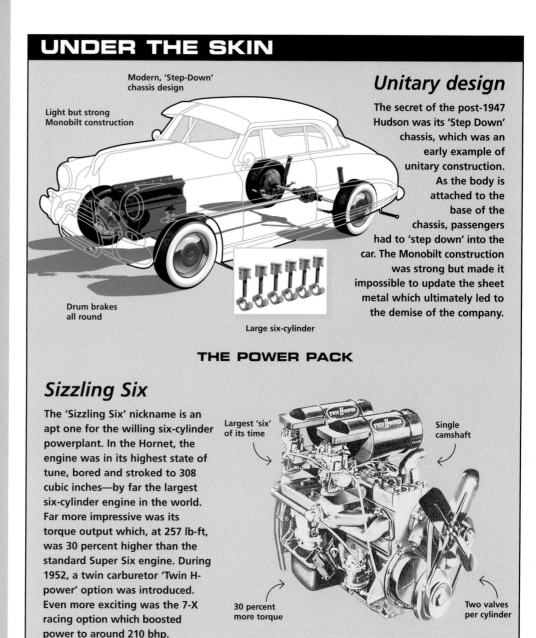

Modern, 'Step-Down' chassis design

Light but strong Monobilt construction

Drum brakes all round

Large six-cylinder

Unitary design

The secret of the post-1947 Hudson was its 'Step Down' chassis, which was an early example of unitary construction. As the body is attached to the base of the chassis, passengers had to 'step down' into the car. The Monobilt construction was strong but made it impossible to update the sheet metal which ultimately led to the demise of the company.

THE POWER PACK

Sizzling Six

The 'Sizzling Six' nickname is an apt one for the willing six-cylinder powerplant. In the Hornet, the engine was in its highest state of tune, bored and stroked to 308 cubic inches—by far the largest six-cylinder engine in the world. Far more impressive was its torque output which, at 257 lb-ft, was 30 percent higher than the standard Super Six engine. During 1952, a twin carburetor 'Twin H-power' option was introduced. Even more exciting was the 7-X racing option which boosted power to around 210 bhp.

Largest 'six' of its time

Single camshaft

30 percent more torque

Two valves per cylinder

Hornet 7-X

The hot, race-winning Hornet is the star of the Hudson family, and all versions have a great image. But if you really want to make an impression, find a Twin H or a rare 7-X engined car with its hot cam, heavy duty crank and cylinder head.

Hornet made its mark on the racetrack with potent Twin H and 7-X versions.

Hudson HORNET

The 'Step-Down' Hudson range was a real revolution. The Hornet's innovative body/chassis construction offered fine handling while its huge engine was highly tunable. It was America's finest from the early 1950s.

Choice of body styles

The Hornet was sold in three basic body styles: a four-door sedan – easily the most popular – a two-door coupe and a two-door Convertible Brougham. The convertible is the rarest, selling only 550 examples in its most popular year (1951).

Straight-six engine

While the 'Big Three' Detroit automakers were discovering the V8 engine, Hudson stuck to its straight-six. It expanded its Super Six engine to 308 cubic inches and provided enough torque and power to challenge and beat the V8 powerplants in NASCAR racing.

'Step-Down' construction

The floorpan of the body sits below the chassis in a semi-unitary construction called Monobilt. Passengers have to step over the chassis rails to get in, leading to the nickname 'Step-Down'. There is still over 8 inches of ground clearance.

Enclosed rear wheels

Because the construction used dual rear chassis outriggers, one either side of each of the rear wheels, it was natural to adopt fully-enclosed rear wheels. Changing wheels is a challenge, though, as they had to drop right down.

Low roofline

The most dramatic part of the Hornet's overall shape is its ultra-low roofline. The windows resemble tapering slits and the sloping line is echoed by a similarly-profiled body side moulding. The low roofline was made possible by keeping the 'Step-Down' floor low.

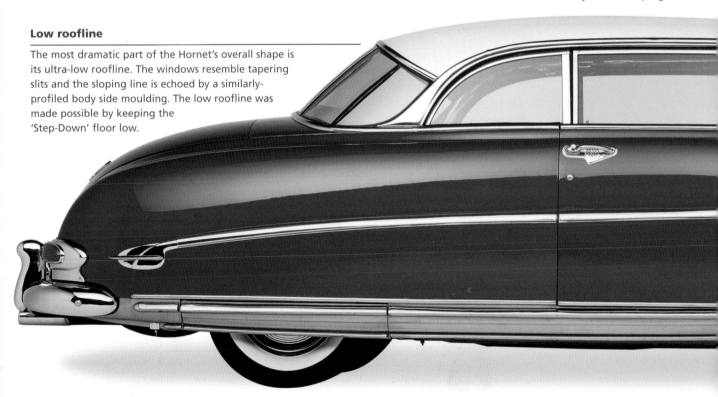

Specifications

1952 Hudson Hornet

ENGINE

Type: In-line six-cylinder

Construction: Cast-iron block and aluminum cylinder head

Valve gear: Two valves per cylinder operated by a single camshaft

Bore and stroke: 3.81 in. x 4.50 in.

Displacement: 308 c.i.

Compression ratio: 7.2:1

Induction system: Single carburetor

Maximum power: 145 bhp at 3,800 rpm

Maximum torque: 257 lb-ft at 1,800 rpm

TRANSMISSION

Four-speed manual or three-speed automatic

BODY/CHASSIS

Steel unitary construction with steel coupe, convertible or four-door sedan body

SPECIAL FEATURES

Twin carburetors gave the powerful 1952 Twin H Hornets their name.

The sun visor was a popular dealer-installed item in the early 1950s.

RUNNING GEAR

Steering: Recirculating ball

Front suspension: Wishbones with coil springs and telescopic shock absorbers

Rear suspension: Live axle with semi-elliptic leaf springs and telescopic shock absorbers

Brakes: Drums (front and rear)

Wheels: Steel, 15-in. dia.

Tires: 5 x 15 in.

DIMENSIONS

Length: 201.5 in.   **Width:** 77.1 in.

Height: 60.4 in.   **Wheelbase:** 123.9 in.

Track: 58.5 in. (front), 55.5 in. (rear)

Weight: 3,600 lbs.

Streamlined shape

Chief designer Art Kibiger knew that the Monobilt body could not easily be updated, so he designed a car that would stay current as long as possible. It was much lower and wider than other Detroit offerings and received a rapturous reception.

Hudson **TERRAPLANE**

By the mid 1930s, Terraplanes were considered to be inexpensive, rugged and reliable automobiles. But that was to ignore the fact that these cars had a number of ingenious design features that set them aside from their more mainstream rivals from Ford and Chevrolet.

"...its appeal is obvious."

"You don't drive a Terraplane to go fast. Revel instead in the comfort of the softly sprung chassis and the refinement from such an apparently crude, simple engine. The side-valve six is surprisingly quiet. Its long stroke gives a large torque output at low rpm so it will pull from incredibly slow speeds in top gear. Add light steering once the car is underway, and very effective brakes and its appeal is obvious."

The spartan cabin includes a speedometer and a unique steering column-mounted semi-automatic gear shift selector.

Milestones

1924 Hudson develops a flathead, side-valve, six-cylinder engine for the new Essex Six.

1932 The first Terraplane appears. It is designed to undercut rivals from Ford and Chevrolet.

The most famous Hudson is the Hornet, made from 1949-1952.

1934 The Terraplane range is improved. The biggest news this year is the introduction of 'Axleflex'— a design that combines a beam front axle and an independent front suspension. The bodies are also restyled.

Dating from 1954, the compact Jet was the last true Hudson.

1947 The last link with the Terraplane comes to an end. The 212-cubic inch, side-valve six engine that began life in the stylish coupe was replaced with a larger 262-cubic inch engine.

UNDER THE SKIN

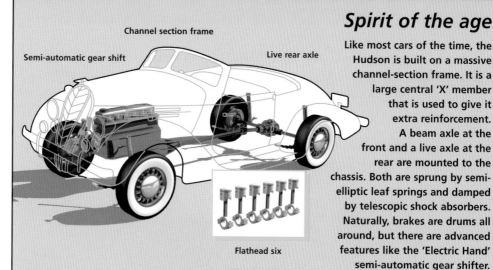

Channel section frame

Semi-automatic gear shift

Live rear axle

Flathead six

Spirit of the age

Like most cars of the time, the Hudson is built on a massive channel-section frame. It is a large central 'X' member that is used to give it extra reinforcement. A beam axle at the front and a live axle at the rear are mounted to the chassis. Both are sprung by semi-elliptic leaf springs and damped by telescopic shock absorbers. Naturally, brakes are drums all around, but there are advanced features like the 'Electric Hand' semi-automatic gear shifter.

THE POWER PACK

Old faithful

Hudson's flathead, six engine was already an old design by 1936 but had been steadily improved since it first appeared in 1924. It is a cast-iron unit with a three-bearing crank-shaft and sidevalves operated upward by block-mounted camshafts. One oddity, even for the time, is the lack of full-pressure lubrication to the bearings, although oiling improvements were made in 1934 when the veteran engine was stretched to 212 cubic inches. This, along with a low 6.3:1 compression ratio, was enough to give the Terraplane 88 bhp and surprising performance—0–60 mph in 23.2 seconds.

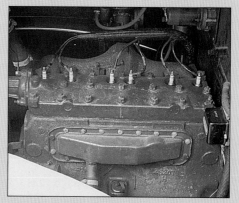

Short-lived

Although they started life under the Essex brand, the Terraplanes soon became a make in their own right. From 1936, they adopted a tasteful wraparound style grill. They were fast too, able to reach 60 mph in under 27 seconds and top 80 mph. Most desirable of all are perhaps the coupes and convertibles. A short production run means rarity today.

The Terraplane lasted only through 1937.

Hudson TERRAPLANE

Even though Terraplanes were not intended to be the most flamboyant and stylish cars on the road, features like the attractive grill helped make these cars stand out in a crowd.

Side-valve engine

In an L-head sidevalve engine like the 3.5-liter Hudson six, both the intake and exhaust valves are on one side of the engine. Effectively, they work upsidedown, compared with an overhead-valve engine, with the combustion chambers in the head but to one side of the engine over the valves.

Low-pressure tires

To make its cars as comfortable as possible, Hudson had a tendency to fit larger, wider tires than its rival companies. These also ran at a relatively low pressure to improve the ride.

Welded-on body

Although the Terraplane had an unusual and immensely strong steel chassis for its time, Hudson made the whole car stiffer by welding on the all-steel bodywork at more than 30 points rather than simply bolting it in place like other manufacturers were doing.

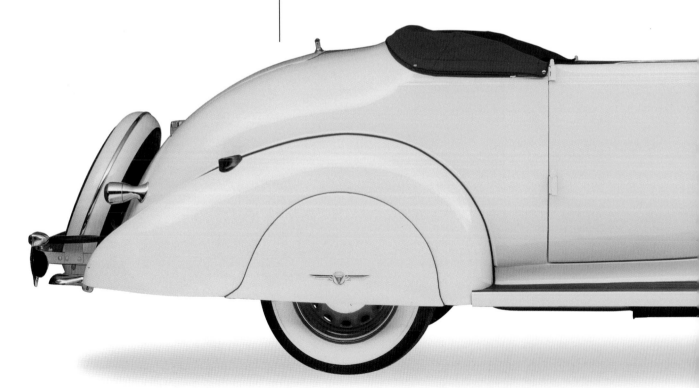

Solid front axle

Hudson's normal front-suspension system was more complicated than most. It fitted a radius arm on each side that was bolted to a solid axle. These ran back from the axle to pivots on the frame and provided better location than the semi-elliptic leaf springs could manage by themselves. They also provide a measure of antidive under severe braking.

Reserve brake system

In case the hydraulic system failed (and these were the days before dual circuits), Hudson developed Duo-Automatic as a safety feature. Should the pedal get near the floor, it operates a cable to activate the rear brakes.

Specifications
1936 Hudson Terraplane

ENGINE

Type: Inline six cylinder

Construction: Cast-iron block and head

Valve gear: Two valves operated by single camshaft mounted on side of block

Bore and stroke: 3.0 in. x 5.0 in.

Displacement: 212 c.i.

Compression ratio: 6.0:1

Induction system: Single downdraft Carter carburetor

Maximum power: 88 bhp at 3,800 rpm

Maximum torque: Not quoted

Top speed: 80 mph

0–60 mph: 23.2 sec.

TRANSMISSION

Three-speed manual

BODY/CHASSIS

Separate channel-section frame with X-brace and welded-on steel body

SPECIAL FEATURES

The Hudson Terraplane was known for its ornate details such as this interesting grill ornament.

A fold-out rear rumble seat can easily accommodate two people in total comfort.

RUNNING GEAR

Steering: Worm-and-sector

Front suspension: Solid axle with radius rods, semi-elliptic leaf springs and telescopic shock absorbers

Rear suspension: Live axle with semi-elliptic leaf springs and telescopic shock absorbers

Brakes: Drums (front and rear)

Wheels: Pressed steel, 16-in. dia.

Tires: 6.00 x 16

DIMENSIONS

Length: 195.0 in. **Width:** 70.0 in.

Height: 70.8 in. **Wheelbase:** 115.0 in.

Track: 56.0 in. (front), 57.5 in. (rear)

Weight: 2,740 lbs.

Kaiser **DARRIN**

Before Chevrolet released the Corvette, Kaiser produced a fiberglass-bodied sports car with distinctive styling. However, based on the Henry J sedan the Darrin was unable to stop the company's financial slide.

"...full of 1950s character."

"Rather than an all-out sports car, the Kaiser Darrin is a glamorous car full of 1950s character. The engine isn't particularly powerful, but because it has a lightweight fiberglass body, performance is lively with sharp acceleration and a top speed of almost 100 mph. The humble underpinnings from the Henry J sedan limit its cornering ability, however. When cruising with the top down, the Darrin offers a glimpse at a bygone age of motoring."

The plush interior of the Darrin perfectly complements its striking body styling.

Milestones

1952 Details of a Kaiser Darrin sports car are first announced.

The elegant K1 special—Kaiser's first production model—was the most modern car of its time.

1953 Prototypes are shown and production begins in September.

1954 The car goes on sale in January but is dropped mid season; Howard Darrin goes on to sell the remaining stock (around 100 cars), some with ferocious Cadillac V8 power.

A striking alligator-style interior was one distinguishing feature of the 1953 Kaiser Dragon.

1955 The last remaining Kaiser Darrins are sold through dealers.

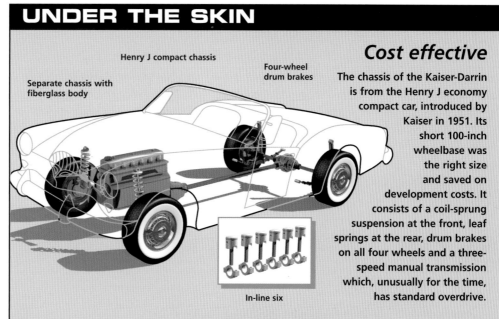

Henry J compact chassis

Separate chassis with fiberglass body

Four-wheel drum brakes

In-line six

Cost effective

The chassis of the Kaiser-Darrin is from the Henry J economy compact car, introduced by Kaiser in 1951. Its short 100-inch wheelbase was the right size and saved on development costs. It consists of a coil-sprung suspension at the front, leaf springs at the rear, drum brakes on all four wheels and a three-speed manual transmission which, unusually for the time, has standard overdrive.

THE POWER PACK

Willys F-head six

As well as the chassis, the engine is derived from the Henry J compact, which used a Willys powerplant. It features an F-head on a six-cylinder block, four main bearings, solid valve lifters, a 161-cubic inch displacement, and a single Carter Type YF single-barrel carburetor. With 90 bhp developed at 4,200 rpm, it has an extra 10 bhp compared with the Henry J motor. Some experi-mental Edmunds alloy L-head engines were fitted: a triple-carburetor unit with 100 bhp and a McCulloch supercharged unit with even more power. The last cars, sold independently by Darrin, had 304-bhp Cadillac V8 engines.

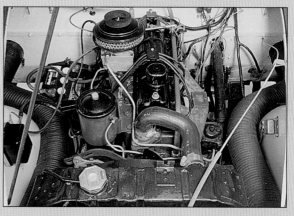

Highly valued

With the exception of the Corvette, the Kaiser Darrin is perhaps the most desirable U.S.-built 1950s sports cars. Its unique styling and novel character make it highly valued in collector circles, especially with the 140-mph V8 engine fitted.

The unique look of the Kaiser Darrin have made it very collectible.

Kaiser DARRIN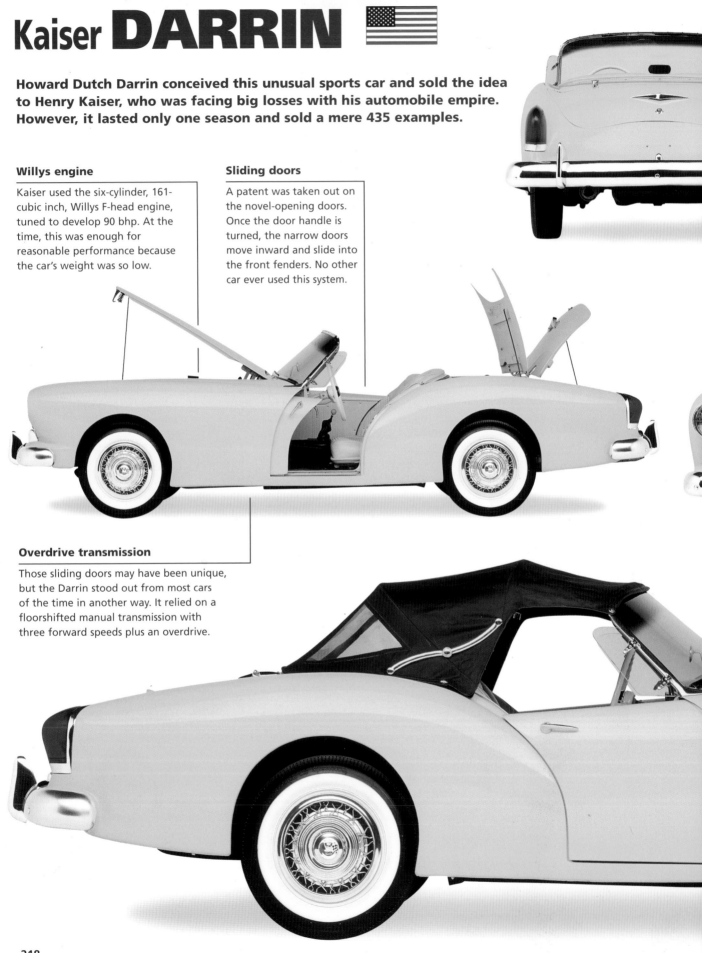

Howard Dutch Darrin conceived this unusual sports car and sold the idea to Henry Kaiser, who was facing big losses with his automobile empire. However, it lasted only one season and sold a mere 435 examples.

Willys engine

Kaiser used the six-cylinder, 161-cubic inch, Willys F-head engine, tuned to develop 90 bhp. At the time, this was enough for reasonable performance because the car's weight was so low.

Sliding doors

A patent was taken out on the novel-opening doors. Once the door handle is turned, the narrow doors move inward and slide into the front fenders. No other car ever used this system.

Overdrive transmission

Those sliding doors may have been unique, but the Darrin stood out from most cars of the time in another way. It relied on a floorshifted manual transmission with three forward speeds plus an overdrive.

Henry J chassis

To get a 100-inch wheelbase suitable for a sports car, Kaiser turned to its Henry J model. This had a conventional specification with coil springs in the front and left springs at the rear. Four-wheel drums safely bring the car to a stop.

Fiberglass bodywork

Howard Darrin was a fiberglass pioneer. He was well ahead of Chevrolet when he produced the prototype for the Kaiser Darrin in 1952. By then, however, companies such as Glasspar had plastic shells in production.

Stylized grill

The distinctive concave grill retains typical Kaiser styling. The very small 'mouth' has vertical chrome teeth, a V at its lower edge and a rounded top that follows the shape of the hood.

Specifications

1954 Kaiser Darrin

ENGINE

Type: In-line six-cylinder

Construction: Cast-iron block and head

Valve gear: Two valves per cylinder operated by a single camshaft

Bore and stroke: 3.12 in. x 3.50 in.

Displacement: 161 c.i.

Compression ratio: 7.6:1

Induction system: Single Carter carburetor

Maximum power: 90 bhp at 4,200 rpm

Maximum torque: 135 lb-ft at 1,600 rpm

TRANSMISSION

Three-speed manual with overdrive

BODY/CHASSIS

Separate chassis with fiberglass two-door convertible body

SPECIAL FEATURES

The sleek rear end incorporates the unusually shaped trunklid.

The front doors completely slide into the front fender. This patented design is the most novel feature of the Kaiser Darrin.

RUNNING GEAR

Steering: Worm-and-roller

Front suspension: A-arms with coil springs and shock absorbers

Rear suspension: Live axle with leaf springs and shock absorbers

Brakes: Drums (front and rear)

Wheels: Steel, 15-in. dia.

Tires: 5.90 x 15

DIMENSIONS

Length: 184.0 in.   **Width:** 67.5 in.

Height: 52.7 in.   **Wheelbase:** 100.0 in.

Track: 54.0 in. (front and rear)

Weight: 2,250 lbs.

Lincoln CONTINENTAL MKII

A good way to describe the alluring Lincoln-built Continental Mark II is a reincarnated Duesenberg. Extremely expensive, it was also superbly built and handsome despite its huge size and satisfyingly powerful engine.

"…effortless to drive."

"Ford wanted the driver to feel special in this expensive two-door coupe, and in that they certainly succeeded. Once settled in behind the typically large steering wheel, your view is superb—a curved windshield opens out onto a hood that seems to go on forever. Fire it up and the V8 rumble is familiar. There is plenty of power, but the best way to enjoy the Continental is to allow the smooth column-shifted automatic transmission to do all the work."

The interior is swathed in leather, has plush carpeting and power seats.

Milestones

1956 The 1956 model year Continental Mark II makes its debut at the 1955 Paris Salon. It is not badged as a Lincoln but is a marque in its own right, reflecting its hand-built nature.

The Mark III couldn't save the Continental marque.

1957 With very few cosmetic changes, the 1957 Continental enters production with a mild power increase to 300 bhp.

By the 1970s the Lincoln Continental had become rather less exclusive.

1958 The all-new and rather overblown Mark III replaces the Mark II, bringing the hand-made Continental era to an end.

1959 The Continental marque is incorporated in the Lincoln-Mercury division. The Mark III becomes the Lincoln Continental Mark IV.

UNDER THE SKIN

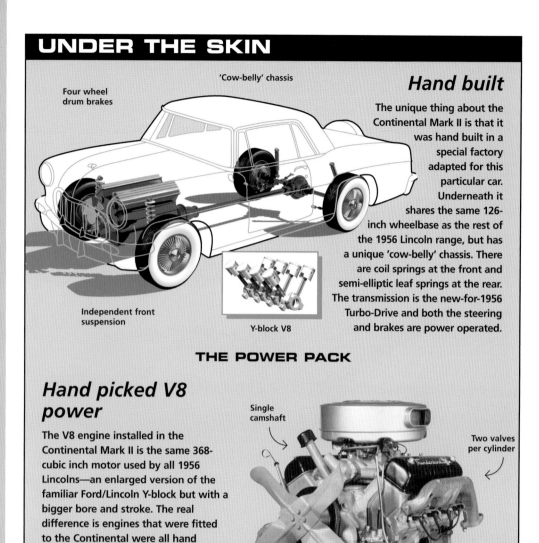

Four wheel drum brakes

'Cow-belly' chassis

Independent front suspension

Y-block V8

Hand built

The unique thing about the Continental Mark II is that it was hand built in a special factory adapted for this particular car. Underneath it shares the same 126-inch wheelbase as the rest of the 1956 Lincoln range, but has a unique 'cow-belly' chassis. There are coil springs at the front and semi-elliptic leaf springs at the rear. The transmission is the new-for-1956 Turbo-Drive and both the steering and brakes are power operated.

THE POWER PACK

Hand picked V8 power

The V8 engine installed in the Continental Mark II is the same 368-cubic inch motor used by all 1956 Lincolns—an enlarged version of the familiar Ford/Lincoln Y-block but with a bigger bore and stroke. The real difference is engines that were fitted to the Continental were all hand picked off the line, ensuring the best and most powerful units were installed. Additionally, every engine was adjusted prior to being fitted. The power output in 1956 was 285 bhp, which increased to 300 bhp in 1957 due to a higher compression ratio.

Single camshaft

Two valves per cylinder

Cast-iron construction

Carefully tuned before fitting

Rare 1957

Because it was made for only two seasons, the Mark II is extremely rare, but the 1957 model is by far the more scarce (444 cars compared with 2,556 of the 1956 model). The ideal find would be an untouched original car with air conditioning.

The hand-built Mark II is a real collector's item.

221

Lincoln CONTINENTAL MK II

William Clay Ford's brain storm, the Continental Mark II, was a brave attempt to outdo even Cadillac. Certainly the car was more expensive than any Cadillac, and Ford lost a reputed $1,000 on every car sold.

Hand picked mechanicals

The V8 engines in the Continental were hand picked off the assembly line to deliver the best possible performance. The same was true of the three-speed Turbo-Drive automatic transmission and rear axle.

Hand-tailored build

The bodies of the Mark II were trial fitted to the chassis and then painted, sanded and polished by hand. All cars were given a 12-mile road test followed by an in-depth inspection and tuning as necessary.

Lush cabin

The styling is simple and engineering-inspired, rather than juke-box glamorous. The gauges are quality crafted and very easy to read. It is garnished with cloth seat covers, or Scottish 'Bridge of Weir' leather.

Cow-belly chassis

In order to free up as much headroom in the low-roof coupe cabin, chief engineer Harley Copp gave it a unique 'cow-belly' chassis that drops down between the front and rear axles. This allows the seats to be positioned lower in the bodyshell and makes the cabin impressively roomy.

Specifications

1956 Continental Mark II

ENGINE
Type: V8

Construction: Cast-iron block and heads

Valve gear: Two valves per cylinder operated by a single camshaft via pushrods and rockers

Bore and stroke: 4.00 in. x 3.66 in.

Displacement: 368 c.i.

Compression ratio: 9.0:1

Induction system: Single carburetor

Maximum power: 285 bhp at 4,800 rpm

Maximum torque: 401 lb-ft at 2,800 rpm

TRANSMISSION
Three-speed Turbo-Drive automatic

BODY/CHASSIS
Separate chassis with steel two-door coupe body

SPECIAL FEATURES

The hallmark 'Continental'- style spare wheel on the trunk echoed the great Lincolns of the past.

The front uses much chrome, but the design is remarkable for its simplicity.

RUNNING GEAR
Steering: Recirculating ball

Front suspension: Independent with coil springs and telescopic shock absorbers

Rear suspension: Live axle with semi-elliptic springs and telescopic shock absorbers

Brakes: Drums (front and rear)

Wheels: Steel, 16-in. dia.

Tires: 16-in. dia.

DIMENSIONS
Length: 218.4 in. **Width:** 77.5 in.

Height: 56.0 in.   **Wheelbase:** 126.0 in.

Track: 58.6 in. (front), 60.0 in. (rear)

Weight: 4,825 lbs.

Electric gadgets

The Continental is certainly filled with its share of electrical components such as power seats. The only listed option was air conditioning.

Lincoln CONTINENTAL MK IV

Ford's luxury division revealed one of its largest cars ever for 1958. The following year, the Continental returned as a separate Lincoln sub series offered in coupe, convertible, town car and limousine forms. Priced at just over $7,000, it was not, surprisingly, rare and exclusive.

"...unparalleled level of opulence."

"It's apt to describe this car as huge! The Mark IV is longer and wider than just about any of its contemporaries. Although it has 350 bhp on tap, this Continental is more of a cruiser than muscle car, but it still remains effortless to drive and extremely smooth on the open road. The power steering is very light and taking corners at speed can produce some interesting results. The cabin has an unparalleled level of opulence."

Dominating the interior are the jumbo-sized steering wheel and unique instruments.

Milestones

1958 Lincoln issues its largest car

yet for public consumption. It is offered in Capri and Premiere series and both are powered by a 375-bhp, 430-cubic inch V8. In a recession year, sales are a modest 17,134. A similar, separate machine, the Continental Mk III, priced much economically than its predecessor is also offered; 12,500 are sold.

The first Continental arrived for 1940 as an upmarket Zephyr.

1959 Continental Mk IV

becomes part of the Lincoln line with its own range of models. It is priced above the Capri and Premiere. Power on the 430-cubic inch V8 drops to 350 bhp. Production reaches 15,780.

A much smaller and neater Continental debuts for 1961.

1960 The 131-inch wheelbase

Lincolns make their final appearance this year. Production falls yet again to below 15,000. A new, smaller Continental bows for 1961.

UNDER THE SKIN

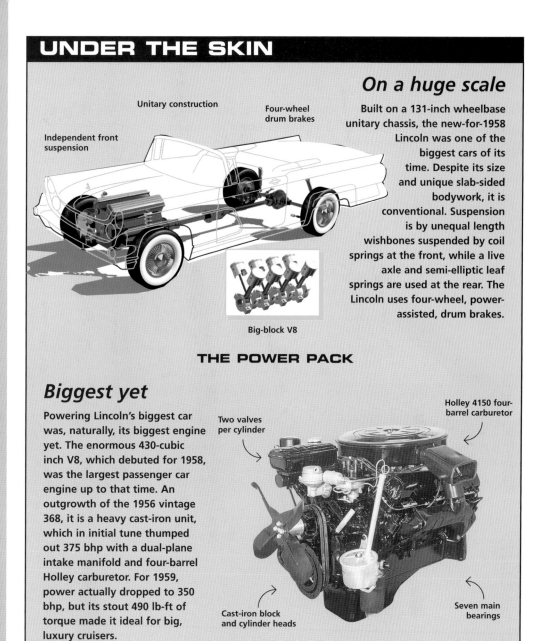

Unitary construction

Four-wheel drum brakes

Independent front suspension

Big-block V8

On a huge scale

Built on a 131-inch wheelbase unitary chassis, the new-for-1958 Lincoln was one of the biggest cars of its time. Despite its size and unique slab-sided bodywork, it is conventional. Suspension is by unequal length wishbones suspended by coil springs at the front, while a live axle and semi-elliptic leaf springs are used at the rear. The Lincoln uses four-wheel, power-assisted, drum brakes.

THE POWER PACK

Biggest yet

Powering Lincoln's biggest car was, naturally, its biggest engine yet. The enormous 430-cubic inch V8, which debuted for 1958, was the largest passenger car engine up to that time. An outgrowth of the 1956 vintage 368, it is a heavy cast-iron unit, which in initial tune thumped out 375 bhp with a dual-plane intake manifold and four-barrel Holley carburetor. For 1959, power actually dropped to 350 bhp, but its stout 490 lb-ft of torque made it ideal for big, luxury cruisers.

Two valves per cylinder

Holley 4150 four-barrel carburetor

Cast-iron block and cylinder heads

Seven main bearings

Slow seller

Making its debut on the eve of a recession, these big Lincolns were never built in large numbers. Among Continental Mk IVs, the convertible is the most valuable—only 2,195 were built. Good examples are highly sought after by collectors today.

Despite its huge size, the Mk IV has surprisingly clean lines.

Lincoln CONTINENTAL MK IV

At 227 inches long and weighing 5,192 lbs., the Continental Mk IV was no lightweight. In fact, it was so big that owners in certain parts of the country were required to place clearance lights on their cars for use on the road.

Power top

The Lincoln's power-operated soft top retracts behind the rear seats and is hidden under a metal tonneau cover, giving it a neat top-down appearence. An unusual option was available in 1958. If the car was parked outside with its top down and it started to rain, the top would automatically raise. Ford had many problems with this option which resulted in its ultimate demise in 1959.

Monster big-block V8

Weighing more than 5,000 lbs., the Mk IV needed a massive engine to move it around. Nestling between the fenders is a monster 430-cubic inch V8, producing 350 bhp and an earth-moving 490 lb-ft of torque.

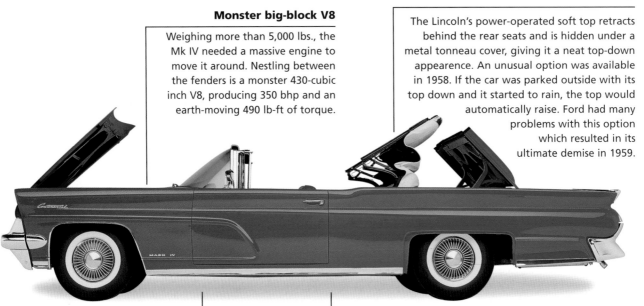

Automatic transmission

By 1959, most buyers expected automatic transmissions. Thus, the Mk IV came with a Ford Turbo-drive three-speed automatic operated with the column-shifter.

Unitary construction

A surprising feature for 1958-1960 Continentals and Lincolns was the adoption of unitary construction, making them stiffer and stronger than rival luxury cars.

Breezway rear window

With the top up, the 'Breezway' rear window gives a distinctive inverted profile. This style feature allows a smaller window, plus it reduces glare from sunlight and helps to keep the interior cool.

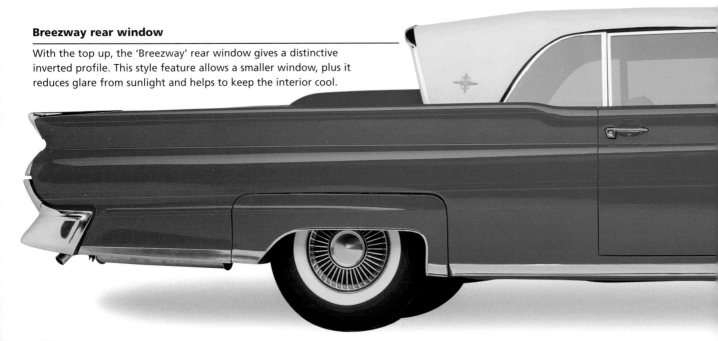

Independent front suspension

The Mk IV uses typical 1950s Detroit suspension at the front, with unequal length wishbones, coil springs and telescopic shocks. Air suspension was offered for 1958, but few buyers chose it.

Panoramic windshield

First seen on the 1953 Cadillac Eldorado, the panoramic windshield was a feature of most U.S.-built cars by 1959. These provide excellent forward vision due to moving the A-pillars further back.

Specifications

1959 Lincoln Continental Mk IV

ENGINE
Type: V8

Construction: Cast-iron block and heads

Valve gear: Two valves per cylinder operated by a single camshaft with pushrods and rockers

Bore and stroke: 4.30 in. x 3.70 in.

Displacement: 430 c.i.

Compression ratio: 10.0:1

Induction system: Holley 4150 four-barrel carburetor

Maximum power: 350 bhp at 4,400 rpm

Maximum torque: 490 lb-ft at 2,800 rpm

TRANSMISSION
Turbo-drive three-speed automatic

BODY/CHASSIS
Unitary monocoque construction steel coupe body

SPECIAL FEATURES

A 'Breezway' power window allowed open air driving for the rear passengers.

Compared to rival 1959 luxury cars, the fins on the Mk IV are quite modest.

RUNNING GEAR
Steering: Recirculating ball

Front suspension: Unequal length wishbones with coil springs and telescopic shock absorbers

Rear suspension: Live axle with semi-elliptic leaf springs and telescopic shock absorbers

Brakes: Drums (front and rear)

Wheels: Steel disc, 14-in. dia.

Tires: 9.50 x 15 in.

DIMENSIONS
Length: 227.1 in **Width:** 80.1 in.

Height: 56.7 in. **Wheelbase:** 131.0 in

Track: 61.0 in. (front and rear)

Weight: 5,192 lbs.

Lincoln ZEPHYR

Introduced as a 'junior' Lincoln, the Zephyr was the car that saved the division during the late 1930s. It revitalized the range and brought a combination of style and V12 power at a price rivals could not match.

"...relaxed performance."

"Effortless, relaxed performance sums up the Zephyr. The V12 is silky-smooth and pulls from extremely low revs yet still has enough top-end power to move the car to a relaxed 87 mph. With its synchromesh gears and a light clutch, gear shifts are easy. The steering is light thanks to the low-geared ratio, with 4.5 turns lock to lock. Despite having a fairly dated suspension, the ride is smooth, making long-distance journeys an enjoyable experience."

A distinctive feature of the Zephyr is its large-faced, center-mounted speedometer.

Milestones

1934 Briggs exhibits
a concept car designed by John Tjaarda at the Chicago World's Fair. It has a rear-mounted V8 engine, fully independent suspension, unitary construction and radically new streamlined body styling.

The Zephyr was initially offered in two- and four-door sedan forms.

1936 A production Zephyr
goes on sale. It is powered by a 267-cubic inch V12 and is styled is by Bob Gregorie.

1938 Zephyrs get a longer
wheelbase and styling changes including a mouth organ grill.

A restyle for 1938 set a styling trend for the rest of the decade.

1940 The Zephyr gains an
all-new body and a V12 stroked to 292 cubic inches. The convertible sedan is dropped, but production reaches 21,944.

1942 Civilian auto production
is suspended.

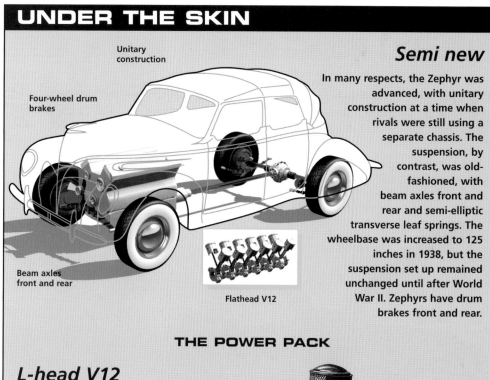

Unitary construction

Four-wheel drum brakes

Beam axles front and rear

Flathead V12

Semi new

In many respects, the Zephyr was advanced, with unitary construction at a time when rivals were still using a separate chassis. The suspension, by contrast, was old-fashioned, with beam axles front and rear and semi-elliptic transverse leaf springs. The wheelbase was increased to 125 inches in 1938, but the suspension set up remained unchanged until after World War II. Zephyrs have drum brakes front and rear.

THE POWER PACK

L-head V12

Although originally intended to be powered by a V8, the Zephyr was actually fitted with a V12 on the orders of Edsel Ford. It is a four-main-bearing L-head unit based on the flathead V8, but with a 75-degree angle. Initially, it produced only 110 bhp, and early versions suffered from overheating, warped bores and oil sludge buildup due to inadequate crankcase ventilation. The addition of hydraulic lifters in 1938 and cast-iron heads in 1941 improved reliability.

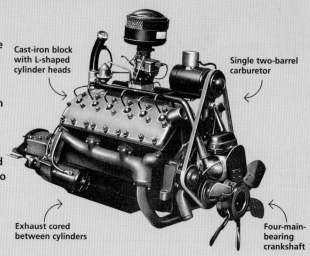

Cast-iron block with L-shaped cylinder heads

Single two-barrel carburetor

Exhaust cored between cylinders

Four-main-bearing crankshaft

Open air

For its day, the Zephyr was revolutionary in many ways, with its unitary construction and trend-setting styling. Perhaps the most desirable of all body styles is the four-door convertible, built only in small numbers and lasting through 1939.

Convertible Zephyr sedans were offered only in 1938 and 1939.

Lincoln **ZEPHYR**

The Zephyr was a curious mixture of new technology—with unitary construction and smooth styling—combined with the old, including mechanical drum brakes and beam axle suspension front and rear.

V12 engine

The Zephyr V12 is a compromise as it is based on the flathead V8. Quiet and refined, it is tuned for torque, not horsepower. The biggest problem is reliability and, consequently, many owners chose to replace the V12 with later Mercury flathead V8s.

Beam axles

Due to the stubbornness of Henry Ford, the Zephyr retained beam-axle suspension with transverse leaf springs. To improve the handling, adjustable hydraulic shocks were offered.

Three-speed transmission

Geared more for torque than power, the V12 is perfectly mated to the three-speed manual transmission. Synchromesh is fitted to second and top gear to make shifting easier.

Unitary construction

Adopting aircraft techniques, the Zephyr has a light, steel-covered girder-like framework onto which the body is welded. This results in a lighter structure than most rival luxury cars of the time.

Vacuum wipers

There is no electric motor for the windshield wipers, so they are powered by the inlet manifold vacuum. The speed of the wipers varies with engine load, resulting in a slower wiper speed up hills.

Steel disc wheels

By 1936, most American automobile manufacturers had abandoned wire wheels in favor of discs, and the Zephyr was no exception.

Two-speed axle

From 1936 to 1940 a two-speed Columbia rear axle was offered. This effectively doubles the number of gears, giving six forward speeds.

Specifications
1939 Lincoln Zephyr

ENGINE

Type: V12

Construction: Cast-iron block and alloy heads

Valve gear: Two sidevalves per cylinder operated by a side-mounted camshaft

Bore and stroke: 2.75 in. x 3.75 in.

Displacement: 267 c.i.

Compression ratio: 7.2:1

Induction system: Single two-barrel downdraft carburetor

Maximum power: 110 bhp at 3,900 rpm

Maximum torque: 180 lb-ft at 3,500 rpm

Top speed: 87 mph

0–60 mph: 16.0 sec.

TRANSMISSION

Three-speed manual

BODY/CHASSIS

Unitary steel construction with four-door convertible sedan body.

SPECIAL FEATURES

A special V12 engine was commissioned for the Zephyr.

The spare tire mount can be hinged outward for easier luggage access.

RUNNING GEAR

Steering: Worm-and-roller

Front suspension: Beam axle with transverse semi-elliptic leaf spring and hydraulic shock absorbers

Rear suspension: Live axle with transverse semi-elliptic leaf spring and hydraulic shock absorbers

Brakes: Drums (front and rear)

Wheels: Steel discs, 16-in. dia.

Tires: 7.00 x 16 in.

DIMENSIONS

Length: 210.0 in.   **Width:** 73.0 in.

Height: 67.0 in.   **Wheelbase:** 122.0 in.

Track: 55.5 in. (front), 58.25 in. (rear)

Weight: 3,790 lbs.

Mercury **COUGAR ELIMINATOR**

A true performance Cougar emerged in 1969 and continued through 1970. Available with a long list of sports options, it posed a considerable threat to the established muscle cars both on the street and at the drag strip. Despite its potential, the Eliminator is often overlooked by enthusiasts today.

"...a gentleman's muscle car."

"With its wood-rimmed steering wheel and full instrumentation, the Cougar appears to be a gentleman's muscle car. Starting up the monster 428 engine reveals a totally different character. The big engine demands high-octane fuel and concentration on the open road. Its greatest asset is the huge amount of mid-range torque. A drag racer's dream, it is enough to humble any would-be challenger. It's quick enough to run the ¼ mile in 14.1 seconds."

This Eliminator has base model trim and is fitted with vinyl seats instead of leather ones.

Milestones

1967 Two years after
Mustang, Mercury launches its own pony car, the Cougar. It features a distinctive front end with a razor-style grill and hidden headlights. Initially it is offered only as a hardtop.

Mercury's other 1969 muscle car was the Cyclone. This one is a Spoiler II.

1969 After minor updates
for 1968, the Cougar is restyled the following year and a convertible is now offered. A high performance model, the Eliminator, is launched mid-year and is available with a host of extra performance options, and was painted with 'high impact' exterior colors such as yellow blue, and orange.

The Cougar share the 302 and 428 engines with the Mustang.

1970 The Eliminator
returns for its second and final season. Its body restyling is more refined than the 1969 model. Just over 2,000 cars are sold and the model is dropped after only two years of production.

UNDER THE SKIN

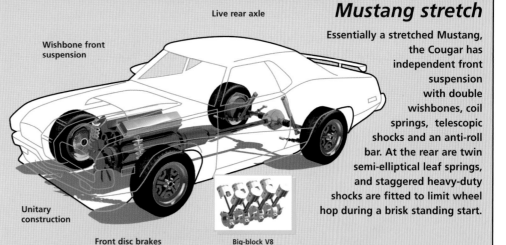

Live rear axle

Wishbone front suspension

Unitary construction

Front disc brakes

Big-block V8

Mustang stretch

Essentially a stretched Mustang, the Cougar has independent front suspension with double wishbones, coil springs, telescopic shocks and an anti-roll bar. At the rear are twin semi-elliptical leaf springs, and staggered heavy-duty shocks are fitted to limit wheel hop during a brisk standing start.

THE POWER PACK

Snake bite

The Eliminator was available with either a 302 V8 or a 428 Cobra Jet V8 (identical to the Mustang engine shown here). The 428 came with or without a ram air system. The engine benefits from a modified crankshaft, stronger connecting rods, and, if the Drag Pak was specified, the owner would receive an oil cooler and 4.30:1 gears. At the time, headers, dual quads, and quadruple Weber carbs could be ordered from dealer parts counters to make the Eliminator more of a street terror than what it already was.

Ram-air induction

Four-barrel carburetor

Heavy duty connecting rods

Oil cooler

Street racer

Since the Eliminator is longer and heavier than the Mustang, it is able get more grip and harness the power from the mighty 428 V8. Though the engine had a factory rating of 335 bhp it actually made closer to 410. The lower rating was to fool insurance companies.

The 1970 Eliminator is offers more refined body panels than the 1969 car.

Mercury COUGAR ELIMINATOR

This is Mercury's version of the high-performance Mustang. More refined than its baby brother, it still keeps the Ford heritage with bright paint, side stripes, spoilers, a hood scoop, and big block power.

Staggered shocks

Axle tramp can be a serious problem with smaller-sized performance Fords from this era, especially those with big engines. The Cougar Eliminator has staggered rear shock absorbers to help overcome this problem.

'High Impact' paintwork

'High Impact' exterior colors was the order of the day in 1970. The Cougar was available in bright blue, yellow and Competition Orange as seen here.

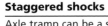

Cobra Jet engine

The Eliminator is available with either the 290-bhp Boss 302 or the more stout 428 Cobra Jet with a conservatively rated 335 bhp. This example is powered by the larger 428, often thought of as one of the finest muscle car engines ever produced.

Interior trim

Although more luxurious than the Mustang, the Eliminator is a base model Cougar and has vinyl upholstery. Full instrumentation is standard and includes a tachometer.

Drag Pak

This Eliminator is garnished with the legendary 'Drag Pak' option, which includes the 428 Super Cobra Jet engine, an oil cooler, and ultra-low rear-end gearing (3.91:1 or 4.30:1). This makes the Cougar one of the fastest accelerating muscle cars.

Restyled front

For 1970 the Cougar received a revised front grill with vertical bars and a more pronounced nose. The tail panel was also slightly altered.

Sequential turn indicators

The rear indicators, which are also combined with the brake lights, flash in sequence when the driver flicks the lever. These are also found on contemporary Shelby Mustangs.

Specifications
1970 Mercury Cougar Eliminator

ENGINE
Type: V8
Construction: Cast-iron block and heads
Valve gear: Two valves per cylinder operated by pushrods and rockers
Bore and stroke: 4.0 in. x 3.5 in.
Displacement: 428 c.i.
Compression ratio: 10.6:1
Induction system: Four-barrel carburetor
Maximum power: 335 bhp at 5,200 rpm
Maximum torque: 440 lb-ft at 3,400 rpm
Top speed: 106 mph
0-60 mph: 5.6 sec

TRANSMISSION
C-6 Cruise-O-Matic

BODY/CHASSIS
Steel monocoque two-door coupe body

SPECIAL FEATURES

The headlights are concealed behind special 'flip-up' panels.

A rear Cougar spoiler is standard Eliminator equipment.

RUNNING GEAR
Steering: Recirculating ball
Front suspension: Unequal length wishbones with coil springs, telescopic shocks and anti-roll bar
Rear suspension: Semi-elliptical multi-leaf springs with staggered rear telescopic shocks
Brakes: Discs (front), drums (rear)
Wheels: Styled steel, 5 x 14 in.
Tires: F60-14 Goodyear Polyglas GT

DIMENSIONS
Length: 191.6 in.   **Width:** 77.6 in.
Height: 52.8 in.   **Wheelbase:** 111 in.
Track: 60 in. (front), 60 in. (rear)
Weight: 3,780 lbs.

Mercury **CYCLONE SPOILER**

Mercury redesigned its intermediates for 1970, which spelled big changes for the Cyclone. Besides the smoother, more flowing contours, it got a new engine. Packing a massive amount of torque, it could run rings around rival muscle cars.

"...unique and distinctive style."

"A four-speed with a Hurst shifter, high-back bucket seats and acres of black vinyl greet you when you take your place behind the wheel. Being a Mercury, the Cyclone rides extremely well on the highway. The Cyclone also has a unique and distinctive style. The steering may feel light and the Spoiler can feel a little unwieldy around sharp corners, but in a straight line it really goes. Accelerating hard from 20 mph, the force is incredible."

A three-spoke steering wheel and a Hurst shifter complete the businesslike cockpit.

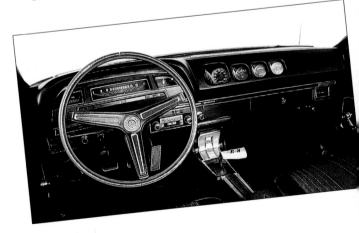

Milestones

1968 The midsize Mercury gets new styling
and a new name—the Montego. A semi-sporty Montego– the GT—is offered, but only 334 are built.

A limited-edition spoiler for 1969 was the Dan Gurney Special.

1969 A new Cyclone CJ appears,
fitted with a standard 428-cubic inch V8 producing 335 bhp. A Spoiler version also arrives but has a standard 351-cubic-inch small-block V8.

Ford's Torino Cobra is a close relative of the Cyclone Spoiler.

1970 Midsize Mercs are rebodied and get a
longer wheelbase. The Cyclone now comes in three different trims: base, GT and Spoiler. The 351 and 390 are offered in lesser Cyclones, but the 370-bhp 429 is standard in the Spoiler. 13,490 Cyclones are built.

1971 The Cyclone returns with few
changes. Production plummets to 3,084 in this, its final year.

UNDER THE SKIN

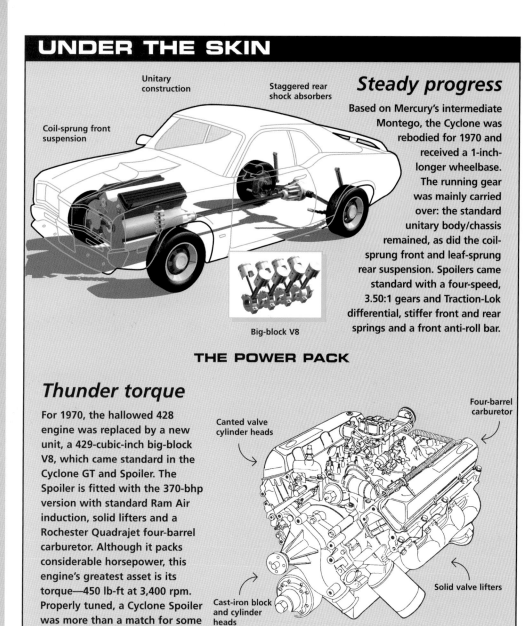

Unitary construction

Staggered rear shock absorbers

Coil-sprung front suspension

Big-block V8

Steady progress

Based on Mercury's intermediate Montego, the Cyclone was rebodied for 1970 and received a 1-inch-longer wheelbase. The running gear was mainly carried over: the standard unitary body/chassis remained, as did the coil-sprung front and leaf-sprung rear suspension. Spoilers came standard with a four-speed, 3.50:1 gears and Traction-Lok differential, stiffer front and rear springs and a front anti-roll bar.

THE POWER PACK

Thunder torque

For 1970, the hallowed 428 engine was replaced by a new unit, a 429-cubic-inch big-block V8, which came standard in the Cyclone GT and Spoiler. The Spoiler is fitted with the 370-bhp version with standard Ram Air induction, solid lifters and a Rochester Quadrajet four-barrel carburetor. Although it packs considerable horsepower, this engine's greatest asset is its torque—450 lb-ft at 3,400 rpm. Properly tuned, a Cyclone Spoiler was more than a match for some of the competition's hottest iron.

Canted valve cylinder heads

Four-barrel carburetor

Cast-iron block and cylinder heads

Solid valve lifters

Unspoiled

The most desired car among the second-generation Cyclones is the 1970 Spoiler, with its Ram Air V8. Add a few other options, such as the Drag Pak with lower rear gearing and the Hurst shifted four-speed, and good ones can cost $15,000.

Cyclone Spoilers are still undervalued muscle cars.

Mercury CYCLONE SPOILER

In 1970, Mercury really came together, launching its best-ever muscle car. The Cyclone Spoiler had its own distinctive style, packing a wallop, which made it a real threat on the street no matter who was driving it.

Luxury interior

The Cyclone boasts a plusher cabin than the closely related Ford Torino. This includes hounds-tooth vinyl seats and a dash with all auxiliary controls angled toward the driver.

Thunder Jet engine

The canted valve-head 429 came with standard Ram Air in the Spoiler, producing 370 bhp and 450 lb-ft of earth-moving torque. It made the Spoiler a strong runner, especially on the street, which is what counted most of all.

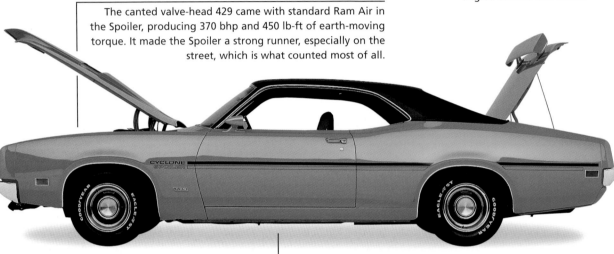

Drag Pak

The Drag Pak option gives the Spoiler even more straight line grunt. This adds an engine oil cooler, stronger bearings and main caps, plus steeper rear axle ratios in the form of 3.91:1 or 4.30:1 cogs.

Swoopy styling

Like its relative the Ford Torino, the Cyclone was rebodied for 1970 with smoother, more flowing lines. A distinctive feature is the projecting snout with gunsight grill treatment. This gave rise to the nickname 'Coffin Nose' and wasn't universally well received. At 209.9 inches overall, the Cyclone is one of the larger 1970 muscle intermediates.

Safety emphasis

Ford was one of the first U.S. manufacturers to seriously market safety features. The Cyclone boasts such items as dual hydraulic braking systems with warning light, glare-reducing dashboard, energy-absorbing steering wheel and column, standard front and rear lap belts, safety rimmed wheels and corrosion-resistant brake lines.

Hidden headlights

By the late 1960s, hideaway headlights were popular in Detroit. The Cyclone's quad circular units are hidden behind flip-up grill panels operated by vacuum tubes. A second set of running lights is mounted astride the grill.

Heavy-duty suspension

In an effort to give the car a more balanced enthusiast flavor, a heavy-duty suspension was standard on the Spoiler. This included stiffer springs, shocks and a front anti-roll bar.

Specifications

1970 Mercury Cyclone Spoiler

ENGINE

Type: V8

Construction: Cast-iron block and heads

Valve gear: Two valves per cylinder operated by a single camshaft with pushrods and rockers.

Bore and stroke: 4.36 in. x 3.59 in.

Displacement: 429 c.i.

Compression ratio: 11.3:1

Induction system: Rochester Quadrajet four-barrel carburetor

Maximum power: 370 bhp at 5,400 rpm

Maximum torque: 450 lb-ft at 3,400 rpm

TRANSMISSION

Borg-Warner T-10 four-speed manual with Hurst shifter

BODY/CHASSIS

Steel unitary chassis with two-door fastback body

SPECIAL FEATURES

A Hurst T-handle was offered with the Borg-Warner T-10 four-speed.

The protruding front end contains a distinctive 'gunsight'-type grill.

RUNNING GEAR

Steering: Recirculating ball

Front suspension: Unequal-length A-arms with coil springs, telescopic shock absorbers and anti-roll bar

Rear suspension: Live axle with semi-elliptic leaf springs and telescopic shock absorbers

Brakes: Discs (front), drums (rear)

Wheels: Steel, 7 x 14 in.

Tires: Goodyear Polyglas, G60-14

DIMENSIONS

Length: 209.9 in. **Width:** 77.3 in.

Height: 52.2 in. **Wheelbase:** 117.0 in.

Track: 60.5 in. (front), 60.0 in. (rear)

Weight: 3,773 lbs.

Mercury **SPORTSMAN**

With the Sportsman, Mercury management created the most collectible car the division would ever build. However, it was based on a pre-WWII design so there weren't many innovative mechanical features and it relied on an old sidevalve V8 engine.

"...quiet and refined."

"The Sportsman was designed for comfort and style. While it may have an ancient suspension, this Mercury can soak up the bumps and potholes without ruffling its occupants. The flathead V8 is quiet and refined offering plenty of torque to compensate for its use of a less-than-desirable three-speed transmission. Hitting 60 mph in just over 21 seconds was fine performance for 1946 and its maximum speed of 82 mph is as fast as you'd want to go back then, too."

The large white plastic steering wheel adds character to the wood-finished dashboard.

Milestones

1939 Spotting a gap in the market, the Ford Motor Company launches the Mercury brand name. It is a success right from its inception. 80,000 cars are sold within a few years.

Chrysler released the wooded Town & Country in 1946, too.

1946 Following the end of World War II, Mercury cars go back into production using updated 1942 models. There isn't time to make fundamental mechanical changes, so the two-door convertible receives some hardwood body paneling. The newly restyled model is know as the Sportsman.

The Ford Sportsman sold very well during the two years it was built.

1947 It is not the end for the Sportsman concept, as the base Ford version carries on the line. Despite strong sales the design is too expensive to build and production ends at the end of the year, although some 1947 cars were sold as 948 models.

UNDER THE SKIN

Three-speed manual transmission

Hydraulic drum brakes

Solid front axle

Sidevalve V8

Old fashioned

Underneath the Sportsman is an old-fashioned Ford chassis. It has a solid front axle, sprung by transverse leaf springs. The rear axle is also located on another transverse spring. Rival GM cars had automatic transmissions available, but the Sportsman had to make do with a three-speed manual. For stopping power, the Sportsman relies on four-wheel, hydraulically-operated drum brakes.

THE POWER PACK

Proven pre-war V8

The design of Ford's classic flathead V8 dates back to 1932. By the time it found its way into the Mercury Sportsman it had grown to 239 cubic inches. The sidevalve layout was the same, with a cast-iron block and cylinder heads. The valves operate upwards into an overhanging head rather than having the combustion chambers directly over the pistons as in modern engines. By this stage the engine's early reliability problems had been long since remedied. It is a long-stroke design with good low-rpm torque. There was no shortage of tuning parts for what was a race-winning engine in its day.

Rare wood

If you can't find a Mercury Sportsman, there's always the Ford version. Also wood trimmed, it has the same engine and performance and almost as much style. However, because the Ford is more common, the Mercury commands quite a premium with collectors.

Rarity ensures the Mercury Sportsman will always be collectable.

Mercury SPORTSMAN

Mercury used the design genius of Bob Gregorie, who had created the look of the famous 1940 Lincoln Continental to make the Sportsman stand apart. He did it with extensive and stylish wood paneling.

V8 engine

It would not be until the 1954 model year that Mercury cars would receive standard overhead-valve V8 engines. The early post-war models used the existing, modest L-head sidevalve V8. The Sportsman managed just 100 bhp from a 239-cubic inch engine.

Drum brakes

Like every other car on sale in the U.S. at the time, the Sportsman has hydraulically-operated drum brakes. Ford introduced these for the 1939 model year.

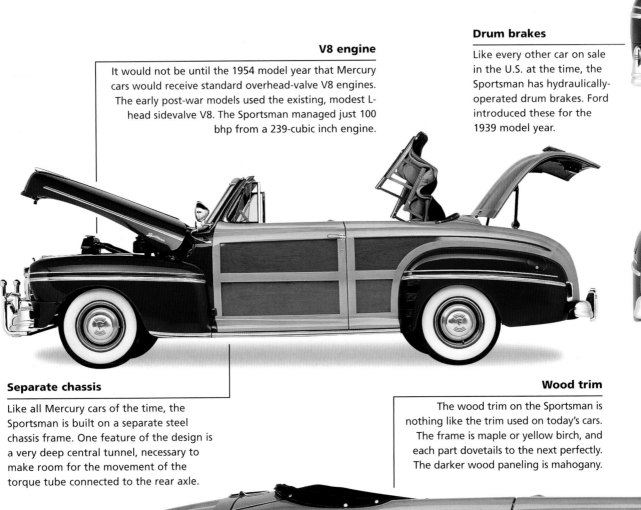

Separate chassis

Like all Mercury cars of the time, the Sportsman is built on a separate steel chassis frame. One feature of the design is a very deep central tunnel, necessary to make room for the movement of the torque tube connected to the rear axle.

Wood trim

The wood trim on the Sportsman is nothing like the trim used on today's cars. The frame is maple or yellow birch, and each part dovetails to the next perfectly. The darker wood paneling is mahogany.

Split windshield

Along with all post-war U.S. auto manufacturers, Ford and Mercury had to make do with flat windshield glass. The only way the windshield could be angled backward was by having a central join.

Three-speed transmission

Mercury offered the Liquamatic automatic transmission before World War II, but it was dropped for the 1946 line. The only transmission was a three-speed manual with a column shifter.

Specifications

1946 Mercury Sportsman

ENGINE
Type: V8
Construction: Cast-iron block and heads
Valve gear: Two valves per cylinder operated in L-head cylinder heads by a block-mounted camshaft with solid lifters
Bore and stroke: 3.19 in. x 3.75 in.
Displacement: 239 c.i.
Compression ratio: 6.75:1
Induction system: Holley 94 two-barrel carburetor
Maximum power: 100 bhp at 3,800 rpm
Maximum torque: Not quoted

TRANSMISSION
Three-speed manual

BODY/CHASSIS
Separate steel channel-section chassis with two-door convertible body

SPECIAL FEATURES

Adding whitewalls and wood to the 1942 Mercury gave it its classic look.

With so much wood attached to the car's body, it makes sense to have a fire extinguisher on board the Sportsman.

RUNNING GEAR
Steering: Worm-and-sector
Front suspension: Solid axle with transverse semi-elliptic leaf spring and hydraulic lever-arm shock absorbers
Rear suspension: Live axle with transverse semi-elliptic leaf spring, angled trailing arms and hydraulic lever-arm shock absorbers
Brakes: Drums (front and rear)
Wheels: Pressed steel disc, 15 in. dia.
Tires: Crossply 6.50 x 15

DIMENSIONS
Length: 201.8 in.   **Width:** 73.1 in.
Height: Not quoted   **Wheelbase:** 118.0 in.
Track: 58.0 in. (front,) 60.0 in. (rear)
Weight: 3,407 lbs.

Oldsmobile 4-4-2

While the 1968 4-4-2 had plenty of power with its 400-cubic inch V8 engine, this stock-looking Oldsmobile street machine has been modified with a massive 455 V8 that makes the kind of power found only in the limited edition Hurst-modified cars.

"...fast and fun street machine."

"The 1968 Oldsmobile 4-4-2 came with a W-30 360-bhp 400-cubic inch engine with the new, forced-air option. This custom example, however, has a full-size 455-cubic inch Rocket motor with added performance parts, similar to the Hurst/Olds introduced that same year. With a 410 bhp under the hood and a convertible top, this 4-4-2 is a fast and fun street machine. It accelerates like a rocket and handles better than most cars of its era."

The interior remains relatively stock, but the engine under the hood is a different story.

Milestones

1964 The 4-4-2
nameplate debuts as a package option on the mid-size F-85™.

1965 The standard
4-4-2 engine is a destroked and debored 425 V8 creating the new 400-cubic inch V8.

Early 4-4-2s have more square bodywork than the later cars.

1967 Tri-power
induction is offered for one year and the engine makes 360 bhp.

1968 A restyled body
gives the 4-4-2 a more elegant look. 3,000 modified versions known as the Hurst/Olds are offered with 455 engines.

The 1970 W-30 came with a big 455 V8 and fiberglass hood.

1970 A 455-cubic
inch engine becomes available with Oldsmobile's "select fit" parts. The W-30 455 makes 370 bhp, but its 14.3 quarter mile time suggests this car made more power. These cars had fiberglass hoods and plastic fender liners.

UNDER THE SKIN

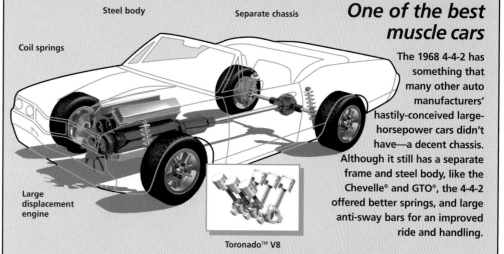

Steel body · Separate chassis · Coil springs · Large displacement engine · Toronado™ V8

One of the best muscle cars

The 1968 4-4-2 has something that many other auto manufacturers' hastily-conceived large-horsepower cars didn't have—a decent chassis. Although it still has a separate frame and steel body, like the Chevelle® and GTO®, the 4-4-2 offered better springs, and large anti-sway bars for an improved ride and handling.

THE POWER PACK

Full-size V8

After 1965 the first '4' in 4-4-2 stood for the size of the standard 400-cubic inch engine. Oldsmobile destroked and debored its full-size 425 V8 engine just for the 4-4-2. For 1966, Olds™ offered a tri-carburetors boosting power to 360 bhp (right). In 1970, its size was increased again to 455. It was the biggest and most powerful engine Olds ever offered. The owner of the model featured here has replaced the factory 400 V8 engine with a 455-cubic inch Rocket motor that makes 410 bhp thanks to special modifications.

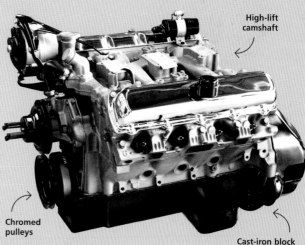

High-lift camshaft · Chromed pulleys · Cast-iron block

Convertible

The new 1968 range of 4-4-2 models updated the earlier cars. At the top of the new range, above the hardtop coupe, was the convertible. It offered incredible value for this type of car, not to mention loads of fun with the top down in the summer.

The convertible top and stock wheels give this 4-4-2 a stealth-like look.

Oldsmobile 4-4-2

The 4-4-2 was one of the best muscle cars of the 1960s. It has incredible performance and, unlike many of its rivals, it also has the agility and braking to match the speed.

Custom paint

The bodywork has been sprayed with a base coat of Infinity White paint, followed by a clear coat to give a deep, high gloss finish.

4-4-2 badging

By 1968 the 4-4-2 nameplate had become familiar and sought-after property. Badging in the grill announced that you were driving something special.

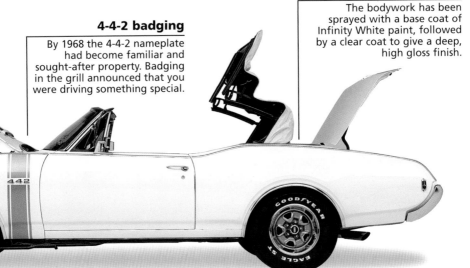

Uprated wheels and tires

The 1968 4-4-2 had 14-inch diameter wheels, but the owner of this car has chosen to upgrade to 15-inch Super Stock II rims, shod with Goodyear Eagle ST tires.

Improved cabin

As well as 1970 Gold Madrid interior, this particular car features full GM and AutoGauge instruments and a 'Rallye' steering wheel.

Heavy-duty suspension

The rear end has been beefed up by replacing the stock coil springs with heavy-duty springs from a station wagon. Modern polyurethane bushings and $1^7/_8$-inch thick front and rear anti-roll bars have also been added to tighten the suspension further.

Sharp steering

To improve handling, the owner installed a quick-ratio steering box. This means the wheel has to be turned less when cornering.

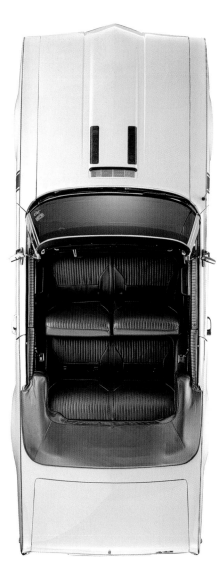

Big 455 V8

Although the 455 V8 engine was not offered in the 1968 4-4-2, it was available in a special edition called the Hurst/Olds. It became standard for all 4-4-2 models in 1970.

Specifications

Oldsmobile 4-4-2 Convertible

ENGINE
Type: V8
Construction: Cast-iron cylinder block and cylinder heads
Valve gear: Two valves per cylinder operated by a single camshaft
Bore and stroke: 4.12 in. x 4.25 in.
Displacement: 455 c.i.
Compression ratio: 10.5:1
Induction system: Four-barrel carburetor
Maximum power: 410 bhp at 5,500 rpm
Maximum torque: 517 lb-ft at 3,500 rpm
Top speed: 134 mph
0-60 mph: 6.2 sec.

TRANSMISSION
Turbo HydraMatic 350 three-speed automatic

BODY/CHASSIS
Separate chassis with two-door convertible steel body

SPECIAL FEATURES

The interior has been taken from a 1970 Oldsmobile and features Gold Madrid vinyl upholstery.

On this modified car, the exhaust tips exit behind the rear tires rather than out of the back as on the standard 4-4-2s.

RUNNING GEAR
Steering: Recirculating ball
Front suspension: Wishbones with coil springs, shocks, and anti-roll bar
Rear suspension: Rigid axle with coil springs, shocks, and anti-roll bar
Brakes: Discs front, drums rear
Wheels: Super Stock II, 15-in. dia.
Tires: Goodyear Eagle ST

DIMENSIONS
Length: 201.6 in.   **Width:** 76.2 in.
Height: 52.8 in.   **Wheelbase:** 112 in.
Track: 59.1 in. (front), 59.1 in. (rear)
Curb weight: 3,890 lbs.

Oldsmobile STARFIRE

Filling Oldsmobile's personal luxury niche in 1961 was the Starfire, a convertible based on the Eighty-Eight™, with a 394-cubic inch engine under the hood.

"...lots of torque."

"Like most early-1960s American cars, the Oldsmobile Starfire has a nautical feel. The feather-light steering and pillow-soft ride make the car ideal for a coast-to-coast cruise on an interstate highway, but it is under the hood where the Starfire really shines. Using a high-output, four-barrel, 394-cubic inch V8, the big Olds has lots of torque, enabling it to leave many other supposed 'sports' cars in its wake."

Quite sporty for its day, the Starfire boasted front bucket seats and a center console.

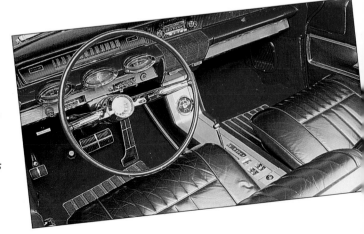

Milestones

1961 Oldsmobile launches the Starfire as a personal luxury car, only available as a convertible.

Pontiac's® Ventura™ shared its chassis with the Starfire.

1962 The Starfire becomes available as a two-door hardtop.

1965 For its fifth season, a total of 15,260 Starfires are built, the majority being hardtops.

The midsize 4-4-2™ became Oldsmobile's® most prominent performance car in 1961.

1966 With the arrival of the front-wheel-drive Toronado™, the Starfire is living on borrowed time, and is consigned to history at the end of the model year.

UNDER THE SKIN

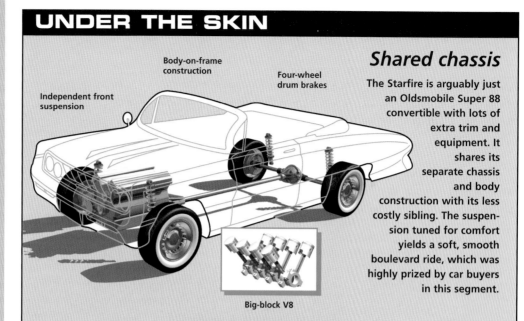

Independent front suspension

Body-on-frame construction

Four-wheel drum brakes

Big-block V8

Shared chassis

The Starfire is arguably just an Oldsmobile Super 88 convertible with lots of extra trim and equipment. It shares its separate chassis and body construction with its less costly sibling. The suspension tuned for comfort yields a soft, smooth boulevard ride, which was highly prized by car buyers in this segment.

THE POWER PACK

Four barrels and high compression

The Starfire's engine is a 394-cubic inch V8, which was standard in the Super 88. However, as the Starfire was the division's flagship in 1961, the big V8 was given a tuneup. High-compression pistons yielded a 10.25:1 ratio and a need for high-octane fuel. Sitting above the dual-plane, cast-iron intake is a four-barrel Rochester 4GC carburetor, and with 330 bhp and a 440 lb-ft of torque, the big V8 makes the Starfire quite a mover. Considering the Starfire weighs in at 4,305 lbs., it boasts 0-60-mph times in the 9-second range.

About time

As the horsepower wars heated up in the early 1960s, Oldsmobile needed a sporty flagship to bolster its image. The Starfire, introduced in January, 1961, was the answer. Offered until 1966, the original model remains the most significant.

All 1961 Starfires were convertibles.

Oldsmobile STARFIRE

An Oldsmobile flagship, the Starfire offered all the luxury and performance of the bigger 98 series in a more compact and sporty package.

More powerful engine

For 1961, Oldsmobile enlarged the 371-cubic inch V8 to 394 cubic inches. For the Starfire, this included an improved induction system and a hotter camshaft. To achieve the ultimate performance from the 394, the Starfire utilized the Skyrocket's four barrel carburetor and high-compression pistons.

Style by skegs

Oldsmobiles shared a corporate styling quirk that was used by only one other GM division—the skeg. Skegs are sort of upside-down tailfins, which protrude from the bottom of the rear quarter panels.

Stiffer chassis

In order to boost torsional stiffness, Oldsmobile created a new frame by adding sturdier sections to the front and back of the side rails. To prevent the excessive chassis flex that many larger American cars suffered from, four steel members were triangulated to counteract torsional and bending movement.

Two pipes are nice

Starfires came standard with a dual-exhaust system. Not only functional in increasing horsepower, they also signified the car's presence on the road.

Room for four

As a range of small, sporty pretenders assaulted the U.S.-car market, the Starfire wore its full-size credentials with pride. Just because it was a big car didn't mean it was slow. As sales of other big sportsters like the Chrysler 300 and the Thunderbird showed, car buyers couldn't get enough.

Lavish interior

The Starfire had one of the most luxurious interiors in the Oldsmobile lineup. Bucket seats with power adjustment and a console were standard, as was leather upholstery and a tachometer.

Specifications

1961 Oldsmobile Starfire

ENGINE

Type: V8

Construction: Cast-iron block and head

Valve gear: Two valves per cylinder operated by a single camshaft with hydraulic valve lifters

Bore and stroke: 4.125 in. x 3.688 in.

Displacement: 394 c.i.

Compression ratio: 10.25:1

Induction system: Rochester 4GC four-barrel carburetor

Maximum power: 330 bhp at 4,600 rpm

Maximum torque: 440 lb-ft at 2,800 rpm

TRANSMISSION

Hydramatic three-speed automatic

BODY/CHASSIS

Separate chassis with steel two-door convertible body

SPECIAL FEATURES

Skegs were a prominent feature of the 1961 Starfire.

 **The Starfire was fitted with Oldsmobile's most powerful and highest-compression V8.**

RUNNING GEAR

Steering: Recirculating-ball

Front suspension: Unequal-length upper and lower A-arms with coil springs and telescopic shock absorbers

Rear suspension: Live axle with control arms, coil springs and telescopic shock absorbers

Brakes: Drums (front and rear)

Wheels: Steel, 14-in. dia.

Tires: 8.50 x 14

DIMENSIONS

Length: 212.0 in.   **Width:** 77.0 in.

Height: 55.0 in.   **Wheelbase:** 123.0 in.

Track: 61.0 in. (front and rear)

Weight: 4,305 lbs.

Oldsmobile **TORONADO**

Ultraconservative Oldsmobile produced one of the most innovative cars of the 1960s with its Toronado coupe. The bold styling was just a teaser, for underneath lay Detroit's first front-wheel drive layouts. This endowed the Toronado with first-rate handling finesse.

"...fantastic front wheeler."

"The Toronado was one of the most well balanced drivers that came out of Detroit in the 1960s. The first thing you'll notice about this fantastic front wheeler is the lack of any transmission tunnel. Fire up the engine and the muted Rocket V8 revs happily and is an eager performer on the road. The real revelation comes when you turn your first corner—the car really handles. The payoff is a rather hard ride, but its light steering and easy cruising keep you smiling."

Needles and rocker switches fill the dash-board, but it's all clear and accessible.

Milestones

1966 General Motors turns history on its head with its most radical car of the decade, the front-drive Oldsmobile Toronado.

1967 Optional front disc brakes and radial tires improve the package.

The second generation 1971-1978 Toronado was bigger and heavier.

1968 A semi-notchback rear end is grafted on. Under the hood the engine displacement grows to 455 cubic inches, although standard power output falls by 10 bhp.

E-bodies, including the Toronado, were downsized in 1979.

1970 In its final year before being replaced by an all-new Toronado, fixed headlights replace the pop-up ones.

UNDER THE SKIN

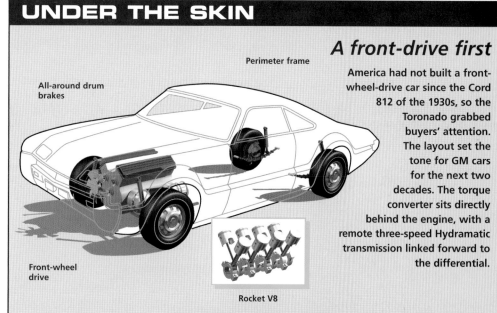

Perimeter frame

All-around drum brakes

Front-wheel drive

Rocket V8

A front-drive first

America had not built a front-wheel-drive car since the Cord 812 of the 1930s, so the Toronado grabbed buyers' attention. The layout set the tone for GM cars for the next two decades. The torque converter sits directly behind the engine, with a remote three-speed Hydramatic transmission linked forward to the differential.

THE POWER PACK

Full-size V8

Originally, chief engineer John Beltz requested an all-alloy transverse V6 engine in the Toronado, but the GM chiefs knew that the market wanted a V8 in a flagship model. So Oldsmobile turned to the familiar full-size Rocket V8. Standard in Olds' big cars, the 425-cubic inch, cast-iron engine was rated at 385 bhp in the Toronado. Engineers mounted it in a rubber-insulated subframe, resulting in less cabin noise and vibration. From 1968, the engine size grew to 455 cubic inches and, though power dropped to 375 bhp, there was an optional W-34 package with twin exhausts and a special cam, capable of 400 bhp.

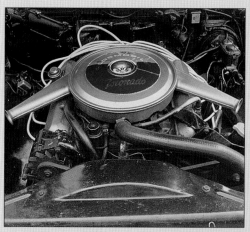

'66 Toronado

The original is the best when it comes to Toronados, and the first fastback body-style is preferred over the semi-notchback form adopted for 1968. And unless you find a modified 400-bhp version, the original 1966 Toronado has more power than later cars.

Today, the earlier models are the most sought after.

Oldsmobile **TORONADO**

Front-wheel drive was one thing, but an innovative engine/transmission layout freed up a lot of space inside and allowed engineers to deliver class-leading handling.

Concealed headlights

In all but 1970 models, the quad headlights are hidden away in pods. These swing up at the press of a button, increasing the sense of drama around the car.

Split transmission

For packaging reasons, the transmission is not an all-in-one unit. Instead, there is a torque converter mounted behind the engine with a two-inch Morse chain running to the Turbohydramatic three-speed.

Beam rear axle

In contrast with the innovative front end, the rear is conventional. The beam axle is suspended on rudimentary single-leaf, semi-elliptic springs. Two sets of shock absorbers are fitted, one pair mounted horizontally.

Bold styling

The Toronado combines European and American styling influences. Its designer, David North, created a clean and dramatic shape dominated by swoopy rear pillars, smooth flanks and heavy chrome bumpers.

1966 Oldsmobile Toronado

ENGINE

Type: V8

Construction: Cast-iron block and heads

Valve gear: Two valves per cylinder operated by a single camshaft with pushrods and rockers

Bore and stroke: 4.13 in. x 3.98 in.

Displacement: 425 c.i.

Compression ratio: 10.5:1

Induction system: Single four-barrel carburetor

Maximum power: 385 bhp at 4,800 rpm

Maximum torque: 475 lb-ft at 3,200 rpm

Top speed: 124 mph

0-60 mph: 9.9 sec.

TRANSMISSION

Turbohydramatic three-speed automatic

BODY/CHASSIS

Separate chassis with steel two-door coupe body

SPECIAL FEATURES

Cornering lights on the front fenders were an option on 1967 Toronados.

The heavily chromed rear bumper has cutouts for twin exhaust pipes.

RUNNING GEAR

Steering: Recirculating ball

Front suspension: Wishbones with longitudinal torsion bars, shock absorbers and anti-roll bar

Rear suspension: Beam axle with semi-elliptic springs and shock absorbers

Brakes: Drums, front and rear

Wheels: Steel 15-in. dia.

Tires: 8.85 x 15

DIMENSIONS

Length: 211.0 in.   **Width:** 78.5 in.

Height: 52.8 in.   **Wheelbase:** 119.0 in.

Track: 63.5 in. (front), 63.0 in. (rear)

Weight: 4,655 lbs.

Big cabin

Enormous doors open wide to provide access to a very spacious six-passenger interior. A long, 119-inch wheelbase coupled with the compact drivetrain gives ample room for passengers.

Front-wheel drive

In 1966, front-wheel drive cars were unique to the U.S market. The Toronado was easily the world's biggest example.

Packard CARIBBEAN

In the early 1950s, the Packard company decided its conservative image needed a transformation. One result was an exclusive luxury car, the straight-eight powered, 100 mph Caribbean convertible.

"...a pleasant surprise."

"When mated with the Ultramatic transmission, the big and wonderfully smooth straight eight gives leisurely performance, although it will eventually top 100 mph. Even at low speeds, the car leans through corners, but there is a pleasant surprise in store; as the speed rises the Caribbean steadies itself and can be hustled along quickly and with superb comfort, even over rough roads. The steering is very light, and the brakes need only the slightest touch."

The strawberries-and-cream interior of the Caribbean looks good enough to eat.

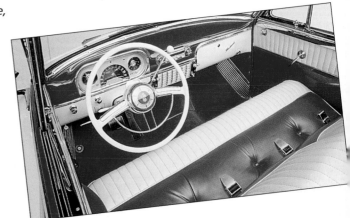

Milestones

1951 Packard

boosts its image with a show car from the Henney Body Co. The car appears the following year as the Pan American.

The top-of-the-range 1956 Clipper was the last of the true Packards.

1953 Reaction to

the Pan American is so strong that Packard decides to go into production with a luxury convertible, the Caribbean.

1954 A facelift

adds new headlight rims, a chromed hood scoop, semi-enclosed rear wheels, two-tone paint, new taillights and a color-keyed interior.

Studebaker's financial troubles contributed to Packard's demise.

1955 An all-new

ribbean arrives with innovative new self-leveling suspension. It lasts for a further year. Financial concerns shift the focus to high-volume models.

UNDER THE SKIN

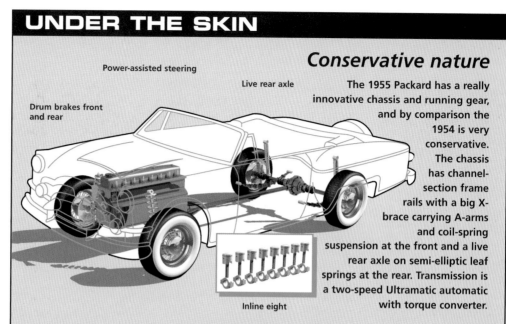

Power-assisted steering

Live rear axle

Drum brakes front and rear

Inline eight

Conservative nature

The 1955 Packard has a really innovative chassis and running gear, and by comparison the 1954 is very conservative. The chassis has channel-section frame rails with a big X-brace carrying A-arms and coil-spring suspension at the front and a live rear axle on semi-elliptic leaf springs at the rear. Transmission is a two-speed Ultramatic automatic with torque converter.

THE POWER PACK

Straight eight

Packard kept faith with inline straight-eight engines while its rivals were making more modern V8s. Engine design was old-fashioned with a long cast-iron block carrying a crankshaft on nine main bearings. On top is an alloy head, but the two inline side valves per cylinder work in an L-head design. The valve lifters are hydraulic, and thus adjustment-free. It is a long-stroke design and output compared well with its V8 rivals. There were very few engines as powerful for the size as the Packard 359 with its 212 bhp.

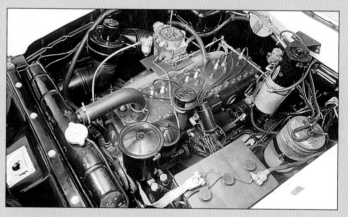

'53 or '54?

Some aficionados prefer the 1953 Carribean, with its fully open rear wheelarch design, but the 1954 version is rarer (400 were built). The later Caribbean, with 212 bhp, also boasts more power than its predecessor.

1954 was the last year for straight eights in Packards.

Packard CARIBBEAN

With two-tone paintwork, lots of chrome and wire wheels, the Caribbean was an impressive showpiece. It was ideally suited for wealthier Americans to cruise around in on Sunday afternoon drives.

Power top

For the price Packard charged, Caribbean buyers were not expected to have to lower the convertible top manually and there was a hydraulically powered system that could raise or lower the roof completely in around 30 seconds. When lowered, the top disappeared completely.

Inline eight cylinder

Prestige and smooth running apart, there were clear disadvantages to the straight-eight design. The design was inherently heavier and larger than a V8. The length of the crankshaft also kept engine speeds down. The 1954 engine was the final flowering of the straight-eight concept and has an alloy head and one of the highest compression ratios of any U.S. engine at the time.

Live rear axle

Packard used a live axle that is both located and suspended by semi-elliptic leaf springs. There are telescopic shock absorbers and an anti-roll bar. Packard was working on a sophisticated system of torsion-bar self-leveling suspension but this would not debut until the following year.

Two-speed Ultramatic

The idea of a two-speed automatic transmission may sound frustrating, but Packard's Ultramatic with torque converter is extremely smooth. It shifts into high gear at speeds ranging from 15 mph to 50 mph depending on how hard the driver accelerates.

Specifications

1954 Packard Caribbean

ENGINE

Type: Inline eight cylinder

Construction: Cast-iron block and alloy head

Valve gear: Two inline side valves per cylinder operated upwards by a single block-mounted camshaft

Bore and stroke: 3.56 in. x 4.50 in.

Displacement: 359 c.i.

Compression ratio: 8.7:1

Induction system: Single Carter WCFB four-barrel carburetor

Maximum power: 212 bhp at 4,000 rpm

Maximum torque: 310 lb-ft at 2,000 rpm

TRANSMISSION

Two-speed Ultramatic automatic

BODY/CHASSIS

Separate box-section steel chassis frame with two-door convertible body

SPECIAL FEATURES

Chrome-plated flat-top rear wheel arches are a feature unique to the 1954 Caribbean.

The spare wheel is neatly incorporated into the rear bodywork and was color-coded, too.

RUNNING GEAR

Steering: Spiral-bevel

Front suspension: A-arms with coil springs and telescopic shock absorbers

Rear suspension: Live axle with semi-elliptic leaf springs, telescopic shock absorbers and anti-roll bar

Brakes: Drums front and rear, 12.0-in. dia. (front and rear)

Wheels: Wire spoke, 15-in. dia.

Tires: 8.00 x 15

DIMENSIONS

Length: 211.5 in.   **Width:** 77.8 in.

Height: 64.0 in.   **Wheelbase:** 122.0 in.

Track: 60.0/60/8 front and rear

Weight: 4,400 lbs.

Power steering

Although the steering gear on the Caribbean is very low-geared and needs a full 4.4 turns to get from lock to lock, it still has power assistance, although the system chosen is slow to self-center after a turn.

Panoz ROADSTER

Despite its youth, the Panoz has made big waves as a superfast, hand-built roadster. Its bare-boned style and advanced aluminum construction make it intriguing and exciting to drive.

"...pure, modern magic."

"To get into the Panoz you have to open a tiny door and step over the sill. The narrow cockpit feels like one of the great sports cars of the 1960s, but when you turn the key and hear the throb of a Mustang V8, you know this has to be a 1990s car. Floor the throttle and you are catapulted off the line at tremendous speed. The pleasure of prowling along twisty roads in the Roadster is pure, modern magic."

The cockpit may be in the spirit of 1960s sports cars, but ergonomically-designed seats and a heater are welcomed modern features.

Milestones

1994 Danny Panoz

sets out to create a car that offers pure driving thrills for the American driver. Having taken over an Irish motorsports company that had an inspired car design, Panoz develops the vehicle to meet U.S. regulations and shows the Roadster this year.

In 1997, Panoz entered the GT endurance series with the sleek new GTR-1.

1995 At the Geneva Motor Show, the Swiss

tuning company Rinspeed presents a mildly-modified version of the Panoz, known as the Rinspeed Roadster.

The latest car from Panoz is the sleek Esperante coupe.

1996 Panoz AIV

Roadster (AIV stands for aluminum-intensive vehicle) debuts in the U.S. to a rapturous reception from the press.

UNDER THE SKIN

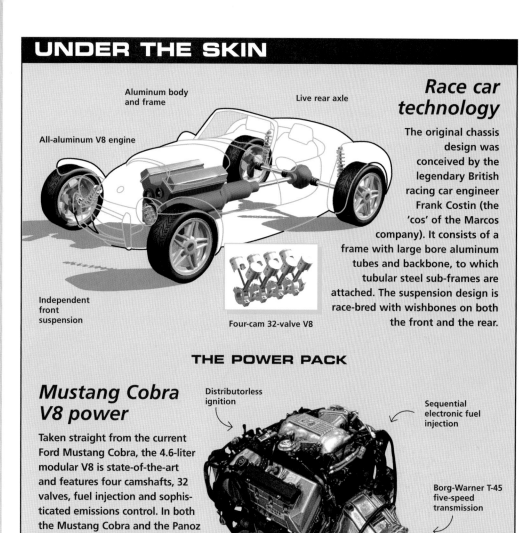

Aluminum body and frame

Live rear axle

All-aluminum V8 engine

Independent front suspension

Four-cam 32-valve V8

Race car technology

The original chassis design was conceived by the legendary British racing car engineer Frank Costin (the 'cos' of the Marcos company). It consists of a frame with large bore aluminum tubes and backbone, to which tubular steel sub-frames are attached. The suspension design is race-bred with wishbones on both the front and the rear.

THE POWER PACK

Mustang Cobra V8 power

Taken straight from the current Ford Mustang Cobra, the 4.6-liter modular V8 is state-of-the-art and features four camshafts, 32 valves, fuel injection and sophisticated emissions control. In both the Mustang Cobra and the Panoz Roadster this engine develops 305 bhp, and when combined with the aluminum construction of the Panoz it produces outstanding performance and refinement. The use of a standard Ford engine also means that the Panoz Roadster can be serviced by Ford dealers.

Distributorless ignition

Sequential electronic fuel injection

Borg-Warner T-45 five-speed transmission

All-aluminum block and cylinder heads

Hand-built

Although it also produces the Esperante Le Mans road-racing car, Panoz offers just one version of its hand-built AIV Roadster. However, there is a range of options to suit an individual's preferences. A sports suspension package is available, as are a trunk-mounted luggage rack and side wind deflectors.

Panoz owners can personalize their cars with factory options.

Panoz ROADSTER

With Ford Mustang Cobra V8 power, awesome performance and few creature comforts, the American-built Panoz AIV Roadster is the true Shelby Cobra of the 1990s.

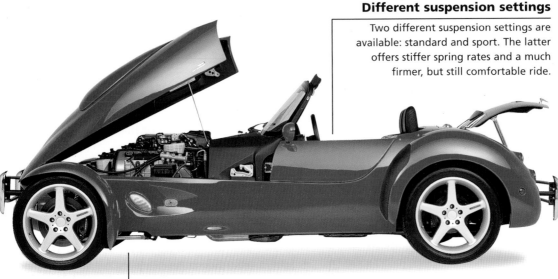

Different suspension settings

Two different suspension settings are available: standard and sport. The latter offers stiffer spring rates and a much firmer, but still comfortable ride.

Ford sub-systems

Choosing standard Ford parts for the engine, drivetrain, and electrics results in excellent reliability and servicing that can be carried out by Ford dealerships.

Race car chassis

The chassis is descended from an original design by the ex-Marcos and Lotus engineer Frank Costin. The integrity of Costin's original aluminum frame is retained, despite modifications to house the drivetrain.

Ultra-low profile tires

The wide, 18-inch alloy wheels are fitted with ultra-low profile BF Goodrich Competition T/A tires—245/40 at the front and 295/35 at the rear.

Classically simple interior

Inside, in classic sports car fashion, form follows function. Interior choices are burr walnut or carbon fiber trim, and dark- or beige-colored leather upholstery. Air-conditioning and a monster stereo are available as options.

Elemental styling

The original style of the Panoz was co-created by Danny Panoz and Freeman Thomas, and draws on many influences, particularly the Jaguar E-type and Austin Healey, as well as traditional American hot rods.

Aircraft-technology body

The Roadster's aluminum body panels are built for safety and strength and are similar to those used on aircraft.

Vented disc brakes

The Roadster has one of the world's most effective braking systems, consisting of large diameter vented disc brakes on all four corners. The front discs also boast twin-piston calipers.

Specifications

1997 Panoz AIV Roadster

ENGINE

Type: V8
Construction: Aluminum cylinder block and heads
Valve gear: Four valves per cylinder operated by two chain-driven overhead camshafts per cylinder bank
Bore and stroke: 3.55 in. x 3.54 in.
Displacement: 4.6 liters
Compression ratio: 9.9:1
Induction system: Fuel injection
Maximum power: 305 bhp at 5,800 rpm
Maximum torque: 300 lb-ft at 4,800 rpm

TRANSMISSION

Borg-Warner T-4S five-speed manual

BODY/CHASSIS

Aluminum space frame with two-door roadster body

SPECIAL FEATURES

Small 'cycle-wing' fenders turn with the front wheels to prevent debris from being thrown over the car and driver.

Extensive use of aluminum results in a very light, but strong, frame.

RUNNING GEAR

Steering: Power rack-and-pinion
Front suspension: Unequal length wishbones, with coil spring/shock units, and anti-roll bar
Rear suspension: Unequal length wishbones with coil/spring shock units, and anti-roll bar
Brakes: Vented disc brakes all around
Wheels: Aluminum, 18-in. dia.
Tires: 245/40 ZR18 (front), 295/35 ZR18 (rear)

DIMENSIONS

Length: 155 in.   **Width:** 76.5 in.
Height: 47 in.   **Wheelbase:** 104.5 in.
Track: 65 in. (front), 64.2 in. (rear)
Weight: 2,459 lbs.

Plymouth **BARRACUDA**

The Barracuda was the result of Chrysler's determination not to be left out of the 'pony car' market. Plymouth took an existing compact platform from the Valiant, added unique bodywork and options and there it was—Chrysler's very own version of the Mustang.

"...exhilarating experience."

"The 1967 Barracuda was part of the new wave of smaller, more powerful cars that swept across the U.S. during the mid-to-late 1960s. Chrysler followed the trend by providing an exhilarating driving experience, combining compact dimensions with awesome power. The Barracuda has decent handling characteristics. However, with legendary 383 V8 grunt it can be quite a handful when driven at the limit. Nonetheless, it's high on the fun factor."

The Barracuda's large steering wheel dominates the cabin and is typical of the era.

Milestones

1964 The Plymouth Barracuda
is launched on April 1st, two weeks before the Ford Mustang. Though it appears mid-1964, it is branded a 1965 model. It features folding rear seats that are quite novel for the time.

Modified Cudas became a common site on drag strips.

1967 The Barracuda undergoes
its first major restyle, which includes a 2-inch wheelbase extension. Convertible and hardtop coupe models are also introduced.

The Road Runner was Plymouth's full-size muscle car.

1970 Lower, wider and shorter,
the Barracuda begins the new decade with a total redesign. The legendary Hemi engine is now available.

1974 Production of the Barracuda
comes to an end—a victim of the fuel crisis and emissions controls.

UNDER THE SKIN

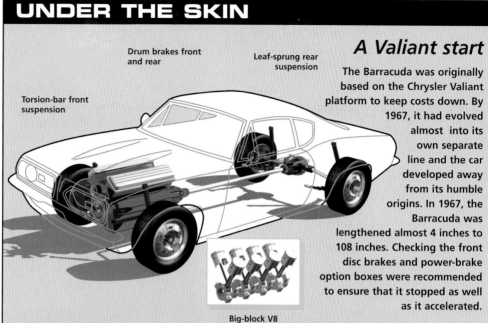

Drum brakes front and rear

Leaf-sprung rear suspension

Torsion-bar front suspension

Big-block V8

THE POWER PACK

A Valiant start

The Barracuda was originally based on the Chrysler Valiant platform to keep costs down. By 1967, it had evolved almost into its own separate line and the car developed away from its humble origins. In 1967, the Barracuda was lengthened almost 4 inches to 108 inches. Checking the front disc brakes and power-brake option boxes were recommended to ensure that it stopped as well as it accelerated.

Solid performance

The big-block, 383-cubic inch engine dates back to 1960, when the Golden Commando unit, complete with 'Ram Induction' was created for the Fury/Sport Suburban models. It is a simple design with a cast-iron block and cylinder heads. Hemi-engined Plymouths may have offered the ultimate in power output, but with Carter four-barrel carburetors, the 383-equipped Barracuda pumps out 280 bhp and an impressive 400 lb-ft of torque at 2,400 rpm. The 383 is a very flexible motor and can be easily tuned or modified with components from other Chrysler engines.

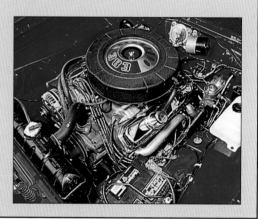

Formula S

Starting in 1968, Barracudas were available with a performance option package called 'Formula S.' These cars were available with a four-speed manual transmission, dual exhaust, anti-roll bars, wider tires and, of course, Formula S badging.

The stylish lines of the Barracuda are some of the finest seen on a Plymouth.

Plymouth **BARRACUDA**

The Barracuda, along with the Mustang, is in many ways the quintessential pony car. It offered the buyer a practical car that could be driven every day, yet had awesome performance potential—especially with the 383 engine.

Engine options

In 1967, buyers could choose either the base 145-bhp, 225-cubic inch slant-six engine or the 273- or 383-cubic inch V8. The following year, Plymouth offered another V8, the 340-cubic inch, to fill the gap between the earlier engines.

Transmission choices

Barracudas may have come as standard with a three-speed manual, but the options list also included a four-speed manual, as well as a TorqueFlite three-speed automatic transmission.

Restyled rear window

Although the first-generation Barracuda sported a distinctive wraparound rear window, the styling cue could not entirely disguise its Valiant origins. New bodystyles for 1967 included a convertible and a hardtop.

Stretched chassis

For 1967, the Barracuda's wheelbase was stretched by 2 inches and the car grew by about 4 inches overall. It still remained in proportion, however, and the motoring press universally applauded its modest, yet distinctive, good looks.

Sporty options

Buyers could specify a range of options to give the car a sporty feel, from cosmetic items—such as bucket seats, consoles and stripes—to real performance hardware—like a Sure-Grip differential or the 383 V8 engine.

Specifications

1967 Plymouth Barracuda

ENGINE

Type: V8

Construction: Cast-iron block and heads

Valve gear: Two valves per cylinder operated by a single camshaft

Bore and stroke: 4.25 in. x 3.38 in.

Displacement: 383 c.i.

Compression ratio: 10.0:1

Induction system: Carter four-barrel carburetor

Maximum power: 280 bhp at 4,200 rpm

Maximum torque: 400 lb-ft at 2,400 rpm

Top speed: 120 mph

0-60 mph: 7.0 sec.

TRANSMISSION

Three-speed manual/four-speed manual or three-speed auto

BODY/CHASSIS

Unitary construction with steel body panels

SPECIAL FEATURES

The rear seats fold down to create cavernous luggage space.

The race inspired style of the fuel-filler cap is unique to the Barracuda.

RUNNING GEAR

Steering: Worm-and-roller

Front suspension: A-arms with torsion bars and telescopic shock absorbers

Rear suspension: Live axle with semi-elliptic leaf springs and telescopic shock absorbers

Brakes: Drums (front and rear)

Wheels: Steel, 14-in. dia.

Tires: Firestone wide ovals, D70 x 14

DIMENSIONS

Length: 192.8 in.   **Width:** 69.6 in.

Height: 52.7 in.   **Wheelbase:** 108.0 in.

Track: 57.4 in. (front), 55.6 in. (rear)

Weight: 2,940 lbs.

Plymouth ROAD RUNNER

By the late 1960s, many muscle cars were beyond the financial reach of their would-be buyers. To corner this segment of the market, Plymouth offered the Road Runner. It was a no-frills coupe with a 383 V8 engine as standard power. The result proved to be an instant sales success and owners were well respected on the street.

"...back to the basics."

"Getting back to the basics is what the Road Runner is all about. It is all business, from the steel wheels to the rubber floormats. The 383 is a strong engine and thrives at low rpm. With the four-speed shifter in your right hand and your foot on the gas, its acceleration is unreal. Because it was a bare-bones muscle car its weight was kept as low as possible for an even better power-to-weight ratio. With 335 bhp, this was a car that really lived up to its name."

The 1968 model is the Road Runner in its purest form with a no-frills interior.

Milestones

1968 With a growing number of enthusiasts wanting a no-frills factory hot rod, Plymouth decides to take the plunge and offer the Road Runner—a two-door coupe with a standard 383-cubic inch V8. Chrysler pays Warner Bros. $50,000 to use the Road Runner name. Projected sales are 2,500, but in the end, 44,589 are sold.

The Super Bee was Dodge Division's equivalent to the Road Runner.

1969 The Road Runner goes upmarket. A convertible model is added to the range. Mid-year, a new 440-cubic inch Six-Barrel joins the 383 and 426 Hemi engine options.

The sporty Road Runner was extensively revamped for 1971.

1970 A new loop-type grill and revised taillights mark the 1970 edition. Fifteen inch Rallye wheels are now a popular option.

UNDER THE SKIN

Unitary body and chassis

Four-wheel drum brakes

Torsion-bar front suspension

Big-block V8

Belvedere based

Essentially a two-door Belvedere fitted with a huge engine, the Road Runner follows Chrysler engineering practice for the period, with a unitary body/chassis and a separate front subframe. Double A-arm suspension is carried up front, sprung by torsion bars, while the live axle at the rear rides on semi-elliptic leaf springs. Standard rear gearing is 3.23:1, although higher ratios were available.

THE POWER PACK

Big block brawler

While other muscle cars relied on increasingly complex engines for propulsion, Plymouth decided that simplicity was essential to the Road Runner. For maximum effect and in order to keep costs down, the division decided to install the 383-cubic inch big-block as the standard engine. This cast-iron V8 had been in production since the 1950s, but for the Road Runner it received some upgrades. The heads, exhaust manifolds, camshaft, heavy-duty valve springs, and crankshaft windage tray are all from the 440. With a four-barrel carburetor and a low-restriction air cleaner, it makes 335 bhp at 5,200 rpm.

Hemi first

The first-generation Road Runner is an undisputed muscle car classic, and the first-year (1968) model is its purest form. Collectors prefer the 426 Hemi-engined cars. They can easily run 13-second ¼-mile ETs, but only 1,019 were built.

Steel wheels were standard on 1968 Road Runners.

269

Plymouth ROAD RUNNER

The Road Runner was so successful that it inspired rival manufacturers to offer budget muscle cars of their own. Anyone who drove a Road Runner was soon mesmerized by its incredible performance.

Torsion-bar front suspension

A typical 1960s Chrysler feature is a torsion-bar front suspension. Twin longitudinal bars provide springing for the front wishbones and give a smoother ride than coil setups. Road Runners have bigger front bars in an attempt to improve handling.

Big-block V8

Inexpensive to build, yet with a few simple tweaks mightily effective, the 383 V8 was the ideal engine for Plymouth's budget muscle-car. Packing 335 bhp and a monster 425 lb-ft of torque, even in stock trim it was a street terror.

Drum brakes

Most muscle cars are about going fast in a straight line and little else. Stopping the Road Runner could be quite entertaining, with the standard four-wheel drums, so ordering front discs was a wise option.

Hardtop styling

When introduced, the Road Runner was only available in one body-style—a pillared coupe. A hardtop version appeared mid year and a convertible was introduced in 1969.

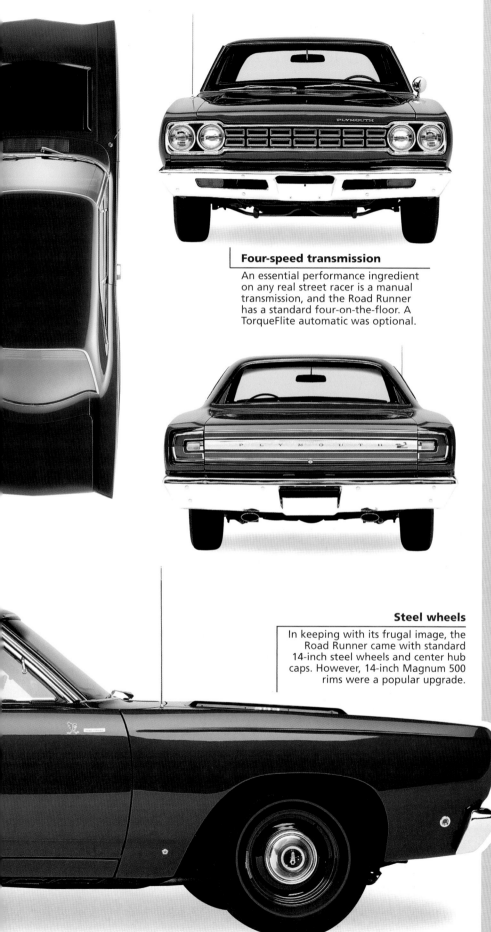

Specifications

1968 Plymouth Road Runner

ENGINE

Type: V8

Construction: Cast-iron block and heads

Valve gear: Two valves per cylinder operated by a single camshaft

Bore and stroke: 4.25 in. x 3.38 in.

Displacement: 383 c.i.

Compression ratio: 10.0:1

Induction system: Carter AFB four-barrel downdraft carburetor

Maximum power: 335 bhp at 5,200 rpm

Maximum torque: 425 lb-ft at 3,400 rpm

Top speed: 130 mph

0-60 mph: 6.7 sec.

TRANSMISSION

Four-speed manual

BODY/CHASSIS

Unitary steel construction with stamped steel body panels

SPECIAL FEATURES

To extract the most power out of the engine, Road Runners were equipped with standard dual exhaust.

The flat black hood center gave this potent Plymouth a very aggressive look.

RUNNING GEAR

Steering: Recirculating-ball

Front suspension: Unequal-length A-arms with torsion bars, telescopic shock absorbers and anti-roll bar

Rear suspension: Live axle with semi-elliptic leaf springs and telescopic shock absorbers

Brakes: Drums (front and rear)

Wheels: Pressed steel, 14-in. dia.

Tires: F70-14

DIMENSIONS

Length: 202.7 in.   **Width:** 81.7 in.

Height: 56.3 in.   **Wheelbase:** 116.0 in.

Track: 59.5 in. (front and rear).

Weight: 3,400 lbs.

Four-speed transmission

An essential performance ingredient on any real street racer is a manual transmission, and the Road Runner has a standard four-on-the-floor. A TorqueFlite automatic was optional.

Steel wheels

In keeping with its frugal image, the Road Runner came with standard 14-inch steel wheels and center hub caps. However, 14-inch Magnum 500 rims were a popular upgrade.

Pontiac CHIEFTAIN

In the immediate post-war years, buyers were hungry for new cars. The straight-eight Chieftain helped GM's sole surviving companion marque achieve more than 300,000 sales during the 1949 model year.

"...smooth riding cruiser."

"With only 104 bhp from its straight-eight and weighing over 3,500 lbs., the Chieftain is definitely not a sports car. What it is, though, is a smooth-riding cruiser. Soft spring settings help smooth out the bumps without causing wallowing under normal driving conditions. Attempting high-speed cornering results in extreme body lean and the narrow tires squeal under the weight. For relaxing summer drives, this Poncho is hard to beat."

Column-mounted shifters were almost universal in most cars by 1949.

Milestones

1949 Replacing the Torpedo

line is the Chieftain. Beneath the new styling is the venerable straight-six or eight and 'Knee-Action' front suspension. Front fenders are now integrated with the body.

Only a mild facelift was made for its sophomore year in 1950.

1950 The Chieftain line is

expanded with the addition of a Super Deluxe Catalina two-door hardtop. The straight-eight's displacement is enlarged to 268.4 cubic inches and power is up to 108 bhp.

The 1953 Pontiac is longer and now has power steering.

1952 The Business Sedan and Coupes

are dropped. Korean war restrictions and a steel strike limit Pontiac's output to 271,000 units.

1953 One piece windshields

and power steering are fitted.

UNDER THE SKIN

120-inch wheelbase, separate steel chassis

Four-wheel drum brakes

Coil-sprung front suspension

Straight-eight

Cautious update

For 1949 Pontiac revised its long-running separate chassis by adding an 'X'-braced box section, enabling a lower body line. GM's Knee Action independent ball joint front suspension with coil springs was standard, while at the rear was a live axle with semi-elliptic leaf springs. Drum brakes were fitted both front and rear. Although a three-speed transmission was standard, a Hydramatic automatic was optional.

THE POWER PACK

Veteran eight

Designed by Benjamin Anibal, Pontiac's straight-eight engine made its debut in 1933. By 1949 it was still powering Pontiacs, though by this stage it had been enlarged to 248.9 cubic inches. An all-cast-iron design, it was typical of L-head engines with side-valve lay-out that resulted in offset combustion chambers. The use of a long-stroke crankshaft produced 188 lb-ft of torque at 2,000 rpm. The basic engine remained in production until 1954, by which time it had 127 bhp.

6.5:1 compression ratio

Single Carter two-barrel carburetor

Cast-iron block and cylinder head

Five main bearing crankshaft

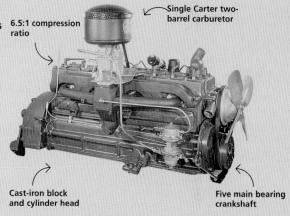

Deluxe

For 1949 all Pontiacs got a single A-body chassis and were both longer and lower. The most expensive of all was the Deluxe Chieftain Eight convertible. The basic design continued through 1954. Today, good examples sell for serious money.

A pristine Deluxe convertible is worth up to $30,000 today.

Pontiac CHIEFTAIN

It took until 1949 before Pontiac offered its first new post-war cars. Longer, lower and wider than pre-war models, with cleaner, more integrated styling, they were also offered with more luxury features.

Side-valve, in-line eight

Although rival Oldsmobile® got a V8 for 1949, Pontiac stuck with its tried and tested L-head six and eight engines. Steady improvement, however, saw the power increase every year during the early 1950s as the horsepower race intensified. In 1949, it put out 104/106 bhp, but by 1954 it was up to 127.

Whitewall tires

Classy whitewall tires became increasingly popular on medium-priced cars during the 1940s. In 1952, due to the conflict in Korea, supplies of whitewalls were restricted along with supplies of copper, used on bumpers and chrome trim.

Power convertible top

Deluxe Chieftain convertibles came with a mohair-lined, power-operated top and a small glass rear window. Plexiglas windows did not become popular until the late 1950s.

Sealed beam headlights

GM had pioneered sealed beam lights in the late 1930s and these were still standard for 1949. Three years later, the famous Autotronic Eye arrived. This system dimmed the headlights automatically at oncoming traffic.

Drum brakes

Drum brakes were the industry standard in 1949. The Chieftain's were hydraulically operated and could stop the car in just over over 200 feet from 60 mph—more than adequate by contemporary standards.

Specifications

1950 Pontiac Chieftain

ENGINE

Type: In-line eight-cylinder

Construction: Cast-iron block and head

Valve gear: Two side-mounted valves per cylinder driven by a single, block-mounted camshaft with solid lifters

Bore and stroke: 3.25 in. x 3.75 in.

Displacement: 248.9 c.i.

Compression ratio: 6.5:1

Induction system: Single Carter WCD two-barrel carburetor

Maximum power: 104 bhp at 3,800 rpm

Maximum torque: 188 lb-ft at 2,000 rpm

Top speed: 86 mph

0-60 mph: 19.0 sec.

TRANSMISSION

Four-speed Hydramatic automatic

BODY/CHASSIS

Separate steel chassis with two-door convertible body

SPECIAL FEATURES

The Pontiac Indian Chief hood ornament illuminates when the headlights come on.

Rear fender skirts were dealer-installed options in 1949.

RUNNING GEAR

Steering: Worm-and-sector

Front suspension: Double wishbones with coil springs and telescopic shock absorbers

Rear suspension: Live axle with semi-elliptic leaf springs and telescopic shock absorbers

Brakes: Drums (front and rear)

Wheels: Stamped steel, 15-in. dia.

Tires: 7.10 x 15

DIMENSIONS

Length: 202.5 in. **Width:** 75.8 in.

Height: 63.3 in. **Wheelbase:** 120.0 in.

Track: 58.0 in. (front), 59.0 in. (rear)

Weight: 3,670 lbs.

Pontiac GTO

Taking a huge engine and putting it into a smaller vehicle was the concept behind the GTO. Pontiac's original muscle car grew larger for 1966 but retained the essential performance ingredients that made it a winner from day one.

"...few cars are cooler."

"Even today, there are few cars as cool as the 1966 GTO. The front bucket seats may be lacking support by today's standards, but the dash is a delight and the interior tastefully restrained. Once on the road, acceleration is tremendous, and the four-speed shifter is well mated to the 389 V8. However, on damp surfaces wheelspin is almost unavoidable if you're heavy on the gas pedal. The GTO is no corner-carver and tends to oversteer if you don't take care."

A two-spoke steering wheel is standard, although a three-spoke one was available.

Milestones

1964 A new, larger and more conventional
Tempest® line arrives. The biggest news is the debut of the GTO (Gran Turismo Omologato), with a standard 389-cubic inch V8 and sporty touches. 32,450 GTOs are sold in the first year.

The GTO got a crisp restyle for 1965, that included vertical headlights.

1966 The GTO gets a larger, curvier
body, but the basic style and performance remain the same. By this stage muscle car competition is getting tougher. However, the GTO sets an all-time muscle car production record with 96,946 cars built.

In 1969 Pontiac releases The Judge™ option to strike more interest in perspective buyers.

1967 Pontiac turns its attention to
improving the car. The grill and taillights are altered, and the V8 is bored out to 400 cubic inches.

UNDER THE SKIN

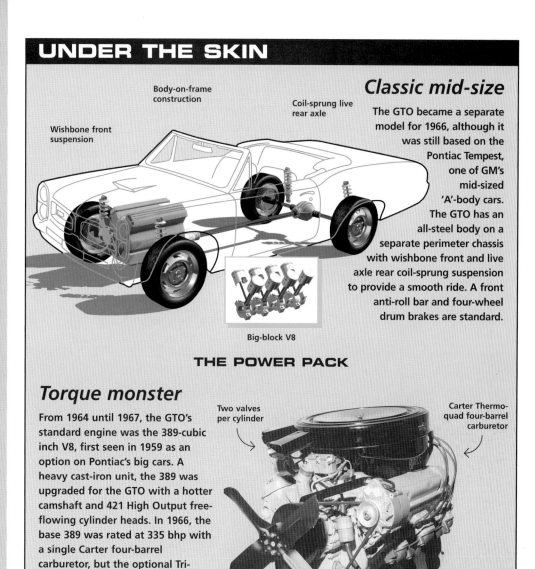

Body-on-frame construction

Wishbone front suspension

Coil-sprung live rear axle

Classic mid-size

The GTO became a separate model for 1966, although it was still based on the Pontiac Tempest, one of GM's mid-sized 'A'-body cars. The GTO has an all-steel body on a separate perimeter chassis with wishbone front and live axle rear coil-sprung suspension to provide a smooth ride. A front anti-roll bar and four-wheel drum brakes are standard.

Big-block V8

THE POWER PACK

Torque monster

From 1964 until 1967, the GTO's standard engine was the 389-cubic inch V8, first seen in 1959 as an option on Pontiac's big cars. A heavy cast-iron unit, the 389 was upgraded for the GTO with a hotter camshaft and 421 High Output free-flowing cylinder heads. In 1966, the base 389 was rated at 335 bhp with a single Carter four-barrel carburetor, but the optional Tri-Power set up with three two-barrel carburetors was rated at 360 bhp. However, mid-year GM outlawed multi-carb set ups.

Two valves per cylinder

Carter Thermo-quad four-barrel carburetor

Seven main-bearing crankshaft

Cast-iron block and cylinder heads

Loaded Goat

Among muscle car aficionados, the 1966 GTO ranks as an all-time great. Desirable options include Rally I wheels, a four-speed transmission and Tri-Power carb set-up. Add these to a convertible body and you've got one fantastic summer cruiser.

The 1966 GTO is one of the most desirable muscle cars of all time.

Pontiac **GTO**

Pontiac set an all-time production record with the 1966 GTO, thanks to the car's combination of outstanding performance, eye-catching looks and attractive pricing.

Ram Air kit

The standard hood scoop was purely for decoration, but a dealer-installed Ram Air kit was also available. Quoted horsepower remained unchanged, but fresh air induction would probably add a few additional bhp.

Big-block V8

In 1966, the GTO could be ordered with the 389-cubic inch engine in two different states of tune. This car is one of 19,045 ordered with the optional Tri-Power set up, which boosted power output to 360 bhp.

Power convertible top

The GTO, if ordered in convertible form, was available with a power top.

Coil-sprung suspension

Like the other General Motors 'A'-body intermediates of the time, the GTO has coil springs front and rear. This results in a much smoother ride than rival Ford and Chrysler muscle cars.

Four-speed transmission

In order to extract maximum performance from the big-block V8, a four-speed manual was the hot ticket, although a TurboHydramatic automatic was offered.

Promotional license plate

GTOs quickly became known on the streets and at the race tracks for their unbelievable performance. One of Pontiac's campaign slogans compared the car's power with that of a tiger, hence the 'growling' license plate.

Restyled body

Still Tempest-based, the GTO grew dimensionally larger for 1966 with a longer body and more flowing lines. It was offered in pillared coupe, hardtop and convertible forms. The hardtop was by far the most popular model.

Fluted taillights

Although base model Tempests and Le Mans have simple rear lights, the GTO has a unique tail end treatment with fluted taillight lenses. These are unique to this model year, as the rear end was revised for 1967.

Optional axle gearing

Since the GTO was after all a muscle car it had to have considerable torque to get it out ahead of the competition. Naturally, Pontiac offered it with a variety of rear axle ratios ranging from econo-wise 3.08:1 gears to the tire-frying 4.33:1s.

1966 Pontiac GTO

ENGINE

Type: V8

Construction: Cast-iron block and heads

Valve gear: Two valves per cylinder operated by a single camshaft with pushrods and rockers

Bore and stroke: 4.06 in. x 3.75 in.

Displacement: 389 c.i.

Compression ratio: 10.75:1

Induction system: Three Rochester two-barrel carburetors

Maximum power: 360 bhp at 5,200 rpm

Maximum torque: 424 lb-ft at 3,600 rpm

Top speed: 125 mph

0-60 mph: 6.2 sec.

TRANSMISSION

Muncie M21 four-speed manual

BODY/CHASSIS

Steel perimeter chassis with separate steel convertible two-door body

SPECIAL FEATURES

1966 was the last year for Tri-Power carburetion on all GM mid-size cars.

Its sinister look is attributed to the vertical headlights and split front grill.

RUNNING GEAR

Steering: Recirculating ball

Front suspension: Unequal length wishbones with coil springs, telescopic shock absorbers and anti-roll bar

Rear suspension: Live axle with coil springs and lower control arms

Brakes: Drums (front and rear)

Wheels: Steel Rally I, 14-in. dia.

Tires: Uniroyal 155/F70 14

DIMENSIONS

Length: 199.0 in. **Width:** 79.8 in.

Height: 54.8 in. **Wheelbase:** 116.0 in.

Track: 53.8 in. (front), 50.1 in. (rear)

Weight: 3,555 lbs.

Pontiac **TORPEDO EIGHT**

Before World War II, Pontiac was fighting to beat Buick in the intermediately-priced car market. In 1940 the company had a new weapon, the Torpedo, and because of its huge success rate, it was built through 1948.

"...beautifully relaxed."

"Don't underestimate the attractions and abilities of a big, sidevalve, 4.1-liter, straight eight. It revs almost silently, producing 190 lb-ft of torque at a very low rpm that wafts along the massive Custom Torpedo in a beautifully relaxed way. Its weight guarantees an incredibly smooth ride, there's hardly any roll through corners, and the handling characteristics are nearly neutral. The interior and dashboard have typical 1940s styling.

Hand-crafted embellishments give the Pontiac's interior real charm.

Milestones

1940 Pontiac introduces

a new name into its lineup, the Torpedo or the Series 29. It is only built as a four-door sedan or two-door coupe. Both bodies are new and built on a longer chassis. The L-head, straight-eight engine has its compression ratio increased to 6.5:1.

The 1934 Pontiac 8 was advanced in using coil-spring suspension.

1941 The Torpedo range

is extended with a wide range of bodies, including a convertible and a six-window, four-door sedan. There is also a sleek fastback body style for the Streamliner Torpedo.

Pontiacs, such as this Chieftain, used straight eights until 1955.

1946 Post-war production

continues with basically the same models as before the war, until more modern styling is introduced in 1949. For 1950, the L-head is stretched and continues until Pontiac's V8 appears for 1955.

UNDER THE SKIN

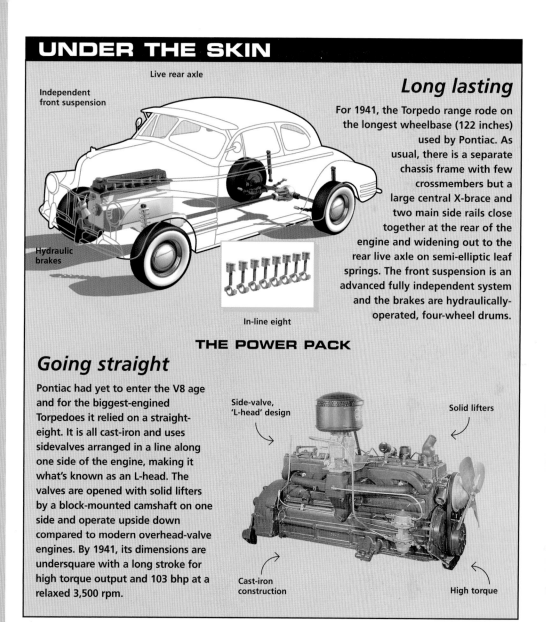

Live rear axle

Independent front suspension

Hydraulic brakes

In-line eight

Long lasting

For 1941, the Torpedo range rode on the longest wheelbase (122 inches) used by Pontiac. As usual, there is a separate chassis frame with few crossmembers but a large central X-brace and two main side rails close together at the rear of the engine and widening out to the rear live axle on semi-elliptic leaf springs. The front suspension is an advanced fully independent system and the brakes are hydraulically-operated, four-wheel drums.

THE POWER PACK

Going straight

Pontiac had yet to enter the V8 age and for the biggest-engined Torpedoes it relied on a straight-eight. It is all cast-iron and uses sidevalves arranged in a line along one side of the engine, making it what's known as an L-head. The valves are opened with solid lifters by a block-mounted camshaft on one side and operate upside down compared to modern overhead-valve engines. By 1941, its dimensions are undersquare with a long stroke for high torque output and 103 bhp at a relaxed 3,500 rpm.

Side-valve, 'L-head' design

Solid lifters

Cast-iron construction

High torque

Super soft top

The most desirable of all the Torpedoes is the two-door convertible. But it's worth considering either of the two coupes in the range, the two-door Business Coupe or two-door Sports Coupe, even if their performance is slightly less impressive.

The Sports Coupe has conservatively sophisticated styling.

Pontiac TORPEDO EIGHT

The Custom Torpedo might lack the dramatic flowing lines of the fastback Streamliner Torpedoes but it still showed the way of things to come in body design, marking an end to separate headlights.

In-line eight-cylinder

Sidevalve engines seem very old-fashioned now, particularly in-line, eight-cylinder units, but they did have their advantages. At moderate engine speeds they run very smoothly and with a long stroke produce large amounts of torque.

Sealed beam headlights

In 1940, General Motors pioneered the sealed beam-type headlight in which the glass, reflector and bulb came as one unit and were replaced together instead of changing a separate bulb. They were regarded as a great advancement giving more light than standard headlights during the 1940s.

Integrated headlights

It was only a few years before the Torpedo that Pontiac had separate headlights mounted on the fenders, so the evolution of faired-in headlights built right into the fenders came very quickly.

Separate chassis

The chassis is of the perimeter type with two main outer box-section sidemembers and a central X-brace. The body is held on to the chassis by rubber mounts.

Rectangular grill

The switch to an almost rectangular radiator grill for 1941 was a sign of things to come as the old-fashioned upright grills gave way to lower, wider ones through the 1950s and 1960s.

Live rear axle

Like virtually all contemporary American cars the Torpedo uses a live rear axle. Pontiac gave it a name—'Duflex'—and promoted its telescopic shocks that reduced sway.

Specifications

1941 Pontiac Torpedo Eight

ENGINE

Type: In-line eight-cylinder

Construction: Cast-iron block and head

Valve gear: Two in-line side valves per cylinder operated by a single block-mounted camshaft

Bore and stroke: 3.25 in. x 3.75 in.

Displacement: 249 c.i.

Compression ratio: 6.5:1

Induction system: Single, twin-choke, Carter carburetor

Maximum power: 103 bhp at 3,500 rpm

Maximum torque: 190 lb-ft at 2,000 rpm

Top speed: 88 mph

0-60 mph: 18.9 sec

TRANSMISSION

Three-speed manual

BODY/CHASSIS

Separate box-section steel chassis frame with central X-brace and steel two-door coupe body

SPECIAL FEATURES

Pontiac's distinctive Indian's head mascot adorns the hood of this Torpedo.

Some critics termed the rectangular radiator grill the 'tombstone' grill.

RUNNING GEAR

Steering: Worm-and-sector

Front suspension: Double wishbones with coil springs and telescopic shocks

Rear suspension: Live axle with semi-elliptic leaf springs and telescopic shock absorbers

Brakes: Hydraulically-operated drums

Wheels: Pressed steel disc, 16-in. dia.

Tires: 6.0 x 16

DIMENSIONS

Length: 201.0 in   **Width:** 64.5 in.

Height: 65.0 in.   **Wheelbase:** 122.0 in.

Track: 58.0 in. (front), 61.5 in. (rear)

Weight: 3,325 lbs.

Pontiac TRANS AM SD455

By 1974, only GM could offer anything even vaguely approaching the performance machines of the late 1960s and early 1970s, with the Chevrolet Corvette and the more powerful Pontiac Trans Am SD-455.

"...raucous take-offs."

"The 1974 Trans Am was strictly 'old school' American muscle in the performance and handling departments. Like its predecessors a decade earlier, it was great in a straight line. The massive 455-cubic inch engine plays a part in the car's front-heavy handling, although it gives fantastic midrange acceleration. Standard disc brakes up front and a limited-slip differential for raucous take-offs are major plus points."

There is a comfortable feel to the interior, which is unmistakably 1970s.

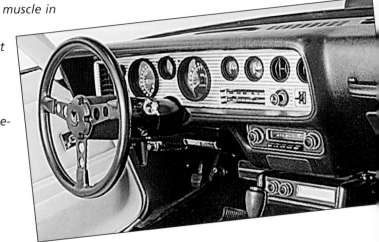

Milestones

1967 Pontiac introduces the Firebird, it shares its basic shell with the Chevrolet Camaro, which debuted a few months earlier. Both are aimed at the 'pony market' created by the Mustang.

Chevrolet dropped the Camaro in 1975, leaving the Trans Am as GM's only muscle car.

1969 The Trans Am is offered for the first time in the Firebird lineup as the top-of-the-line performance Firebird. Standard was the Ram Air III, 335 bhp 400 HO engine.

The Trans Am had a bold redesign for 1979.

1974 First major body and engineering restyle for the Firebird/Trans Am series.

1976 Last year of the Pontiac 455-c.i. engine, only available in the Trans Am as a limited edition.

UNDER THE SKIN

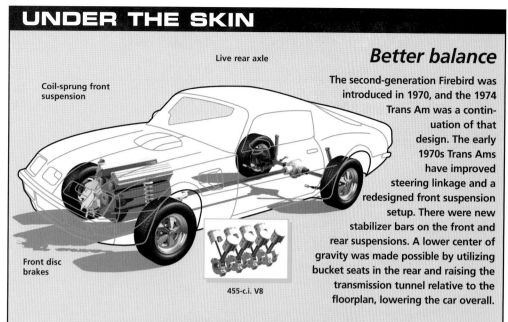

Live rear axle

Coil-sprung front suspension

Front disc brakes

455-c.i. V8

Better balance

The second-generation Firebird was introduced in 1970, and the 1974 Trans Am was a continuation of that design. The early 1970s Trans Ams have improved steering linkage and a redesigned front suspension setup. There were new stabilizer bars on the front and rear suspensions. A lower center of gravity was made possible by utilizing bucket seats in the rear and raising the transmission tunnel relative to the floorplan, lowering the car overall.

THE POWER PACK

Super-Duty punch

Pontiac's Super Duty 455 was the last bastion of big-cube power for the performance enthusiast. With a compression ratio of 8.4:1, output was down as the first of the mandatory emissions controls began to sap power. Nonetheless, the engine still sported all the performance features of the soon-to-be-gone muscle car era. This includes a lot of displacement, four-bolt mains, forged-aluminum pistons and an 800-cfm Quadrajet carb. There was even built-in provision for dry-sump lubrication. Earlier 1974 cars make use of the Ram IV camshaft and are capable of 310 bhp; later 1974 cars do not and are rated at 290 bhp.

Last of its kind

If you wanted a muscle car in 1974, there was only one choice: the Trans Am SD-455. Big-block Camaros had been discontinued and MOPAR, the purveyor of some of the hot muscle car property, had pulled the plug on performance.

For 1974, Pontiac gave the Trans Am new front-end treatment.

Pontiac **TRANS AM SD455**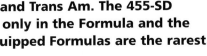

Pontiac Firebirds were offered in four series for 1974: Firebird, Esprit, Formula and Trans Am. The 455-SD engine could be ordered only in the Formula and the Trans Am. Super-Duty equipped Formulas are the rarest.

Special dash

Trans Ams featured a special steering wheel, a faux metal dash and a rally gauge cluster, which included a clock and dash-mounted tachometer. As a sign of the times, a new 'fuel economy' gauge was introduced later in the year.

LSD

Standard on the Trans Am was a limited-slip differential, ensuring minimal wheelspin and consistent launches.

New tires

For 1974, all General Motors cars had to use steel-belted radials. Hence, the old Firestone Wide-Oval F60-15 bias-belted tires were replaced with new Firestone 500 F60 x 15 steel-belted radials.

'Soft' bumpers

New for 1974 was a soft bumper treatment front and rear, utilizing molded urethane foam. These were faced with black rubber front bars to absorb parking bumps.

Scoops galore

Pontiac made sure that the Trans Am looked aggressive and powerful with flared wheel arches and front fender air extractors. The menacing-looking, rear-facing Shaker hood scoop finishes off the whole effect with SD-455 decals on the side.

Restyled rear end

The rear-end treatment includes a full-width rear spoiler. Taillights are wider, in a horizontal casing, giving a more integrated appearance.

Specifications
1974 Trans Am SD455

ENGINE
Type: V8

Construction: Cast-iron cylinder block and cylinder head

Valve gear: Two valves per cylinder

Bore and stroke: 4.15 in. x 4.21 in.

Displacement: 455 c.i.

Compression ratio: 8.4:1

Induction system: 800-cfm Quadrajet four-barrel carburetor

Maximum power: 310 bhp at 4,000 rpm

Maximum torque: 390 lb-ft at 3,600 rpm

Top speed: 132 mph

0-60 mph: 5.4 sec

TRANSMISSION
Three-speed automatic M40 Turbo Hydramatic

BODY/CHASSIS
Steel unibody construction

SPECIAL FEATURES

The SD-455 logos are seen only on Trans Ams and Formulas.

A holographic applique on the dash perfectly reflects mid-1970s style.

RUNNING GEAR
Steering: Variable-ratio, ball-nut

Front suspension: A-arms with coil springs and telescopic shock absorbers

Rear suspension: Live rear axle with leaf springs and telescopic shock absorbers

Brakes: Discs (front), drums (rear)

Wheels: Steel, 15-in. Rally II

Tires: F60 x 15 (raised white letters) Firestone steel belted

DIMENSIONS
Length: 196.0 in.   **Width:** 73.4 in.

Height: 50.4 in.   **Wheelbase:** 108.0 in.

Track: 61.6 in. (front), 60.3 in. (rear)

Weight: 3,655 lbs.

Shelby **MUSTANG GT500**

Softer, roomier and more practical than the original stark GT350, the GT500 still boasted masses of brute strength with over 350 bhp and a gigantic 420 lb-ft of torque from its 428-cubic inch V8.

"...so much power and torque."

"With so much power and torque available, anyone can get stunning performance from the GT500, particularly with the automatic. There are two surprises in store: You expect it to be faster than a 15.6-second quarter mile suggests, but you don't expect it to handle as well as it does. Despite the huge engine making it front heavy, the power steering makes sure the GT500 goes where you want it to. The ride isn't bad for a late-'60s muscle car and the engine isn't very temperamental, although it does throw out an awful lot of heat, making the air conditioning option a must."

The dashboard has a special 140-mph speedometer and 8,000-rpm tachometer as well as plenty of extra gauges.

1965 First Shelby GT350s appear as 1966 models, but sell slowly.

1966 Efforts to make it more of a street car lead to the specifications being toned down: The exhaust is quieter, the limited slip differential is an option and Koni shocks are left off.

1968 was the first year you could get a GT500 convertible.

1967 The last year before Ford takes over building the Shelby Mustang. The GT350 is restyled and the bigger engined GT500 is introduced.

1968 GT500 is joined by the GT500KR (King of the Road). It has a 428-cubic inch engine—the Cobra Jet rather than the Police unit.

Ford's own Mach 1 Mustang killed off the GT500.

1969 Whole Mustang range is restyled, including the GT500 to the big, flatter looking Mach 1 style.

UNDER THE SKIN

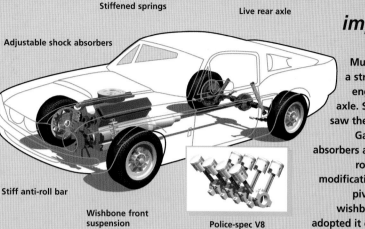

Stiffened springs

Live rear axle

Adjustable shock absorbers

Stiff anti-roll bar

Wishbone front suspension

Police-spec V8

Suspension improvements

Like all performance Mustangs, the GT500 had a straightforward front V8 engine driving a live rear axle. Shelby's improvements saw the springs stiffened and Gabriel adjustable shock absorbers added, and a stiff anti-roll bar at the front. The modification which lowered the pivot for the front upper wishbone was so good Ford adopted it on the stock Mustang.

THE POWER PACK

Simply big

Don't confuse the 428-cubic inch unit installed in the GT500 with the fierce 427 engine in Shelby's Cobras. The 428 has a different bore and stroke and, although it shares the same all-iron pushrod V8 layout, it is a less sophisticated design, and less powerful. It was designed for lower engine speeds and for long sustained use, often in the police chase cars in which it was used. Later the police-spec unit was replaced with the Cobra Jet version which was rated with an extra five bhp but no increase in torque.

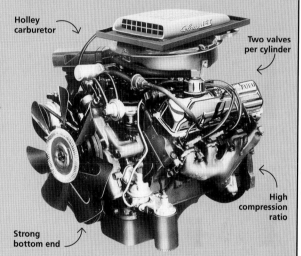

Holley carburetor

Two valves per cylinder

High compression ratio

Strong bottom end

Early or open?

Although the GT500 continued until the 1970 model year, by that stage there was very little to set it apart from the rest of the Mustang range. So if you're after one of the big-engined Shelby Mustangs, it's best to go for an earlier, more subtle car or one of the rare convertibles, which are highly collectible and often faked.

The rarest of the GT500s is the factory convertible.

Shelby **MUSTANG GT500**

If bigger was better, the GT500 was the best of the Shelby Mustang line. There was no way you could have added a bigger engine to the car, and that made sure it was the most powerful of all.

Fiberglass hood

A new fiberglass hood with functional air scoops helps to accommodate the big engine and also reduces the car's weight.

Power steering

With so much weight over the nose and with wide tires, power steering was a very good idea. In fact you had no choice—it was a standard feature, as were the power brakes and shoulder harnesses.

Front heavy

That huge cast-iron V8 naturally made the GT500 front heavy, with a weight distribution of 58 percent front and 42 percent rear. It was just as well that the hood was fiberglass.

V8 engine

With the GT500, Shelby went for the biggest engine he could fit in the bay, the Police Interceptor type 428-cubic inch V8. It filled the engine compartment so fully you couldn't even see the spark plugs.

Wide tires

The GT500 needed to put as much rubber on the road as possible to cope with its power. Shelby opted for Goodyear Speedway E70-15s, a popular choice for muscle cars of the era that were rated at 140 mph.

Alloy wheels

Steel wheels were a standard feature, but these Shelby alloys were available as an option. They are very desirable today.

Adjustable shocks

The standard shocks were thrown out and replaced by Gabriel adjustables. However, the car left the Shelby works with what was considered the optimum settings.

Unique tail lights

The back of the car was distinguished from the standard Mustang fastback by different tail lights, two very wide ones replacing the two sets of triple lights. Above the lights, the trunk lid was another Shelby fiberglass part.

Specifications
1967 Shelby Mustang GT500

ENGINE
Type: V8
Construction: Cast-iron block and heads
Valve gear: Two valves per cylinder operated by single block-mounted camshaft via pushrods, rockers and hydraulic lifters
Bore and stroke: 4.13 in. x 3.98 in.
Displacement: 428 c.i.
Compression ratio: 10.5:1
Induction system: Two Holley four-barrel carburetors
Maximum power: 355 bhp at 5,400 rpm
Maximum torque: 420 lb-ft at 3,200 rpm
Top speed: 132 mph
0-60 mph: 7.0 sec.

TRANSMISSION
Ford Cruise-O-Matic three-speed automatic or four-speed manual

BODY/FRAME
Unitary steel with two-door coupe body

SPECIAL FEATURES

The hood scoops added by Shelby were changed with each model year. They became more prominent after these rather subtle scoops on this 1967 car.

1967 Shelby GT500s were equipped with two extra driving lights but were spread farther apart toward the end of the 1967 model year.

RUNNING GEAR
Steering: Recirculating ball
Front suspension: Double wishbones with adjustable Gabriel shock absorbers and 1-inch dia. anti-roll bar
Rear suspension: Live axle with semi-elliptic leaf springs
Brakes: Discs, 11.3 in. dia. (front), drums, 10 in. dia. (rear)
Wheels: Shelby alloy, 7 in. x 15 in.
Tires: E70-15 (front and rear)

DIMENSIONS
Length: 186.6 in.　**Width:** 70.9 in.
Height: 49 in.　**Wheelbase:** 108 in.
Track: 58 in. (front and rear)
Weight: 3,520 lbs.

Studebaker AVANTI

Looking quite unlike any other American car, the Avanti was an attempt to bolster Studebaker's flagging fortunes. Raymond Loewy's swoopy styling and sports-car feel won many friends.

"...potent road car of its day."

"All Avantis are powerful, and the top versions are among the most potent road cars of their day, with a gutsy V8 engine, suspension tuned for sports-car driving, a low roof line and a long hood stretching out ahead. The ride is hard and the car doesn't roll much because of its anti-roll bars. It's also heavy to drive despite its power-assisted steering. Its overall sensation tells you the Avanti is a special car. After all, it survived for more than three decades with very few changes."

Styling of the Avanti's smart and very functional interior is surprisingly European in design.

Milestones

1962 Studebaker stuns America with its bold new sports coupe, but production is delayed.

1964 The Avanti is dropped after disappointing sales.

Loewy's original Avanti is an all-time design classic.

1965 Two dealers acquire the rights to produce Loewy's design. The Avanti II now uses a Chevrolet engine.

Avanti IIs were hand-built in very small numbers.

1982 The company changes hands, and there are further changes of ownership in 1986 and 1988.

1988 A four-door sedan Avanti is presented, following Raymond Loewy's desire for such a car.

1992 The Avanti finally goes out of production.

UNDER THE SKIN

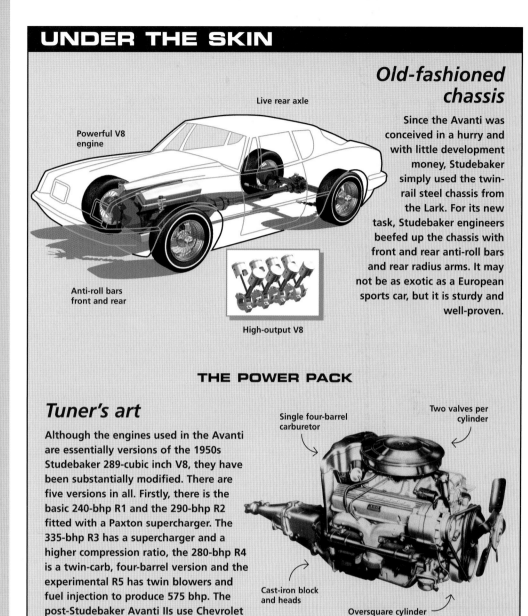

Live rear axle

Powerful V8 engine

Anti-roll bars front and rear

High-output V8

Old-fashioned chassis

Since the Avanti was conceived in a hurry and with little development money, Studebaker simply used the twin-rail steel chassis from the Lark. For its new task, Studebaker engineers beefed up the chassis with front and rear anti-roll bars and rear radius arms. It may not be as exotic as a European sports car, but it is sturdy and well-proven.

THE POWER PACK

Tuner's art

Although the engines used in the Avanti are essentially versions of the 1950s Studebaker 289-cubic inch V8, they have been substantially modified. There are five versions in all. Firstly, there is the basic 240-bhp R1 and the 290-bhp R2 fitted with a Paxton supercharger. The 335-bhp R3 has a supercharger and a higher compression ratio, the 280-bhp R4 is a twin-carb, four-barrel version and the experimental R5 has twin blowers and fuel injection to produce 575 bhp. The post-Studebaker Avanti IIs use Chevrolet engines like the unit shown here.

Single four-barrel carburetor

Two valves per cylinder

Cast-iron block and heads

Oversquare cylinder dimensions

Going strong

Despite its 1960s design and its fluctuating economic fortunes, the Avanti survived well past its sell-by date. Later, post-Studebaker models lacked the crispness of the original design and attempts to modernize its appearance never looked right.

Late Avantis had color-coded bumpers and alloy wheels.

Studebaker **AVANTI**

The Avanti has all the credentials of a hand-built European sports coupe, yet it's 100 percent American made. Nothing else looks like it and, in 1962, very few cars went as fast.

Four-seat interior

Opening up the fiberglass doors reveals an interior which is spacious by the standards of contemporary sports coupes. The rear seats can easily accommodate two adults.

Supercharged V8 engine

Some versions of the Avanti's V8 engine have Paxton superchargers. One experimental version, the R5, has two superchargers and fuel injection, and is claimed to develop 575 bhp and an amazing 196 mph.

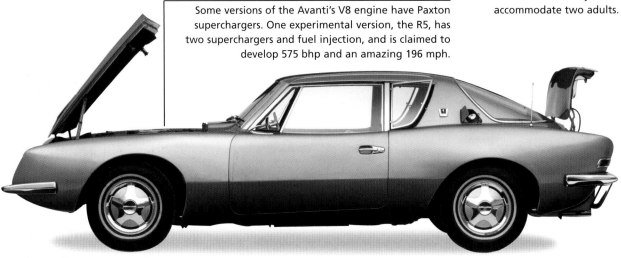

Sturdy chassis

The simple, twin-rail, box-section ladder chassis is a development of Studebaker's standard sedan car chassis, which dates back to 1953.

Antiquated suspension

Although beefed up with anti-roll bars, the suspension belonged to a previous era. The semi-elliptic leaf springs at the rear are typical of conservative American engineering at the time.

Fiberglass bodywork

To minimize time and tooling costs, Studebaker opted for fiberglass bodywork. The Molded Fiberglass Company had quality problems, however, so Studebaker decided to manufacture its own bodyshells after a critical delay.

Front disc brakes

The Avanti was the first American road car to have standard front disc brakes. They are a Dunlop design with servo assistance.

Loewy styling

The fantastic and unusual styling of the Avanti was the responsibility of famous designer Raymond Loewy, who also created another design icon—the Coke bottle.

Specifications

1963 Studebaker Avanti R2

ENGINE

Type: V8

Construction: Cast-iron cylinder block and heads

Valve gear: Two overhead valves per cylinder operated by a single camshaft via pushrods and rockers

Bore and stroke: 3.56 in. x 3.62 in.

Displacement: 289 c.i.

Compression ratio: 10.3:1

Induction system: Single four-barrel carb

Maximum power: 290 bhp at 5,200 rpm

Maximum torque: 330 lb-ft at 3,500 rpm

TRANSMISSION

Four-speed manual or automatic

BODY/CHASSIS

Steel twin-rail box-section ladder chassis with two-door fiberglass coupe body

SPECIAL FEATURES

Highly unusual for an American car of its day, the Avanti has no grill on its nose. The air intake is underneath the front bumper.

To aid cabin ventilation, the Avanti's unusually-shaped rear side windows are hinged at the front edge.

RUNNING GEAR

Steering: Recirculating ball

Front suspension: Wishbones with coil springs, shocks and anti-roll bar

Rear suspension: Live axle with semi-elliptic leaf springs, shocks, upper torque arms and anti-roll bar

Brakes: Discs (front), drums (rear)

Wheels: Steel, 15-in. dia.

Tires: F78 x 15 in.

DIMENSIONS

Length: 192.5 in.   **Width:** 70.4 in.

Height: 53.9 in.   **Wheelbase:** 109 in.

Track: 57.4 in. (front), 56.6 in. (rear)

Weight: 3,405 lbs.

Studebaker **GOLDEN HAWK**

The supercharged, 275-bhp Golden Hawk was an unusually fast car. However, it was so much more expensive than the normally aspirated version that sales were low despite its outstanding performance.

"...extremely stable."

"With the supercharger boosting power and torque, performance is strong. The driving position is excellent and the steering very direct, although without power assistance, it's heavy. At high speeds, the Hawk is extremely stable, and with revised front anti-roll bar and spring rates compensating for the extra weight of the V8 and supercharger, handling is good. Add effective brakes and a smooth ride and the package is near perfect—aside from the price."

The comfortable and functional interior belies the Golden Hawk's performance.

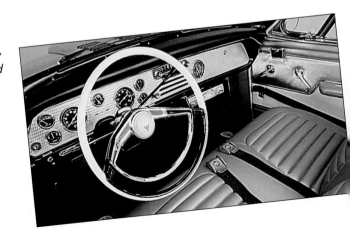

Milestones

1956 Studebaker
introduces the Hawk in coupe and hardtop forms. Engines range from a sidevalve inline six, used in the Flight Hawk, to a Packard 275-bhp, 352-cubic inch V8, used in the flagship Golden Hawk.

Packard offered a Hawk for 1958, also with supercharged power.

1957 Studebaker
reverts to its own 289-cubic inch engine, adding a belt-driven supercharger to bring power up to 275 bhp.

The Lark compact introduced for 1959 could also get a 289-c.i. V8.

1959 After poor
sales, the Hawk range is simplified. Only the 180-bhp Silver Hawk is offered.

1963 The Avanti is
launched with the supercharged 289-cubic inch unit.

1964 The final
Hawk is built—the Gran Turismo.

UNDER THE SKIN

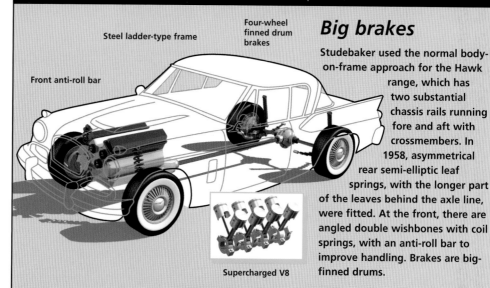

Steel ladder-type frame

Four-wheel finned drum brakes

Front anti-roll bar

Big brakes

Studebaker used the normal body-on-frame approach for the Hawk range, which has two substantial chassis rails running fore and aft with crossmembers. In 1958, asymmetrical rear semi-elliptic leaf springs, with the longer part of the leaves behind the axle line, were fitted. At the front, there are angled double wishbones with coil springs, with an anti-roll bar to improve handling. Brakes are big-finned drums.

Supercharged V8

THE POWER PACK

Supercharged flyer

Studebaker introduced its first V8 engine in 1951, which helped boost the company's sales by 50 percent. For 1955, the V8 (standard on the Commander) got a power increase to 140 bhp despite being destroked to 224 cubic inches. A bigger 259 arrived as standard on the President. Debuting as the flagship in 1956, it was only natural that the Golden Hawk packed the largest engine—a 352-cubic inch V8 with 275 bhp, sourced from Packard. This was short-lived; for the following year, the Golden Hawk got Studebaker's own 289 V8 with a belt-driven Paxton supercharger producing 275 bhp.

Hard charger

Silver Hawks proved to be far more popular than Golden ones in 1958—4,485 coupes were built against just 878 blown Golden Hawks. But the passage of time changes things, and the latter is more collectible today simply because it is the rarer of the two.

Supercharged Golden Hawks were built for only three model years.

297

Studebaker GOLDEN HAWK

After the Ford Thunderbird had been restyled, the Golden Hawk emerged as just about the best-looking two-door coupe on the market in 1958. And it had the performance to match its styling.

Auto anti-creep

Another option offered by Studebaker was an anti-creep device for the optional automatic transmission. As its name suggests, this stops the car from creeping forward without the driver needing to keep his foot on the brake at the lights or stop signs.

V8 engine

Studebaker developed a V8 engine before Packard (which took over the company in 1954) and so continued to use its own V8. The biggest version, the 289-cubic inch unit, was supercharged for the 1957 Golden Hawk.

Power windows

For the first time with the 1958 models, Studebaker made power front windows available. It was a $102 option and, curiously, power seats cost less than half that price.

Power brakes

Disc brakes were still a rarity in the late 1950s, and so Studebaker used large drums all around. They were given finned casings to help dissipate heat and maintain braking efficiency. At this time, Studebaker charged $38 for power-assisted brakes.

Wraparound rear window

One of the keys to the Golden Hawk's good looks is the wraparound rear window, which permitted the front and rear roof pillars to be set at almost the same angle.

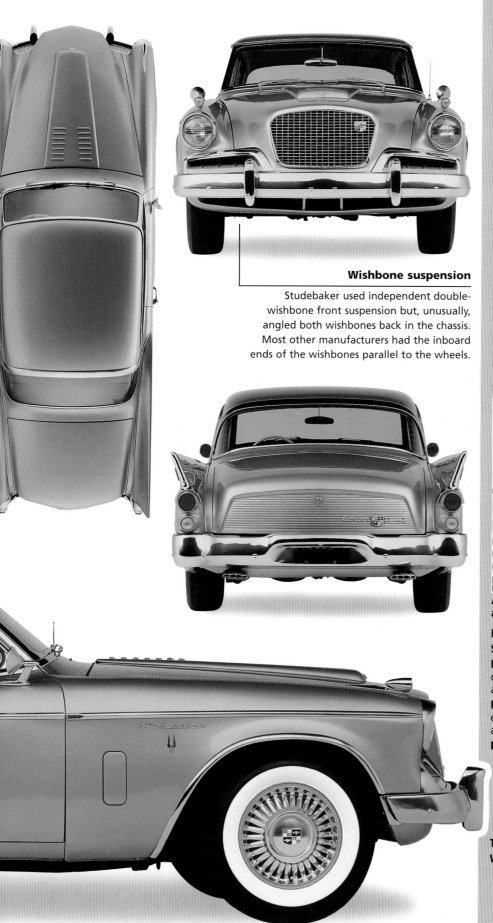

Specifications

1958 Studebaker Golden Hawk

ENGINE

Type: V8

Construction: Cast-iron block and heads

Valve gear: Two overhead valves per cylinder operated by a single centrally-mounted camshaft with pushrods, rockers and solid valve lifters

Bore and stroke: 3.56 in. x 3.63 in.

Displacement: 289 c.i.

Compression ratio: 7.8:1

Induction system: Single Stromberg two-barrel WW carburetor with supercharger

Maximum power: 275 bhp at 4,800 rpm

Maximum torque: Not quoted

TRANSMISSION

Three-speed Flightomatic

BODY/CHASSIS

Separate steel ladder frame with steel two-door coupe bodywork

SPECIAL FEATURES

The distinctive fins on the Hawks were originally made in fiberglass and later in steel.

A machined aluminum dash was quite a novelty on a 1958 Detroit car.

RUNNING GEAR

Steering: Recirculating ball

Front suspension: Double wishbones with coil springs, telescopic shock absorbers and anti-roll bar

Rear suspension: Live axle with semi-elliptic leaf springs and telescopic shock absorbers

Brakes: Finned drums (front and rear)

Wheels: Pressed steel disc, 14-in. dia.

Tires: 8.00 x 14

DIMENSIONS

Length: 204.0 in.   **Width:** 71.3 in.

Height: 55.5 in.   **Wheelbase:** 120.5 in.

Track: 57.1 in. (front), 56.1 in. (rear)

Weight: 3,470 lbs.

Wishbone suspension

Studebaker used independent double-wishbone front suspension but, unusually, angled both wishbones back in the chassis. Most other manufacturers had the inboard ends of the wishbones parallel to the wheels.

Stutz BEARCAT

Developed from an Indianapolis 500 racing car, the Stutz Bearcat has style and charisma but most of all, a huge engine that could take it far beyond the performance of most cars on the roads in the U.S.

"...antique supercar of its time."

"A maximum of 60 bhp doesn't sound like much to get excited about, but the Stutz's big 390-cubic inch four has an enormous amount of torque. Like its maximum power, it seems to be produced right off-idle. The hefty bellowing Bearcat, with its barn-like aerodynamics, could turn a top speed of 80 mph, making it an antique supercar of its time. It'll cruise effortlessly at 60 mph and the sensation of speed is something even a Ferrari driver would be impressed by. It's surprisingly easy to drive, too: the controls are light and the gearshift simple."

It doesn't come more basic than this. Stutz drivers have a bare minimum of instruments and controls.

Milestones

1911 Harry Clayton Stutz
builds a car for the first Indianapolis 500. It finishes 11th out of a field of 44 and inspires Stutz to start production.

In 1915 the Stutz White Squadron team dominated racing in the U.S.

1912 Stutz begins
to build six- and four-cylinder cars.

1914 A Stutz car
finishes fifth in the Indy 500.

1915 Erwin 'Cannonball' Baker
breaks the U.S. coast-to-coast record driving a Bearcat over 3,700 miles at an average speed of 13.7 mph. It sounds slow, but there were no proper roads across the country at this time.

Later Stutz cars were more civilized than the Bearcat, but still offered good performance.

1916 Stutz introduces
its own 360-cubic inch 'T' head engine giving a top speed of 71 mph. Production continues into the 1930s progressing into a more civilized car.

UNDER THE SKIN

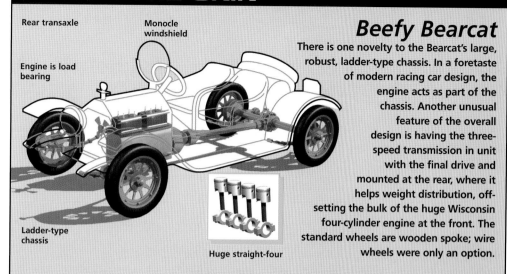

Rear transaxle

Monocle windshield

Engine is load bearing

Ladder-type chassis

Huge straight-four

Beefy Bearcat

There is one novelty to the Bearcat's large, robust, ladder-type chassis. In a foretaste of modern racing car design, the engine acts as part of the chassis. Another unusual feature of the overall design is having the three-speed transmission in unit with the final drive and mounted at the rear, where it helps weight distribution, off-setting the bulk of the huge Wisconsin four-cylinder engine at the front. The standard wheels are wooden spoke; wire wheels were only an option.

THE POWER PACK

'T' head

Stutz bought its engine from the Wisconsin company. It is a large four-cylinder 'T' head side-valve design, so called because the valves are below the cylinder head working up into the combustion chambers, with the intake manifold on one side, and the exhaust manifold on the other. The engine itself is made up of two cast-iron blocks of two cylinders each, mounted on an alloy crankcase. Two plugs per cylinder are used and it produces its maximum power at a very low 1,500 rpm.

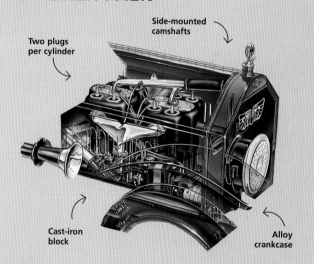

Side-mounted camshafts

Two plugs per cylinder

Cast-iron block

Alloy crankcase

Stutz racer

The Bearcat was a direct development of the Stutz racing car that finished in 11th position in the first Indy 500 in 1911. The production car's minimal bodywork reflects its racing origins. Bearcats used the same 'T' head engines as the original racer.

Stutz racer developed into the Bearcat.

Stutz BEARCAT

Before World War I, both Stutz and Mercer defined their American sports cars—the Bearcat and the Raceabout—as big, brash and fast.

'T' head Wisconsin engine

All Bearcats were built with a Wisconsin 'T' head in-line four. It's much bigger than the side-valve four used in the Mercer Raceabout but only fractionally more powerful.

Bucket seats

Bucket seats were developed to keep the occupants from falling out of the car since it didn't have any doors.

Twin spark ignition

With large cylinders there's an advantage in two spark plugs per cylinder, but they are there for reliability and not to improve the efficiency of the engine.

High ground clearance

With tall wheels and the semi-elliptic leaf springs mounted on top of the axles, the Bearcat has a lot of ground clearance, keeping the transaxle far above the road.

Optional wire wheels

Standard equipment for the Bearcat was wooden wheels with detachable rims. Lightweight wire-spoke wheels, such as these, were optional.

Rear transaxle

Harry Clayton Stutz saw the advantage of mounting the transmission to the rear along with the transaxle to improve weight distribution.

Shift and handbrake levers

In the early days of motoring there was no place for the gearshifter inside the cockpit. It stayed outside, in this case mounted alongside the handbrake lever.

Advance/retard mechanism

The driver adjusted the engine timing with a control on the steering wheel. The ignition could be advanced as the engine speed rose.

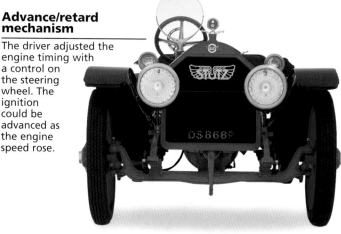

Rear drum brakes

As usual with pre-World War I cars, there are brakes on the rear wheels only, although there is a manual handbrake also acting on the rear wheels.

Specifications

1914 Stutz Bearcat

ENGINE

Type: Wisconsin four-cylinder side valve
Construction: Alloy crankcase with two cast-iron blocks and alloy pistons
Valve gear: Two side valves per cylinder operated by side-mounted camshafts on either side of the block
Bore and stroke: 4.76 in. x 5.51 in.
Displacement: 390 c.i.
Compression ratio: 4.0:1
Induction system: Single updraft Stromberg HA carburetor
Maximum power: 60 bhp at 1,500 rpm
Maximum torque: Not quoted
Top speed: 80 mph
0-60 mph: Not quoted

TRANSMISSION

Rear-mounted three-speed manual

BODY/CHASSIS

Steel ladder frame chassis with the engine acting as stressed chassis member. Open speedster-type bodywork

SPECIAL FEATURES

The monocle windshield gave the driver protection from the slipstream.

A radiator-mounted 'Boyce Motometer' is used to monitor water temperature.

RUNNING GEAR

Steering: Worm-and-nut
Front suspension: Beam axle with semi-elliptic leafs and friction shocks
Rear suspension: Live axle with semi-elliptic leafs and friction shocks
Brakes: Rear drums only, 16 in. dia.
Wheels: Wire spoke, 4.5 in. x 34 in.
Tires: 4.5 in. x 34 in.

DIMENSIONS

Length: 160 in. **Width:** 65.9 in.
Height: 63.4 in. **Wheelbase:** 120 in.
Track: 55.9 in. (front and rear)
Weight: 2,500 lbs.

Tucker **TORPEDO**

Preston Tucker had a dream to make the most advanced, the safest and one of the fastest cars ever seen in the U.S. But along the way, he made enough enemies in the business to doom the project.

"...ahead of its time."

"It would have taken drivers of the 1940s a while to get used to the rear-engined Torpedo. This is a fast car and its torquey flat-six gives acceleration to match. It is quiet, due in part to the rear engine. The assisted steering is far more direct than most cars of the time, so if the back end does break traction and step out, it can be easily controlled. The advanced suspension is firm and high-speed stability is good. This car was way ahead of its time"

For safety reasons, all the controls are deeply recessed behind a padded dash.

Milestones

1946 Preston Tucker assembles a team to help him design and build a car. He also sponsors a car in the Indianapolis 500—a Miller-engined Gulf Oil Special—and renames it the Tucker Torpedo Special to gain exposure for his new road car. Tucker acquires the immense Dodge plant in Chicago.

MGM released a movie about Tucker 40 years after his Torpedo.

1947 Built in an amazingly short time, the prototype Tucker is ready in June.

The next U.S. production car with a rear-mounted engine was the Chevrolet Corvair.

1949 Development problems delay the car and Tucker is investigated for fraud. It is thought that vested interests among Detroit car companies are behind the allegations.

1950 Tucker is cleared, but the damage is done. The company folds after just 51 cars have been made.

UNDER THE SKIN

Unique features

A massive chassis of box-section steel tubes makes the Tucker extremely strong. A separate chassis is about the only ordinary part of this car, with its rear-mounted engine and novel rubber-sprung wishbone suspension. In addition, the center headlight turns with the steering wheel and automatically lights up when darkness falls. The proposed torque-converter transmission was discarded in favor of the complex preselector from a pre-war Cord.

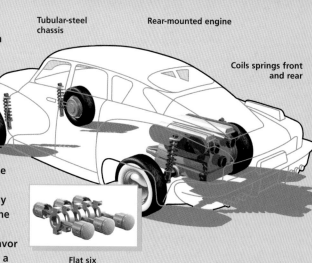

Tubular-steel chassis

Rear-mounted engine

Coils springs front and rear

Flat six

THE POWER PACK

Helicopter engine

Tuckers went into production with a 334-cubic inch, flat-six, helicopter engine. To suit air duty, it was light and designed to run for long periods of time at a relatively low rpm for reliability. Although the engine was converted from air cooled to water cooled, it is still a low-revving engine with a low compression ratio. It produces its 166 bhp maximum power output at only 3,600 rpm. Designed for torque, rather than outright power or fast running, it has side valves in L-head cylinder heads, yet is also advanced in having an alloy block when virtually all car engines were cast iron.

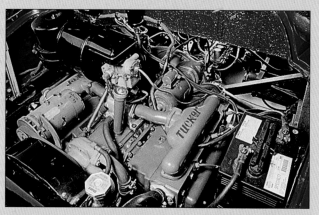

Refined looks

Even if thousands of Tuckers had been built as planned, it would still be much more collectible than the majority of 1948 U.S. production cars. Nothing else built at the time could match its looks and refinement, handling and performance.

From any angle, the Torpedo is a stunning machine.

Tucker **TORPEDO**

Preston Tucker hired Alex Tremulis, one of the best car designers, to style the Torpedo. He had worked on the great pre-war Cords and produced an elegant and aerodynamic design years ahead of its rivals.

Flat-six engine

When his own engine proved impossible to develop, Tucker turned to a converted 5.5-liter, flat-six, water cooled, helicopter engine produced by Air Cooled Motors of Syracuse.

Rear radiator

The prototype Tucker was intended to have a front-mounted radiator connected to the rear engine by copper tubes. When the converted helicopter engine was fitted, the radiator moved behind the engine.

Wishbone suspension

Tucker wanted to use a double-wishbone suspension up front with rubber in torsion for springing. The rear was intended to have trailing links, again with rubber springs. This proved troublesome in the prototype because the alloy suspension arms were too fragile and had to be reengineered. Later cars had coil springs fitted both front and rear.

Safety features

Tucker was obsessed with safety so the Torpedo was years ahead of its time in making the interior safe. The dashboard rail is padded, the steering column is collapsible, and the passenger side footwell is large enough to act as a survival cell.

24-volt electrics

The prototype engine had hydraulic valve gear. The valves remained closed until the engine finally turned over during start ups. Therefore, a 24-volt starter was required.

Specifications

1948 Tucker Torpedo

ENGINE

Type: Air cooled flat six
Construction: Alloy block and heads
Valve gear: Two sidevalves per cylinder in an L-head operated by single block-mounted camshaft per bank of cylinders
Bore and stroke: 4.57 in. x 3.56 in.
Displacement: 334 c.i.
Compression ratio: 7.0:1
Induction system: Single Autolite carburetor
Maximum power: 166 bhp at 3,200 rpm
Maximum torque: Not quoted

TRANSMISSION

Four-speed manual preselector

BODY/CHASSIS

Separate steel-perimeter chassis with steel four-door sedan bodywork

SPECIAL FEATURES

The column-mounted gearshift is an unusual design, in keeping with the rest of the interior.

No fewer than six exhaust pipes stick out from the rear of the car, three for each bank of the flat-six engine.

RUNNING GEAR

Steering: Recirculating-ball
Front suspension: Double wishbones with coil springs and telescopic shock absorbers
Rear suspension: Twin wishbones with rubber springs and telescopic shock absorbers
Brakes: Drums (front and rear)
Wheels: Pressed steel disc, 15-in. dia.
Tires: 7.00 x 15

DIMENSIONS

Length: 219.0 in.   **Width:** 79.0 in.
Height: 60.0 in.   **Wheelbase:** 130.0 in.
Track: 64.0 in. (front), 65.0 in. (rear)
Weight: 4,235 lbs.

Vector W8-M12

The best way of describing the exotic Vector is that it's America's answer to Lamborghini. It boasts phenomenal power output and has the performance to make it a contender for the title of the fastest car on earth.

"...American exotica."

"If you have ever wondered what a fighter pilot must feel like, slide into the Vector and you'll have a good idea. Everything is designed for ultra-high speeds. Its controls resemble those of a jet fighter and the overall ride is the same. As for the acceleration, it's American exotica that can compete with Italian supercars. The Vector offers unearthly performance and is a pleasure to drive—especially in the three digit mph range."

The Vector is by no means your everyday car. Inside it is more like a Space Shuttle than a conventional car.

Milestones

1977 Gerald A. Wiegert's Vector W2 is presented in Los Angeles as "the fastest car in the world."

1990 After years of preparation, the W8 is launched using a Donovan small-block Chevy®-designed engine.

Originally, Vectors were built with domestic drivelines.

1992 A WX3 model has a new aerodynamic body, twin turbos and makes up to 1100 bhp.

1993 After a power struggle, Megatech eventually emerges as the new owner and the company moves to Florida. Since they also own Lamborghini, future plans include building the car with the Diablo's V12. By using the underpowered Italian engine, the Vector will no longer be a full-blooded and extremely powerful U.S. supercar.

On looks, the Vector is a match for any Lamborghini or Ferrari.

1995 With a Diablo 492 bhp V12 engine and a much cheaper price tag, the new M12 model is marketed.

UNDER THE SKIN

Like an aircraft

Based in a part of California well known for its advanced aerospace industry, Vector took full advantage of its location. Under the super-lightweight composite bodywork there is an aircraft-inspired aluminum chassis which is both light and very strong. The Vector's running gear may be state of the art, but it is also practical. The front end boasts independent double-wishbone suspension, while the rear end consists of a well-located de Dion tube and coil/shock units.

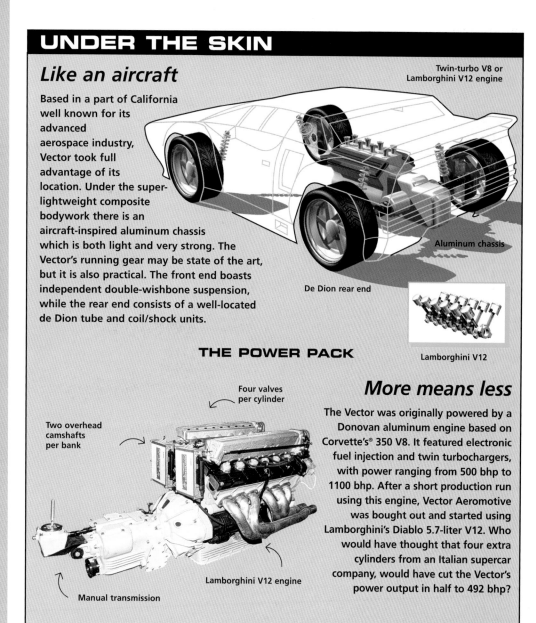

Twin-turbo V8 or Lamborghini V12 engine

Aluminum chassis

De Dion rear end

Lamborghini V12

THE POWER PACK

Four valves per cylinder

Two overhead camshafts per bank

Lamborghini V12 engine

Manual transmission

More means less

The Vector was originally powered by a Donovan aluminum engine based on Corvette's® 350 V8. It featured electronic fuel injection and twin turbochargers, with power ranging from 500 bhp to 1100 bhp. After a short production run using this engine, Vector Aeromotive was bought out and started using Lamborghini's Diablo 5.7-liter V12. Who would have thought that four extra cylinders from an Italian supercar company, would have cut the Vector's power output in half to 492 bhp?

Vector M12

When Megatech acquired Vector Aeromotive, it restyled its body and gave it an Italian supercar engine. While the new body panels bring the car into the 1990s, it should have kept the 1,100-bhp Chevy-designed V8. In comparison, the new V12 only makes 492 bhp.

The M12 uses Lamborghini's bigger but less powerful V-12 engine.

Vector **W8-M12**

Originally marketed as an all-American supercar using a Chevy-designed engine and a Toronado® transmission, the Vector W8 pulled the rug out from under both Lamborghini and Ferrari.

Advanced bodywork

Years before other manufacturers began using sophisticated composites in cars, the Vector's bodywork contained Kevlar, fiberglass and carbon fiber.

Aircraft-influenced design

As well as using aerospace materials and construction methods, the Vector's styling also recalls aircraft practice.

Honeycomb chassis

The advanced chassis is a semi-monocoque structure. Like an aircraft frame, it is constructed from tubular steel and bonded aluminum honeycomb, and is extremely light and incredibly strong.

Turbocharged Chevy V8

In a bid to make this an all-American supercar, the engine was derived from a Corvette V8 unit. To produce enough power to make this the fastest car in the world, Vector used twin intercooled Garrett H3 turbochargers.

Exotic 'scissor' doors

The large gull-wing doors open up in scissor fashion, similar to the Lamborghini Countach and Diablo.

Oldsmobile® transmission

To transfer the immense power of the mid-mounted engine, Vector selected a suitably modified Toronado automatic transmission.

Powerful braking

With performance as breathtaking as the Vector's, brakes that can deal with speeds of up to 218 mph are required. The Vector has vented four-wheel discs measuring a massive 13 inches in diameter. Naturally, there is a sophisticated ABS system.

Specifications
1992 Vector W8

ENGINE
Type: V8
Construction: Cast-iron cylinder block and head
Valve gear: Two valves per cylinder operated by a single camshaft
Bore and stroke: 4.08 in. x 3.48 in.
Displacement: 5,973 cc
Compression ratio: 8.0:1
Induction system: Tuned port electronic fuel injection
Maximum power: 625 bhp at 5,700 rpm
Maximum torque: 630 lb-ft at 4,900 rpm
Top speed: 195 mph
0–60 mph: 4.1 sec.

TRANSMISSION
Three-speed automatic

BODY/CHASSIS
Semi-monocoque honeycomb chassis with two-door coupe body in composite materials

SPECIAL FEATURES

Twin Garrett turbochargers can boost power up to 1100 bhp, a figure the Diablo engine could never match.

The radiator is mounted horizontally in the nose of the car, leaving little space for luggage up front.

RUNNING GEAR
Steering: Rack-and-pinion
Front suspension: Double wishbones with coil springs and shocks
Rear suspension: De Dion axle with longitudinal and transverse arms and coil spring/shock units
Brakes: Four-wheel discs
Wheels: Alloy, 16-in. dia.
Tires: 255/45 ZR16 front, 315/40 ZR16 rear

DIMENSIONS
Length: 172 in.   **Width:** 76 in.
Height: 42.5 in.   **Wheelbase:** 103 in.
Track: 63 in. (front), 65 in. (rear)
Weight: 3,572 lbs.

Willys **65-KNIGHT**

The combination of excellent workmanship and quality, coupled with the refined sleeve-valve engine and the pricing made the four-cylinder Willys 65-Knight a very popular choice in the 1920s.

"...wonderfully quiet engine."

"The four-cylinder sleeve-valve Willys engine is wonderfully quiet: because of its internal balancer system, few four-cylinder motors come close. It is also torquey for its 3-liter size, so you can get away with the minimum of gearchanging. These cars are solidly built, ride comfortably, and handle well, helped by light and low-geared steering. Braking is adequate though, as front brakes had yet to appear on the four-cylinder."

The plain and simple fascia of the Willys 65-Knight is reflective of the period.

Milestones

1914 Willys-Overland
begins to produce a four-cylinder in a new plant at Elyria in Ohio. To begin with, the car is too expensive and sales are slow.

The 6/90 continued Willys' low-priced tradition into the 1930s.

1915 The Willys Knight
is moved down market and sold in the $1,000 range. Sales rapidly climb.

Willys is most famous for its World War II Jeep.

1919 John North Willys
loses financial control after overextending himself with moves such as buying the Duesenberg plant in New Jersey.

1922 Willys buys
himself back into control.

1926 A new six-cylinder
model means that the company stops production of the four. By 1932, all sleeve-valve production comes to an end.

UNDER THE SKIN

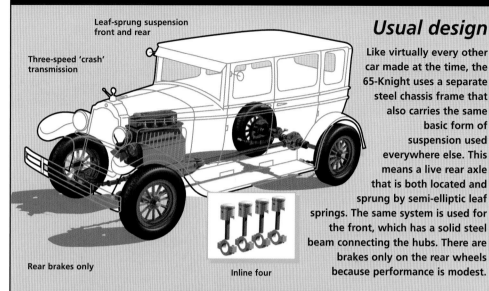

Leaf-sprung suspension front and rear

Three-speed 'crash' transmission

Rear brakes only

Inline four

Usual design

Like virtually every other car made at the time, the 65-Knight uses a separate steel chassis frame that also carries the same basic form of suspension used everywhere else. This means a live rear axle that is both located and sprung by semi-elliptic leaf springs. The same system is used for the front, which has a solid steel beam connecting the hubs. There are brakes only on the rear wheels because performance is modest.

THE POWER PACK

Complex design

The Willys sleeve-valve engine is a complex design in which two sleeves around the pistons move up and down. Each has a connecting rod joined to a shaft, which acts in the same way as the camshaft in an ordinary engine. Ports are cut in the sleeves, and the movement of the sleeves cover and uncover them, acting like the valves in a conventional engine. This design allows an excellent combustion chamber shape with the spark plug centrally mounted. Another advantage is that it is extremely quiet-running. The design was reasonably powerful for the time, producing 40 bhp at a very low 2,600 rpm.

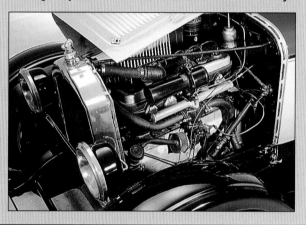

Tourer

For 1925, there was a choice of five different models in the four-cylinder range, but the most sought after now is the five-passenger tourer. Next is the two-door coupe while the ordinary sedan (built in the greatest numbers) is the least valuable.

Back in the 1920s, the Sedan was the most popular model in the range.

Willys 65-KNIGHT

Some 1925 Willys cars, such as the coupe and roadster, were extremely attractive and stylish. The sedan, however, was built on upright lines designed to maximize interior space rather than look elegant.

Thermo-siphon cooling

There is no water pump for the engine. It relies on the thermo-siphon effect of the water moving around the engine and radiator as it heats and cools.

Engine vibration damper

To make the four-cylinder engine smoother, a Lanchester balancer was added. This uses two rotating cylinders geared together to rotate in different directions. As they rotate, they counteract the movement of the pistons, thereby giving the effect of a smoother engine with more cylinders.

Wooden-spoke wheels

Standard equipment for the four-cylinder Willys were wooden spoke wheels. The smooth disc-type wheel could be ordered as an option and was more suited to the formal-looking sedan.

Rear brakes

Four-cylinder Knights were not designed with high performance in mind, so they rely on mechanically operated brakes on the rear wheels only. These are the external-contracting type.

Sleeve-valve engine

One of the advantages of the sleeve-valve engine was that it improved with use. Carbon built up between the sliding sleeves after some miles, improving the sealing. As a result, the power output rose, as genuine independent tests proved.

Live rear axle

The standard form of rear suspension was used on the Willys 65-Knight, namely a live rear axle, which like the front beam axle, uses long, semi-elliptic leaf springs to locate and suspend it. The leaves are 2.25 inches wide and more than four feet long.

Specifications

1925 Willys 65-Knight

ENGINE

Type: Inline four sleeve valve

Construction: Cast-iron block, cylinders and sleeves

Valve gear: Inlet and exhaust ports cut in sliding sleeves

Bore and stroke: 3.63 in. x 4.50 in.

Displacement: 186 c.i.

Compression ratio: N/A

Induction system: Single MS2B carburetor

Maximum power: 40 bhp at 2,600 rpm

Maximum torque: N/A

TRANSMISSION

Three-speed manual

BODY/CHASSIS

Separate steel chassis frame with sedan bodywork

SPECIAL FEATURES

Brakes lights were a novel feature for the 1920s.

Rear opposite opening doors give access for the driver and passengers.

RUNNING GEAR

Steering: Worm-and-gear

Front suspension: Beam axle with semi-elliptic leaf springs

Rear suspension: Live axle with semi-elliptic leaf springs

Brakes: External contracting drums on rear

Wheels: Wooden spoke

Tires: 5.77 x 30

DIMENSIONS

Length: 183.8 in.   **Width:** 75.6 in.

Height: 77.0 in.   **Wheelbase:** 124.0 in.

Track: 55.5 in. (front), 56.5 in. (rear)

Weight: 3,060 lbs.

Glossary of Technical Terms

A

A-pillar Angled roof supports each side of the front windscreen

ABS Anti-lock braking system

Acceleration Rate of change of velocity, usually expressed as a measure of time over a given distance such as a quarter of a mile, or from rest to a given speed, such as 0–60mph

Aerodynamic drag Wind resistance, expressed as a coefficient of drag (Cd); the more streamlined a vehicle, the lower the figure

Aftermarket Accessory fitted to a vehicle after purchase, not always offered by the manufacturer

Air-cooled engine Where ambient air is used to cool the engine, by passing directly over fins on the cylinders and cylinder head

Air dam Device at the front of a car to reduce air flow underneath the vehicle and thus reduce lift at high speeds

Aluminium block Engine cylinder block cast from aluminum, usually with cast iron sleeves or liners for the cylinder bores

Anti-roll bar Transverse rod between left and right suspension at front or rear to reduce body roll

B

B-pillar roof and door frame support behind the driver

bhp Brake horse power, 1 bhp = raising 550 foot-pounds per second; 1 bhp = torque x rpm/5252 with torque measured in foot-pounds

Blown engine or "blower" Engine fitted with a system of forced air induction such as a supercharger or turbocharger

Bucket seat Seat with added support in leg and shoulder area to secure the driver while cornering, used in rally sport

C

C-pillar Side pillar to the rear of the rear seats supporting the roof

Camshaft Engine component which controls the opening and closing of valves via lobes, either directly or indirectly

Carburetor Device for vaporizing fuel and mixing it with air in an exact ratio ready for combustion, via the inlet manifold

Chassis Component to which body, engine, gearbox and suspension are attached

Close ratio Gearbox with closely spaced ratios, used in competition

Clutch Device for controlling the transmission of power from the engine to the gearbox, usually by means of friction materials

Coil spring Helical steel alloy rod used for vehicle suspension

Column change Gearchange lever mounted on the steering column

Con rod Connecting rod that links the piston and the crankshaft, the little end connecting to the piston and the big end connecting to the crankshaft

Cylinder chamber in which piston travels, usually cylindrical in shape

Cylinder head Component which carries the sparkplugs, valves, and sometimes camshafts

D

Differential Arrangement of gears in the drive axle which allows the drive wheel on the outside of a bend to travel faster than the one on the inside

Disc brake System of braking by which friction pads are pressed against a flat, circular metal surface

Double wishbone Method of suspension where each wheel is supported by an upper and lower pivoting triangular framework

Downdraft carburettor Carburetor with a vertical barrel

Driveshaft Shaft that transmits drive from the differential to the wheel, especially on front wheel drive cars with independent rear suspension

Drivetrain Entire power transmission system from the engine's pistons to its tyres

Dry sump Where lubricating oil is contained in a separate reservoir rather than being held in the crankcase; often used in competition to prevent oil surge/starvation

E

Exhaust Device, usually of metal pipe construction, to conduct spent combustion gases away from the engine

F

Fascia A car's dashboard or instrument panel

Flathead Style of engine where the valves are mounted in the cylinder block, and the cylinder head has a flat surface

Flat twin/flat four Boxer engine configuration where cylinders are horizontally opposed to each other, such as in the VW Beetle

Floorpan Structural floor to a car, part of the chassis

Fluid clutch Clutch using a fluid coupling, flywheel, or torque converter

Forced induction Engine using a turbocharger or supercharger to pressurize the induction system to force air and hence more fuel, giving more power

Fuel injection Direct metered injection of fuel into the combustion cycle by mechanical or electro-mechanical means, first devised in 1902

G

Gearbox Component of the transmission system that houses a number of gears of different ratios that can be selected either automatically or manually by the driver. Different gears are selected to suit a variety of road speeds throughout the engine's rev range

Gear ratio The revolutions of a driving gear required to turn the driven gear through one revolution, calculated by the number of teeth on the driven gear divided by the number of teeth on the driving gear

Grand tourer Term originally used to describe an open-top luxury car, now typically a high performance coupé

Grill Metal or plastic protection for the radiator, often adopting a particular style or design of an individual manufacturer to make their car recognizable

GT Gran Turismo; Italian term used to describe a high performance luxury sports car or coupé

Gullwing Doors that open in a vertical arc, usually hinged along the centre of the roofline

H

H-pattern Conventional gear selection layout where first and third gear are furthest from the driver and second and fourth are nearest

Helical gears Gear wheel with its teeth set oblique to the gear axis which mates with another shaft with its teeth at the same angle

Hemi engine An engine with a hemispherical combustion chamber

Hydrolastic suspension System of suspension where compressible fluids act as springs, with interconnections between wheels to aid levelling

I

Independent suspension System of suspension where all wheels move up and down independently of each other, thus having no effect on the other wheels and aiding stability

Intercooler Device to cool supercharged or turbocharged air before it enters the engine to increase density and power

K

Kamm tail Type of rear body design developed by W. Kamm, where the rear end of the car tapers sharply over the rear window and is then cut vertically to improve aerodynamics

L

Ladder frame Tradition form of chassis with two constructional rails running front to rear with lateral members adding rigidity

Limited slip differential Device to control the difference in speed between left and right driveshafts so both wheels turn at similar speeds. Fitted to reduce the likelihood of wheelspinning on slippery surfaces

Live axle Axle assembly patented by Louis Renault in 1899. The axle contains shafts which drive the wheels

M

Manifold Pipe system used for gathering or dispersal of gas or liquids

Mid-engine Vehicle with its engine mounted just behind the driver and significantly ahead of the rear axle to provide even weight distribution, thus giving the car better handling characteristics

Monobloc An engine with all its cylinders cast in one piece

Monocoque Body design where the bodyshell carries the structural strength without conventional chassis rails (see "unitary construction")

O

Overdrive Additional higher ratio gear(s), usually on the third or fourth gear selected automatically by the driver

R

Rack and pinion System of gearing typically used in a steering box with a toothed rail driven laterally by a pinion on the end of the steering column

Radiator Device for dissipating heat, generally from the engine coolant

Rocker arms Pivoting arm translating rotational movement of the camshaft into linear movement of the valves

Roll bar Strong, usually curved bar either internally or eternally across a vehicle's roof then secured to the floor or chassis to provide protection in the event of the car turning over. Used on some open-top sportcars

Running gear General description of a vehicle's underbody mechanicals, including the suspension, steering, brakes, and drivetrain

S

Semi-elliptic spring Leaf spring suspension used on the rear axle of older cars in which the spring conforms to a specific mathematical shape

Semi-independent suspension System on a front-wheel drive car where the wheels are located by trailing links and a torsioned crossmember

Sequential gearbox Gear selection layout in which the selection is made by a linear movement rather than in the conventional H-pattern, used on some sportscars and rally cars

Servo assistance Servo powered by a vacuum, air, hydraulics, or electrically to aid the driver to give a powerful output from minimal input. Typically used on brakes, steering and clutch

Shock absorber Hydraulic device, part of the suspension system typically mounted between the wheel and the chassis to prevent unwanted movement, to increase safety and aid comfort. More correctly known as "damper"

Spark plug Device for igniting combustion gases via the arcing of current between two electrodes

"Split driveline" layout An extra set of epicyclic gears to provide a closer interval between the standard set of ratios, so an eight speed gearbox will actually have 16 gears

Spoiler Device fitted to the front of the car, low to the ground, to reduce air flow under the car and increase down-force, thus improving roadholding at higher speeds

Straight 6, 8 An engine with six or eight cylinders in a single row

Supercharger Mechanically-driven air pump used to force air into the combustion cycle, improving performance

Synchromesh Automatic synchronization using cone clutches to speed up or slow down the input shaft to smoothly engage gear, first introduced by Cadillac in 1928

T

Tachometer device for measuring rotational speed (revs per minute, rpm) of an engine

Torque The rotational twisting force exerted by the crankshaft

Traction control Electronic system of controlling the amount of power to a given wheel to reduce wheelspin

Transmission General term for the final drive, clutch and gearbox.

Transverse engine Engine type where the crankshaft lies parallel to the axle

Turbocharger Air pump for use in forced induction engines. Similar to a supercharger but driven at very high speed by exhaust gases, rather than mechanically to increase power output

U

Unibody Monocoque construction in which the floorpan, chassis and body are welded together to form one single structure

Unitary construction Monocoque bodyshell structurally rigid enough not to require a separate chassis

Unit construction Engine in which the powerplant and transmission are together as one, integrated unit

V

Venturi principle Basis upon which carburetors work: gas flowing through a narrow opening creates a partial vacuum

W

Wheelbase The measured distance between the front and rear wheel spindles

Index